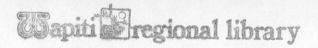

Breakthrough
Business Results
with MVT

A Fast, Cost-Free "Secret Weapon" for
Boosting Sales, Cutting Expenses, and
Improving Any Business Process

CHARLES HOLLAND
WITH **DAVID COCHRAN**

WILEY

John Wiley & Sons, Inc.

Published by John Wiley & Sons, Inc., Hoboken, New Jersey.
Published simultaneously in Canada.

QualPro offers its unique MVT* services to achieve improved client profitability. QualPro's MVT services include a variety of products including MVT experimentation, MVT measurement optimization, MVT process control, and MVT capability analysis. QualPro's MVT seminars, MVT training, and MVT consulting services support all of these products.

* MVT is a trademark of QualPro Inc.

For general information on our other products and services please contact our Customer Care Department within the United States at (800) 762-2974, outside the United States at (317) 572-3993 or fax (317) 572-4002.

Wiley also publishes its books in a variety of electronic formats. Some content that appears in print may not be available in electronic books. For more information about Wiley products, visit our web site at www.wiley.com.

Library of Congress Cataloging-in-Publication Data:

Holland, Charles, 1940–
    Breakthrough business results with MVT : a fast, cost-free "secret weapon" for boosting sales, cutting expenses, and improving any business process / Charles Holland.
       p.   cm.
    ISBN 0-471-69771-0 (cloth : alk. paper)
      1. Industrial management—Statistical methods.   2. Industrial management—Methodology.   I. Title.
    HD30.215.H65 2005

                                                    658.4′03—dc22

Printed in the United States of America.

10 9 8 7 6 5 4 3 2 1

FOREWORD

I feel privileged to be part of this book because I have never come across a more powerful business tool than MVT to identify what needs to be done. My experience with Chuck Holland and the MVT process goes back to the early 1990s when I was the CEO of a multi-billion dollar telecommunications provider. We believed there were many opportunities to apply quality principles to improve our work and, like many companies, were seeking the help of experts. After an intensive search, our company selected Chuck Holland's consulting firm, QualPro, as our process improvement partner. I am still using them over a decade later, now in a different industry, and I am proud to say my education has been enlightening and the financial gains substantial.

QualPro brings a refreshing approach to solving business problems. First, they assume we, the business community, know more about our business than a consultant would. A great start. Next they apply sound statistical principles to test proposed improvement solutions from our own employees.

The MVT statistical process is brilliant. In a nutshell, it enables you to test many business improvement solutions simultaneously and discover those solutions that help, those solutions that make no difference, and those solutions that hurt. Yes, there are many "solutions" that actually make your problem worse. You must read the

book to understand why this is so. I will warn you that the real solutions will many times not be intuitive.

The MVT implementation process is also brilliant. You are encouraged to pick only solutions that are practical, fast, and cost free. This
means you can implement the winning ideas immediately. How many
consultant reports have you commissioned that have great recommendations but require extensive process changes that you cannot afford?

Let me conclude by giving you a few key tips I learned by trial and
error. These will help you over some bumps along the way.

- Whoever authorizes the MVT initiative must be high enough in
  the organization to put a referee shirt on.
- Your people have the answers; let them put their proposed solutions forward and use MVT to test them. Resist your bias to
  squelch those solutions you don't like.
- Choose problems where improvements can be quantified and easily measured. Sounds like a "no brainer," but it can be more difficult than you think.
- If you are the senior executive, stay involved in order to maximize the benefits. There will be no substitute for your personal
  effort. This is not something to delegate.
- Tackle your biggest problems first and expect speed in the testing
  phase.
- Never assume that once you have a successful test that it can be
  exported to another part of your company. If it is to be exported
  to a like operation within the company, do a "refining test" before implementing. Refining is defined in the text to follow.
- Be diligent in the implementation phase. Process change is generally resisted until new habits are institutionalized. My biggest
  MVT challenges have occurred due to my inability to implement
  solutions, not because the solution proven most effective by the
  MVT Process was incorrect.

I predict that as you learn more you too will understand why I am
so passionate about MVT. Good luck and happy reading.

ED MUELLER, CEO
Williams-Sonoma

ACKNOWLEDGMENTS

I would like to thank:

- All the 1,000+ clients of QualPro who have allowed us to be involved in over 13,000 projects utilizing the MVT process since 1982.
- The 400+ client personnel who have presented their MVT process success stories at the annual QualPro Leadership Symposium. There have been 25 to 30 such presentations each year since 1989. Most of the successes discussed in this book came from those presentations.
- David Cochran, without whose help I would never have been able to finish this book. He helped me gather the material, arrange the format, and translate my East Tennessee English into something we hope people can understand. He kept asking, "Do you want to say it that way?" and "Maybe we should include this."
- Debbie Faust who formatted the material, prepared the tables and figures, worked long hours, and smiled through it all.
- Special thanks to Art Hammer and Kieron Dey. They are true MVT Process Improvement Masters, who made significant

contributions to this book and were involved in many of the
13,000+ MVT success stories.

- QualPro consultants, who were involved in the generation of
QualPro MVT successes discussed in this book.
- Bill Leydorf, Jim Brown, Jeff Dolak, and Bill Huckaby, who
helped prepare and format materials for the book.
- Joy Rhea, Shirley Holland, Sandy Holland, Britni Holland, Cara
Holland, Clyde Buck, Randy Conway, Kieron Dey, Jeff Dolak,
and Jim Brown for proofreading the book. Sue Lusk and Joyce
Jones for gathering materials.
- Ken Holland, who made many suggestions on book content.
- Dean Gardenhire, who helped develop the text for several chapters.
- Richard Narramore, who greatly helped shape the book's out-
line. Also, Arlette Ballew for her help in editing the text.
- Dr. W. Edwards Deming, whose input and encouragement helped
me successfully launch QualPro.
- Dr. George Box, who attended QualPro symposiums and made
kind comments about the MVT process and QualPro's work.
- Special thanks to client senior managers such as Carl Bouckaert,
Gordon Cain, Pete DeBusk, Roger Milliken, Ed Mueller, and
Bob Potter, all of whom taught me valuable lessons.

CONTENTS

Introduction: An Outlandish Claim   xi

Part I
THE CASE FOR MVT   1

Chapter 1
The Power of MVT: Practical, Fast, Cost-Free Solutions to
  Any Business Problem   3

Chapter 2
How MVT Works: Using Data to Take the Guesswork,
  Politics, and Emotions Out of Major
  Business Decisions   20

Chapter 3
Using MVT to Increase Sales, Cut Costs, and Improve
  Customer Satisfaction: Stories from Citibank, DuPont,
  Williams-Sonoma, and Others   38

Chapter 4
MVT Compared to Six Sigma and Other
  Popular Improvement Approaches   47

Part II
IMPLEMENTING AN MVT BUSINESS IMPROVEMENT PROJECT IN YOUR COMPANY   55

Chapter 5
Step 1: Choose a High-Payoff Goal and Create
the Environment   57

Chapter 6
Step 2: Define How You Will Measure Success and Validate
Your Measurement System   68

Chapter 7
Step 3: Use Control Charts to Hunt for Good Ideas to Test   79

Chapter 8
Step 4: Use Data Mining and Other Statistical Techniques to
Find Good Ideas to Test   87

Chapter 9
Step 5: Brainstorm for Improvement Ideas with Everyone
Who Could Have Worthwhile Suggestions   96

Chapter 10
Step 6: Select Improvement Ideas That Are Practical, Fast,
and Cost Free   104

Chapter 11
Step 7: Design an MVT Screening Experiment to Test Many
Ideas with Only a Few Tests   112

Chapter 12
Step 8: Execute the MVT Screening Experiment and Measure
Test Results   127

Chapter 13
Step 9: Analyze Screening Test Results to Determine Which
Ideas Help, Hurt, or Have No Impact on Performance (Prepare
to Be Surprised)   142

Chapter 14
Step 10: Design and Execute an MVT Refining Experiment to
   Optimize Results   150

Chapter 15
Step 11: Analyze the Results and Decide Which Ideas Will
   Make the Biggest Impact on Your Business   158

Chapter 16
Step 12: Carefully Implement the Most Powerful Ideas,
   Calculate the Bottom-Line Impact, and Take the Money
   to the Bank!   167

Chapter 17
What It All Adds Up To: Putting the Twelve Steps of the
   MVT Process in Perspective   177

Part III
BREAKTHROUGH MVT SUCCESSES
IN THE REAL WORLD   183

Chapter 18
How Lowe's Reduced Advertising Expenses by $50 Million
   While Increasing Sales   185

Chapter 19
How DuPont Achieved $26 Million in Increased Production
   with No Capital Investment   194

Chapter 20
A Small Company Implements MVT in Its
   Selling Process   201

Chapter 21
How SBC-Ameritech Cut Its Installation and Repair Backlog in
   Half and Eliminated a Public Relations Nightmare   207

Chapter 22
How Progressive Insurance Saved $48 Million by Reducing
  Attorney Involvement in the Claims Process   220

Part IV
USING MVT TO SPREAD BREAKTHROUGH
RESULTS THROUGHOUT YOUR COMPANY   229

Chapter 23
The Keys to Successful Organization-Wide Improvement   231

Chapter 24
Phase I: Complete Two High-Impact MVT Projects with
  Breakthrough Results   242

Chapter 25
Phase II: Commit to an Organization-Wide Rollout—A Senior
  Management Function   251

Chapter 26
Phase III: Execute MVT Projects Throughout
  the Organization   274

Chapter 27
Phase IV: Maintain the Gains, Prioritize MVT Opportunities,
  and Continuously Improve   285

Chapter 28
The Payoff: Higher Revenues, Lower Costs, Improved
  Profitability, and Increased Shareholder Value   293

Appendix: Partial Listing of Presentations from QualPro's Annual
Leadership Symposiums   297

Index   315

Introduction

An Outlandish Claim

Let's start with an outlandish claim: Multivariable Testing (MVT™) is the greatest business improvement methodology ever devised. A lot of evidence will be required to prove that statement, but I think I can make a strong case for it in Parts I and III of this book. Actually, my clients who have implemented MVT will provide much of the evidence. Since 1989, my company QualPro has held an annual symposium in which 25 to 30 of our clients from every industry present case studies on how MVT has improved their businesses. Clients are not allowed to present their case study unless they have achieved at least a fivefold return on their investment during the year in which the MVT project was implemented. Their individual MVT projects typically have a bottom-line impact ranging from a few hundred thousand dollars in small companies to $100 million or more in our Fortune 100 clients.

You may be especially skeptical if, like many, you've never heard of MVT. Maybe all you know is that it was developed by weapons scientists during World War II, further developed in the 1960s, and that it involves advanced statistics. Those who are familiar with MVT, like the diverse group of executives who are our clients, think MVT is pretty amazing, and you will read many stories of companies who have used MVT to generate billions in cost savings and improved profits. MVT has helped all kinds of organizations solve problems, improve processes and quality, and achieve results that seem truly unbelievable. Many of these stories have been presented publicly.

This book describes in detail many real-world MVT experiments conducted by my consulting firm QualPro and by our clients who participated in the actual MVT projects. You will read about the incredible variety of companies and situations to which the MVT methods have been successfully applied, and you will find many opportunities to use these techniques to help you and your company experience the same fantastic results.

Here are some brief examples of the results my clients have achieved with MVT:

- Home-improvement retailer Lowe's wanted to dramatically improve the results of their advertising efforts. With some simple changes to its Sunday circular's graphics and cover content (proven effective by some MVT-based statistical testing), Lowe's saved $50 million in annual advertising costs while increasing sales. This improvement was the result of just a few weeks of structured discovery, experimentation, and implementation using the MVT methodology.
- A DuPont chemical plant was facing fines of $25,000 per day and was in danger of being shut down (which would have cost DuPont about $750,000 per month). The plant discharges wastewater that eventually runs into the Gulf of Mexico, and the Environmental Protection Agency (EPA) measures the cleanliness of this wastewater by determining the mortality rate of shrimp placed in the wastewater. The plant was in trouble because the shrimp in the test samples did not survive in sufficient numbers for the wastewater to pass the test. Five MVT experiments produced results that surprised everyone. The shrimp died, not because of the wastewater, but because the EPA test procedures did not accurately represent the conditions in the Gulf of Mexico. By decreasing the salinity of the test water and using shrimp of the right age, the test results changed. MVT saved the plant and prevented what would have been huge losses by DuPont. DuPont went on to use MVT to streamline operations and improve internal processes in many of its chemical plants, resulting in hun-

dreds of millions of dollars of bottom-line benefits. Amazingly, almost all these benefits required no capital investment. One of the great things about MVT is that it debunks the myth that you have to spend money to make money.

- *The National Enquirer* used MVT experiments to sift through over 500 options for revamping its cover design and subscription renewal mailings. These experiments resulted in significantly increased sales. The MVT process managed the complexities of the project, and *Enquirer* managers were stunned by how often their "gut instincts" or "obviously correct" notions were proven wrong with mathematical precision.

You will see in the following chapters that our clients speak loudly and proudly of the actual results they have experienced from the MVT methods—methods that you can employ, no matter what kind of business you seek to improve.

PART I

THE CASE FOR MVT

CHAPTER 1

THE POWER OF MVT

*Practical, Fast, Cost-Free Solutions to
Any Business Problem*

Over the past 23 years, my company, QualPro, has helped over
1,000 companies (including half of the Fortune 100) conduct over
13,000 business improvement projects using a secret weapon called
Multivariable Testing (MVT). The business results have been hailed
by major companies in every industry and our clients have seen billions
of dollars of positive financial impact. MVT has been praised in almost
every leading business publication including *BusinessWeek, Forbes,*
the *Economist,* and the *Wall Street Journal.* Over time this work has
produced a huge repository of business improvement data and case
studies. This book explains what MVT is, why it is so powerful, and
how leading companies are using it.

THE EXECUTIVE DILEMMA

Every executive wants the same thing—improved results: more profit,
less cost, better quality, higher customer satisfaction, and so on. And
people throughout every organization, including executives, have ideas
to improve results. Unfortunately, there is no agreement as to whose
ideas are the right ones, which ideas are cost effective, or which ideas
will make the biggest impact on the bottom line. For lack of a better
way, most executives, in business areas ranging from marketing and

sales to production and operations, make key business decisions using their judgment, intuition, and gut feeling based on their experience. They may receive suggestions and recommendations from experts and other departments in the organization and may even hire consultants for advice. Finally, they cross their fingers and hope that the solutions they implement will prove to be worth the time and money spent.

QualPro has tested the real-world impact of over 150,000 business improvement ideas over the past three decades and discovered that most business ideas do not work. Our work with over 1,000 companies shows that no matter the source (executives, technical experts, front-line workers, customers, vendors, janitors) 75 percent of their ideas will not improve results, and nobody can accurately predict which 25 percent are the most powerful ideas. Believe it or not, front-line employees are just as likely as CEOs to suggest ideas that make measurable impacts on the bottom line.

The only way to avoid making seat-of-the-pants guesses at which ideas and solutions will make the biggest impact on your organization's performance is to test them. The only way most of us know to test ideas and solutions is to test one idea at a time, measure the results, and hold all other conditions constant. Do this for each idea that you think might improve your business, and you will know with certainty which idea produces the best measurable results. Unfortunately, this method has some severe shortcomings in the real world:

1. *It is highly inefficient.* Testing ideas that could improve any and every area of your business requires significant time, money, and resources. Testing all the reasonable-sounding ideas that you and your organization might generate to solve a business problem or improve performance is just not practical.

2. *It cannot identify synergies.* In the real world, ideas often act differently when they are implemented together than they act separately. If you test only one idea at a time, it is impossible to uncover these synergies between ideas.

3. *Test results often cannot be consistently repeated in the real world.* During one-idea-at-a-time tests, you attempt to hold all conditions constant. Because conditions continuously change in the real world, the tests can not accurately represent reality.

These problems pose such hurdles that most executives, even though they would like to make more rigorous, data-based decisions, do not think they have the time or money to test lots of creative ideas and solutions to key business problems. So they fall back on seat-of-the-pants decision making. Is there any alternative? The answer is MVT.

MVT offers a powerful, inexpensive, efficient way to use statistics to test dozens of business improvement ideas, discover the synergies between them, and prove with certainty which ones are the most powerful and profitable under real-world conditions. Businesses that use MVT regularly generate millions of dollars in cost savings or new revenues as a direct result.

WHAT IS MVT?

MVT basically means testing a lot of different variables/solutions/business improvement ideas all at the same time. When applied to a business problem, it is a 12-step process that starts with dozens of practical, fast, cost-free ideas for improvement and uses advanced statistics to quickly sort out the ideas that will help from the ideas that will hurt or make no difference. Using the MVT process, you can tackle your biggest business problems, test dozens of practical, fast, and cost-free improvement ideas at once, and discover which combinations make the greatest impact on your bottom line.

The essence of an MVT improvement project is *rigorous, quantifiable, accelerated learning*. You do not need to guess about whether a new ad campaign will impact sales or hope that a change to a production line will boost output by 50 percent. You can know, with certainty, which changes will help any area of your business, and you can statistically quantify how much the changes will help.

This knowledge allows organizations to focus their energies on only the actions that matter and to make breakthrough improvements in a short time. Here is how some clients describe MVT:

Dennis Harris, president, SBC/Ameritech: "Some of the ideas that intuitively we'd think would help, didn't; and some that we didn't think would help, did . . . and that's the way it's always been when I get into an MVT project."

Jeff Wells, senior vice president, Circuit City: "The MVT Process . . . What did we learn about ourselves? That our gut stinks."

Carl Bouckaert, CEO, Beaulieu of America: "Learning occurs when an informative event is combined with a perceptive observer. MVT accelerates the occurrence of informative events. . . . I had no idea such a powerful tool existed. . . . If your competition is regularly using MVT and you are not, you are in trouble."

MVT MAKES A $1 BILLION BOTTOM-LINE IMPACT AT SBC

From 1989 into the 2000s, Neil Ismert was one of several people throughout SBC who were involved in quality improvement in the organization. Neil focused on applying the MVT process to improve quality. At QualPro's Leadership Symposium in October 2000, Neil described to over 300 executive attendees how SBC had achieved over $1 billion worth of improvements in the first 10 years of using MVT.

In 1989, Southwestern Bell, now a part of SBC Communications, was a very successful result of the breakup of "Ma Bell" (the original AT&T) into regional telephone companies. New services, new consumer-driven competition, and the opportunity for rapid growth fueled enthusiasm within the company for innovation. Southwestern Bell had more than 66,000 employees and $9 billion in revenue from service offerings in five southwestern states.

Each of the five states acted as a separate organization with its own president, marketing and sales departments, installation and repair operations, and so on. Each state had started internal quality groups with the common goal of improving things—all kinds of things, and each quality group worked independently, applying various techniques that were in vogue at the time, including total quality management (TQM), and other variants of statistical process control (SPC). The results were fragmented and frustrating and eventually led to the decision to implement a single, corporate-wide approach, headed by a Quality Advisory Committee, that could be leveraged across the states. The Quality Advisory Committee took on the mission of finding the best improvement approach or methodology to apply across the entire organization and solicited proposals from the top 10 consulting organizations in the quality improvement field. The committee sought a methodology that could produce immediate breakthrough successes that would help promote future improvement projects around the company. After lively discussion and analysis, the committee chose to work with QualPro because of QualPro's MVT process. The committee liked the fact that MVT was objective and rigorous yet could be learned and applied by internal company resources and, most importantly, that MVT could be applied to any kind of business process, which is exactly what Southwestern Bell proceeded to do.

The Results of MVT

MVT requires an openness to change, and that openness was evident in the support that Southwestern Bell was giving. After training senior managers in the process and selecting a few pressing problems for initial projects, the committee and the QualPro consultants began to implement MVT. By 1992, Southwestern Bell had used MVT to tackle all kinds of improvement challenges. The results were magical. In the first two years, MVT projects generated an estimated $100 million in reduced or eliminated expenses and in increased sales, and Southwestern Bell was just getting started. Over the next eight years, Southwestern Bell and its parent SBC trained thousands of employees and ran hundreds of MVT projects on every aspect of its business. Here are some examples:

- A massive backlog in repairs and installations at SBC/Ameritech was rapidly cut by more than half, slashing customer response time.
- An MVT project focusing on sales in four metropolitan areas in Texas increased sales by $11 million while reducing associated expenses by $4 million.
- A California MVT project, aimed at increasing Caller ID revenues, increased the direct-mail response rate from 3.7 percent to 6.9 percent, with a revenue impact of over $7 million per year.
- An MVT effort in Oklahoma was directed at reducing a $40 million inventory of plug-in circuit boards. The result was a 25 percent reduction, a savings of $430 thousand per year in carrying charges.

- On-time installations were improved from 84 percent to 98 percent through an MVT project completed in less than 90 days for SBC's industrial and inter-exchange business at Pacific Bell.
- An MVT project in Kansas and Missouri saved over $16 million per year on detecting and recovering telephone lines that were incorrectly labeled "defective."
- A Pacific Bell MVT project optimized the communication process associated with the introduction of a new voice-mail service. Over $1 million in marketing costs was saved.
- The timeliness of installation of high-speed Internet access was improved by an SBC MVT project. Orders filled within two days without manual intervention increased from less than 50 percent to over 95 percent.
- An MVT effort that achieved a 19-percent reduction in late installations of high-capacity circuits was valued at $11.95 million annually by SBC's Industry Markets operations.

Neil Ismert summarized SBC's experience with MVT:

> The projects we've done touched all areas of the business . . . installation, repair, dispatches, sales, churn, repeat calls, productivity, cable cuts, once a cable is cut how we restore it, outages, blocked calls, billing, plug-ins (a big part of our inventory and costs), direct mail, and new-product introduction. Literally hundreds of MVTs; we worked with thousands of factors and saved millions of dollars. In fact, the bottom-line impact for the first 10 years is approximately one billion dollars.

This is an amazing story, but it is not at all uncommon. Over the years, MVT has made a significant impact at over 1,000 companies from every industry. The rest of this book, especially Part III, contains many more detailed case studies from a wide range of industries and business functions.

THE ROOTS OF MVT

The core ideas behind MVT were developed during World War II by British statisticians who were devising ways to shoot down German bombers over London. When the Germans began attacking London, the British quickly realized that their antiaircraft artillery were inadequate. The British desperately needed to improve the accuracy of their artillery, but the training and testing required to develop better targeting techniques and artillery were extensive, time consuming, and error prone. The challenge of solving this problem was given to a special British military unit called SR17 that specialized in operations research and reported directly to Prime Minister Winston Churchill. George Barnard, the head of SR17, asked two brilliant mathematical statisticians, R. L. Plackett and J. P. Burman, to find a way to quickly test not only different types of projectiles but also multiple variations on 11 different components in order to find the most accurate and deadly combination. The statisticians devised screening experimental designs that allowed them to test 30 or 40 variables at a time. The net result was a projectile design that greatly improved the English's ability to shoot down German planes. After the war, Plackett and Burman published an influential paper describing their new system ("Multifactorial Experiments," *Biometrika 33,* 1946).

I first heard about the concept of screening designs in 1964 while working for Union Carbide as a statistician in the Nuclear Weapons Manufacturing Division in Tennessee. While attending an American Society for Quality Control (Chemical Division) Convention, I heard a presentation by two chemists who had read the Plackett-Burman paper and developed a way of implementing screening designs in a factory. After listening to their presentation, I was fascinated by the power of the idea. Excited and challenged by my discovery of this powerful tool, I looked for ways to apply screening designs to nuclear weapons development and production.

A Nuclear Weapons Manufacturing Crisis

During the Cold War, the development and production of the U.S. arsenal of conventional and nuclear missiles were national priorities. Enormous sums of money were invested to develop the production facilities and techniques necessary to produce these weapons, and many knowledgeable and influential people thought that the safety and security of the United States was contingent on its ability to produce sophisticated and superior weapons.

I had the opportunity to use screening designs on several weapons manufacturing processes. The tests were done on low-visibility projects involving mid-level personnel, but each one required extensive internal selling to get agreement to even try it. The results were encouraging. We experienced dramatic improvements in the manufacturing process, with increased output and reduced defects.

In 1969, I finally had the opportunity to use screening designs on a very important, high-visibility problem. Despite the efforts of the best engineers and experts in the field, the production of a key component in one of the nation's vital defense programs was failing. Eighty-five percent of the carbon-foam parts produced at the weapons plant in Oak Ridge, Tennessee, were failing to meet quality requirements and were unusable. As a result, the plant simply could not keep pace with production requirements. This problem was stalling the production of the entire weapons system and threatened to become a national security problem. Something had to change soon.

In a meeting to decide what, if anything, could be done, the best minds from Union Carbide's operations, engineering, production, and management departments, and military representatives were gathered in desperation. There was a wide variety of suggestions, including changing the materials involved, retooling parts of the machinery, and other system-level changes. Most of these suggestions entailed high costs and long delays. One of the Research and Development (R&D) engineers who had been involved in the original process development recommended a completely new process and estimated the cost at $48 million. The managers were anxious and frustrated.

I was a statistician working in process control and improvement, and I wanted to get into the debate. My people and I had achieved some previous success in improving complex processes, and we knew how to make fast, cheap improvements with the materials and processes already in place. To make my case, I focused on the time required for the other solutions under consideration. The program could not wait months or even weeks; the security of the nation was at risk. Improvement had to come quickly, and no other quick solutions were being considered.

Fearful that there were no quick or good solutions, the vice president of the nuclear division of Union Carbide, a bright and capable fellow who was highly regarded, decided that, although the company reluctantly had to proceed with the planning for expensive, long-term improvements, there could be no harm in examining what practical, fast, cost-free improvements a statistician might wring out of the current situation. Using a good bit of personal influence, he convinced the others to go along with some limited testing of the existing production process. Unknowingly, he had accepted one of the fundamental tenets of the MVT methodology: *Use practical, fast, cost-free ideas to get more out of what you already have.*

The Birth of the MVT Process: A Practical, Fast, Cost-Free Solution

To begin the testing process, we reviewed all control charts and analyzed the historical data using multiple linear regression and various multivariate methods. Unfortunately, the past data revealed no clues. Next, we collected suggestions for improvement from everyone who touched the process in any way, regardless of level or position. No proposed solution was rejected at this point; most solutions focused on changing the materials or equipment used. About 60 suggestions were identified. Because we had so little time, we reduced the list to 19 suggestions that could be done simply and immediately. *What can be done simply?* and *What can be done right now?* are still two of the three main questions asked when assessing ideas for change in the MVT process.

Most of the remaining 19 suggestions were for simple changes to the process, such as the mixing time for the chemicals that made the foam (30 seconds or 60 seconds), the position of the blade in the mixing can (high or low), and the speed of the turntable during mixing (10 rpm or 40 rpm). Each of these ideas was easily controlled and could be tested immediately.

Our next step was to arrange testing time, which I estimated would require two full shifts for two days, just for the screening experiments. The production manager, already so far behind that he had no time for experiments, was adamant. "No way! You can have one shift, one day." And he wasn't happy about that. At this point, the frustration and anger were mutual. There was no way to test effectively with so many restrictions and limitations. After consulting with my colleagues, I was struck by another reality of business improvement: When a process is this bad, there must be ways to get substantial improvement with just a few simple changes, because almost anything is better than a consistently failing process. If we could increase the acceptance rate of the foam castings from the current 15 percent to a mere 30 percent, we would be considered heroes or magicians and would certainly get more testing time.

So I agreed to proceed into what might be considered the worst possible experimental situation: Our primary variables produced only attributes measurements; we had very limited test time; and, at least in the minds of the experts, we had eliminated all of the best suggestions because they cost too much money or could not be implemented right away.

The Results

The screening experiment involved 16 production runs to test 11 different factors. For each of the 11 factors, two levels, or conditions, were measured: (1) the status quo and (2) the change. To my great relief, the screening experiment identified factors that yielded a reliable increase in the acceptance rate of foam castings from 15 percent to 50 percent—and after only a single shift of testing! The experiment also identified five of the 11 factors that merited further investigation: heating of the mold, distance of the mixing blade from the bottom of the mixing can, time taken for mixing, turntable speed, and speed of pouring the mixture from the can into the mold.

We were heroes and much smarter heroes as well. The vice president of the nuclear division could breathe again. The engineer who had recommended a $48 million overhaul of the production line was suddenly quiet. The shop-floor operators were ecstatic that people were actually listening to their ideas and recognizing their contributions. (Thirty-five years later, these are still common reactions to an MVT implementation.)

After our first big success, senior management admonished the production manager to be cooperative and announced that this process was in experimental mode until we had accomplished all possible improvements. We raised the rate of acceptable foam castings from the manufacturing process to 85 percent, which was formerly the rate of rejection! Without spending any money, changing anything complicated, or changing any of the major steps in the process and using the same people who had always made the castings, we had turned the acceptance rate completely around. This was far beyond what anyone had hoped for when we started using MVT techniques. Additional refining experiments led to a greater than 95 percent rate of acceptable castings, and some fine tuning of the lessons we had learned further raised the rate of acceptable castings to more than 99 percent. During the last five years of the manufacturing line, no bad castings were produced at all.

This effort, which solved a critical problem in a vital weapons system at the height of the Cold War represents the birth of the MVT process. Although we published a white paper on the project for the Atomic Energy Commission, years passed before I formalized and refined the 12-step MVT process described in this book. Nevertheless, most of the 12 steps were utilized in this monumental accomplishment.

Beginning in 1969, we used MVT extensively in production and in research and development at the Nuclear Division of Union Carbide. We also applied MVT to areas such as training effectiveness, maintenance, product certification, and laboratory service. Eventually, I became the head of quality for the nuclear weapons facility in Oak Ridge, Tennessee, a 7,200-person organization.

MVT UNDERMINES CONVENTIONAL BUSINESS WISDOM

The MVT process begins with the idea that you can do better with the people, equipment, and processes you already have and you can do it quickly, without spending any money. In the course of going from 15 percent acceptable castings to 100 percent acceptable castings, we debunked the myth that you have to spend money to make money (or make improvements or progress).

Another common (albeit wrong) rule of thumb for solving critical business problems is to "gather the opinions of the best experts in the field and follow their advice." In this case, the best experts (the design engineers, the production managers, the materials experts) had ideas that would have taken time which we did not have and would have cost much more to implement, and we had no real guarantee that we would realize improved results. We did listen to the experts; but we also listened to everyone else involved in the process, right down to the front-line operators. In an MVT process, good ideas are just as likely to come from front-line employees as they are from experts, managers, or senior managers.

W. EDWARDS DEMING HELPS LAUNCH AN MVT TRAINING COMPANY

In 1982, W. Edwards Deming was the leading quality guru in the United States and was trying to educate American management about the power of statistical process control. I met Dr. Deming at one of his seminars and we became friends. I traveled to his home in Washington, DC, to discuss his philosophy of quality, and we carried on a regular correspondence. Dr. Deming was an intimidating figure, but I engaged him in many discussions on statistical thinking and enjoyed our dialogue. He convinced me to help spread his "gospel of quality" starting with the auto industry, because he felt that it was the most visible and influential industry and that ideas adopted there would be most likely to spread to the rest of the world. On Dr. Deming's recommendation, Ford employed me to train managers and suppliers in statistical thinking and quality improvement methods.

In late 1982, I developed a thick packet of statistical training curriculum that I hoped would be the foundation of a new training company called QualPro and that would allow me to teach statistical thinking and MVT to the business world full time. I drove to Washington, DC, with a friend to show the material to Dr. Deming and get his feedback. We sat nervously in his office on a Saturday morning as Dr. Deming thumbed through the pages. I remember the sinking feeling when he began reviewing the MVT material and his smile turned into a frown. He shook his head and said, "It's too complex." We left, and I worked day and night for six weeks to make the statistics as simple as possible for my future clients and trainees. Dr. Deming approved of the revised materials; he smiled, and QualPro was born.

For the first two years, Dr. Deming's referrals accounted for 90 percent of my business. The first seminars had about 20 attendees; but before the end of 1983, I was holding seminars in ballrooms with 120 to 150 attendees. It was more than I could handle alone, so I hired other process improvement experts who had worked with me at Union Carbide, including Art Hammer. We began teaching the methodology to many manufacturing companies. But, at the end of 1983, we surveyed participants from the seminars and were very disappointed in the findings. We found that while most seminar participants rated the seminars highly and left the seminar full of excitement and good intentions, few actually used the technique when they returned to their companies. Those who did try the technique applied it incorrectly and did not get good results. This was painful because I thought that I had done a good job in teaching these seminars. I knew that the technique was great; how could people not use it? And how could those people who did try to use it fail to succeed?

By the middle of 1984, I had decided that MVT training was not enough. I had to go out and help people use MVT. In 1985 and 1986, I spent at least 48 weeks per year on the road, helping people use the MVT process. I hired more people and trained them to teach the seminars, but I went directly to companies, showing them how to use MVT and generating one success story after another. First, I helped parts manufacturers including many automobile suppliers. I worked with small companies such as Associated Spring and Faber-Castell, and larger companies such as Ford and Boise Cascade. Our client roster later grew to include chemical companies such as Monsanto, Union Carbide, Rogers Corporation, and Copolymer (now DSM).

During this time, I found that it was much easier to train a person to teach a seminar than it was to train a person to improve a real-world process. In fact, I discovered it took years to train a person with a strong quantitative background to improve real-world processes.

Applying Multivariable Testing to Service Businesses

While we were working in the manufacturing plants, we learned that people in service organizations also wanted to improve or the manufacturing people felt that their service organizations needed to improve. We began using the MVT process in service organizations within manufacturing plants and even on human resources projects, logistics and transportation projects, and billing projects. One company's CEO, who had been a long-time friend, said, "You have helped us make better stuff, can you help us sell it better? And how about accounts receivable, can we make that better?" We showed that MVT could work on those processes as well. By 1990, we had many examples of dramatic process improvement on nonmanufacturing processes. In the mid-1990s, we had fantastic successes in the hospital industry. In 1997, we expanded into the retail industry. We now do more business in retail than in any other field. Our business is about 50 percent manufacturing and 50 percent service. Many of our service efforts involve marketing and sales processes.

Over the past 35 years, I have built on the basic concepts and have added many enhancements to the 12-step MVT process. The result is a practical problem-solving technique that is suited for today's dynamic business environment and results in superior business performance. In short, we have demonstrated that MVT can bring practical, fast, cost-free improvements to any process in any organization.

MVT, TAGUCHI METHODS, AND DESIGN OF EXPERIMENTS (DOE)

The MVT process that grew out of the Oak Ridge Nuclear Division has proven to be a breakthrough improvement methodology, but other statisticians and quality improvement experts have done important related work. In the 1980s, I gave many joint seminars at Ford and for Ford suppliers with Shin Taguchi, the son of Genechi Taguchi who developed a form of MVT called the Taguchi Method. Dr. Genechi Taguchi deserves a great deal of credit for getting a lot of experimentation done and producing results. The Taguchi Methods work because experimental design, even if applied inefficiently, is extremely powerful. However, the Taguchi Methods do not work nearly as well as the MVT process. The Taguchi Methods omit key steps that are in the MVT process, such as involving everyone in generating suggestions for improvement, creating the right environment, controlling the measurement system(s), performing the refining experimentation, and implementing the results. Also, what Taguchi presented was so complex that most managers and engineers could not understand the powerful implications and had trouble implementing it in real-world conditions.

Other good work has been done in an area of statistics called design of experiments (DOE), which is related to MVT but is much less powerful. DOE is the term usually used to describe small experiments with five or fewer factors. DOE methods are, in fact, used in one of the 12 steps in the MVT process, and DOE by itself sometimes produces good results. However, because only a small number of factors are investigated and 75 percent of them are likely to hurt or make no difference, the improvement is likely to be small or nonexistent.

BREAKTHROUGH IMPROVEMENTS

The MVT process typically yields dramatic breakthrough improvements—often beyond what anyone imagines. Using the MVT process to redesign one of our retail clients' catalogs produced a 60 percent improvement in sales. Applied to a call center, the MVT process generated a 25 percent increase in revenue per hour per sales representative. In many manufacturing situations, yields and throughput improved 50 percent or more—usually with little or no new money invested in the process. When one retail client utilized MVT on a sales process, it improved so dramatically that the client's stock became the best-performing stock on the New York Stock Exchange over a two-year period.

In more than 13,000 projects involving more than a thousand companies, MVT has never failed to identify actions that measurably improve results. As a famous nuclear scientist, Dr. John Googin, noted in the 1970s, "The only way the MVT process can fail is if there is not a single good idea in the whole organization." Fortunately, our experience indicates that this is never the case.

RAPID SUCCESSES

MVT successes often can be generated in very short periods. In the carbon-foam process mentioned earlier, the initial screening experiment required one shift, one day. Several manufacturing-process improvements in which the work was done in less than a week have been presented at QualPro MVT Symposiums over the years. Even in complex chemical processes, the MVT work can be done within a month.

A GREAT MORALE BOOSTER

Our experience over 22 years indicates that, in general, MVT does wonders for the morale of the organization. The fact that the process allows everyone who could possibly have worthwhile suggestions to make those suggestions is the key. Even if a person's idea is proven not to work, the person still feels as if he or she had a say and is much more likely to support the new findings.

In the 1980s, I utilized MVT in several companies that had militant unions. In every case, once we considered the union workers' suggestions for improvement, their attitudes improved and their interactions with management improved. Many times I have heard from front-line workers, "Well, this is the first time they've ever listened to us around here." In many instances, these employees would not speak up or make suggestions for improvement when management and technical people were present. When I met with them privately, however, they would make suggestions, eagerly await the test results, and invariably support the findings. Many times their ideas proved more effective than those coming from management or engineering. If everybody is allowed to make suggestions for improvement, we always get improved results, and the morale of the people in the organization always improves.

Surprising and Counterintuitive Solutions

We often find that surprising, counterintuitive suggestions provide the biggest sources of improved performance. For example, when we were working with a large chemical company, the workers on the production line said that they got better yields when they had more catalyst in the feed tank. The PhDs from R&D laughed at this, declaring it impossible. Nevertheless, we used the production workers' suggestion in the experiment. The amount of catalyst in the feed tank turned out to be the most important factor in increasing yield. A few months later, I saw the R&D people and several of their colleagues making a presentation on the theoretical reason that increased catalysts in the feed tank improved yields.

We have had hundreds of such examples.

MEET EVERY IMPORTANT BUSINESS CHALLENGE

The MVT process has worked in every organization on every process that we have encountered. We have improved processes such as emergency-room customer satisfaction, corporate Political Action Committee (PAC) contributions, foster-home availability for a state, corporate sales, corporate profits, manufacturing product characteristics, and billing errors using the basic MVT process. Our experience proves that the results of any process can be improved using MVT if two criteria are met: (1) the process has a measurable output and (2) the people in the organization have ideas about how to improve results.

CHAPTER 2

HOW MVT WORKS

*Using Data to Take the
Guesswork, Politics, and Emotions
Out of Major Business Decisions*

Business decisions cause businesses to survive or fail, careers to soar or tumble, shareholders to celebrate or withdraw, and workforces to expand or decrease. Good and bad business decisions do not impact just the businesses themselves; they impact the professional and personal lives of their managers and employees. They impact their shareholders and the customers who rely on their products and services. And yet, the data we have collected in the course of applying MVT show that 75 percent of important business decisions and business improvement ideas either have no impact on performance or actually hurt performance.

Our experience has shown that, when most executives are making big decisions and when they really need big results, the decision-making process typically goes something like this:

We start with an objective that we need to accomplish: raise sales, increase manufacturing throughput, reduce defects, or improve service levels (such as, shortening the time for installations or repairs or improving our overall level of customer satisfaction). So we pull together our staff, including line managers, subject-matter experts, professional staff, and so on; and we identify as many ideas as possible. We take that

list, go through it, and determine which of the potential actions we
have the time, energy, resources, and money to implement. We make
our best judgments. We vote. We express our opinions. . . . Maybe
we have a good, old-fashioned argument. Ultimately, the decision
comes down to a management judgment call based on all the available
information and advice. Gut feeling, the loudest voice, or individual
personalities, or political considerations often play a role. After the
executives and the experts determine the plan, the workforce determines the reality (what actually is done). We all think we are doing
the right thing.

The result? Sometimes our results improve somewhat. Occasionally, we hit a home run. Often, we see no impact. Once in a while,
things get somewhat better for a while and then backslide. The results of our efforts are often disappointing. Our great ideas usually do
not produce the impact which we desired or expected.

MVT and Accuracy of Business Decisions

QualPro and its clients have tested over 150,000 ideas in over 13,000
MVT projects during the past 22 years. Of all the business
improvement ideas that were tested, only about 25 percent (one in
four) actually produced improved results; 53 percent of the ideas
tested (about half) made no difference (and were a waste of everyone's time); and 22 percent (that would have been implemented otherwise) actually hurt the results that they were intended to help (See
Figure 2.1).

The really amazing finding supported by our data is that there is no
correlation between what people in the organization think will work
and what actually does work. In running MVT tests, QualPro has
asked people in an organization to rank proposed ideas from best to
worst. When the experiment is over, we can see the impact of each
idea, and the results are compared to the rankings that people sub-
mitted before the test was run. There is no relationship between their
rankings and the actual results. This does not mean that people in an
organization are not knowledgeable about their processes or that they
are unintelligent. It simply means that the business world is much

Figure 2.1   Of All Business Improvement Ideas . . .

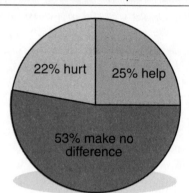

more complicated than most people realize. The lack of correlation between what people think will work and what does work has nothing
to do with the level of the people in the organization who make these
judgments. The experts are no better than the front-line workers or
senior executives in determining which ideas will improve results.
Here is an example:

> When Lowe's, the national home-improvement retailer, began run-
> ning MVT projects, it set up an internal contest. The project was
> aimed at improving the sales power of its advertising flyers in the
> Sunday newspapers. Twenty-eight different flyers were designed to
> test dozens of ideas for improving the sales "pull" of the flyers; these
> flyers were posted in Lowe's headquarters in North Wilkesboro,
> North Carolina. Everyone was given the chance to evaluate which
> flyers were going to be the best and the worst, and in what order
> (from 1 to 28).
>
> Carolina Panthers football tickets were the contest prize. Almost
> everybody participated, including marketing experts, experts from
> various functions throughout the company, administrative assistants,
> and purchasing agents. The winner was not a marketing expert. All
> the experience of the marketing experts did not help them find the
> best approach. The world in general—and the business environment
> in particular—is just too complex.

Here is another typical example of how a manager who was certain his improvement idea would work was proven wrong by MVT.

Bill McBee, the head of the Pactiv Hexacomb organization, makers of honeycomb packaging materials, spoke at a QualPro MVT Symposium in the spring of 2004 and told of an idea that he had come up with for improving results within his sales organization. He was certain that if each of his salespeople reported directly to him each week what their activities and results had been, they would be more disciplined and would improve their sales. The idea was put into an MVT experiment, and the salespeople reported their activities and results for the week to Bill. The test analysis showed that having salespeople report to Bill made their results *worse,* not better. However, Bill could not accept the finding, so another MVT experiment was scheduled. Bill said, "Well, maybe it's not enough for them to report the results to me—they have to know that I actually read their reports. That's what will motivate them." So he added another idea to the next experiment: when salespeople reported their results to him, he would respond to them and make comments or congratulations and encouragement. When the MVT results were tabulated for the second round of experimentation, Bill's idea still had no positive impact on sales performance; it did not help for the salespeople to report to him. Having to report was a hassle for them, and when Bill responded, it made things worse. Bill told us that he learned that no one can predict the results of an improvement idea on a reliable basis; only through testing and objective data are the results confirmed or not.

Even though we cannot know, without testing, which business ideas are the good ones, experience with more than 1,000 companies indicates that there is a virtually unlimited supply of practical, fast, and cost-free ideas in almost all organizations. Implementing just a few of these ideas and eliminating bad or irrelevant ideas and practices will result in enormous benefits.

The good news is that all MVT findings (powerful ideas, bad ideas, and those that do not matter) have great value. The test results precisely show the impact of every idea tested. This allows the one-fourth of the ideas that will actually help the business to become the focus of implementation efforts, avoiding huge amounts of wasted time and money on implementing the ideas that will not work. Eliminating the 22 percent of ideas that typically will produce harmful results will often cause actual improvement in a business process. This improvement is in addition to the tremendous value the business reaps from the good ideas that are implemented. Learning which ideas have no impact on your business can also be a source of powerful cost advantage. If you can do something in more than one way and it has no impact on your results, then you should do it the cheapest way, or the safest way, or the way that requires the least use of organizational energy. Let your competitors keep doing it the more inefficient way.

No one in a business can reliably predict which business ideas will work. MVT is powerful because it eliminates guesswork. The outcome of an MVT project is an objective measure of the impact of each idea and combination of ideas on important business measures. Management can make key decisions based on statistically valid data and facts rather than on opinions, instincts, and organizational clichés. Second, and just as important, MVT eliminates the emotions and politics often involved in decision making. MVT measures the impact of an idea, rather than its source. Because the MVT process solicits ideas from every level of the organization, the whole organization supports the results of the tests. Resistance to change is minimized, and the findings are accepted. Implementation becomes a much easier task than it would have been if the ideas had come from self-proclaimed experts, engineers, or even senior management.

THE 12-STEP MVT PROCESS

The MVT process involves 12 steps, regardless of the business, industry, or process being tested for improvement (Figure 2.2). A brief overview of each step follows.

Step 1: Choose a High-Payoff Goal and Create the Environment

An MVT project starts with someone in management, often senior management, identifying an important business goal—raising sales, increasing production, cutting costs—and deciding, "We are not just

Figure 2.2 QualPro's 12-Step MVT Process

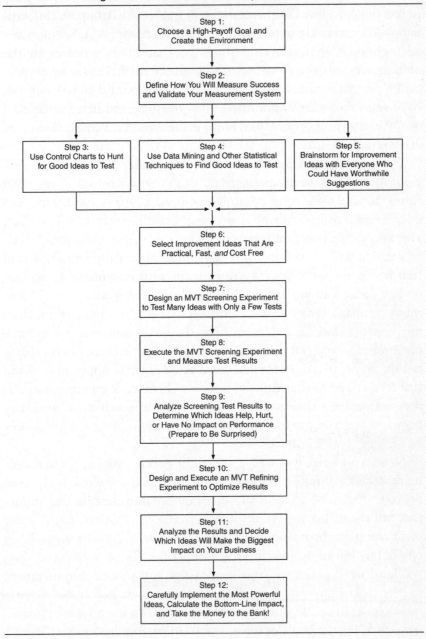

Step 1:
Choose a High-Payoff Goal and Create the Environment

Step 2:
Define How You Will Measure Success and Validate Your Measurement System

Step 3:
Use Control Charts to Hunt for Good Ideas to Test

Step 4:
Use Data Mining and Other Statistical Techniques to Find Good Ideas to Test

Step 5:
Brainstorm for Improvement Ideas with Everyone Who Could Have Worthwhile Suggestions

Step 6:
Select Improvement Ideas That Are Practical, Fast, *and* Cost Free

Step 7:
Design an MVT Screening Experiment to Test Many Ideas with Only a Few Tests

Step 8:
Execute the MVT Screening Experiment and Measure Test Results

Step 9:
Analyze Screening Test Results to Determine Which Ideas Help, Hurt, or Have No Impact on Performance (Prepare to Be Surprised)

Step 10:
Design and Execute an MVT Refining Experiment to Optimize Results

Step 11:
Analyze the Results and Decide Which Ideas Will Make the Biggest Impact on Your Business

Step 12:
Carefully Implement the Most Powerful Ideas, Calculate the Bottom-Line Impact, and Take the Money to the Bank!

going to *hope* we find the best way to meet this goal; we are going to test our best ideas in the real world and let the data pick the winners." To create the environment for a successful MVT, the manager chooses an important objective that really matters to the organization, such as: "We want to improve market share by 10 percent," or "We want to improve plant throughput by 25 percent," or "We want this year's sales to be 20 percent better than last year's," or "We want to improve sales by 20 percent and profitability by 30 percent."

Then, preferably within a few days, the message is relayed to the organization that "We are going to do this!" However, one of the great things about MVT is that you do not need a healthy, receptive, and open organizational culture to successfully implement MVT. In fact, a good organizational culture is often a *result* of successful process improvement with MVT, *not a requirement* for it. In the 1980s, I kept hearing people say, "We have to get our culture right before we can do any process improvement." I thought, "That's ridiculous." I saw many companies put extensive effort into trying to obtain open, flexible, performance-oriented cultures; they expected that process improvement would just follow naturally. But in my experience, that is not the way it works. However, when people help to generate the ideas that MVT uses to dramatically improve their work environment and they realize they have made a major contribution to the effort, they begin to feel and act like members of a winning team. This is how MVT can change cultures.

Next, you need to involve the right people, including management, technical staff, and those who actually do the work within the process. You need to motivate them by communicating the importance of the effort.

Training can be minimal if your organization is not trying to learn MVT but is simply looking for a one-time fix to a problem. You will also need coaching from a statistics and process improvement expert who knows how to design advanced multivariable experiments for testing. If your organization wants to learn how to implement MVT on a broader basis, the training required ranges from a few hours for an executive, to one day for a front-line worker, and up to two three-day sessions for those wanting to learn the method-ology in more depth. Finally, you have to set up an action plan and monitor progress. (There is more detail on this and other steps in Part II of this book.)

Step 2: Define How You Will Measure Success and Validate Your Measurement System

Next, you need to carefully identify and define the key measures of success for your objective. In most instances, there is only one, such as "reduced customer waiting time." Often, there will be other mea-sures that you need to ensure that your process changes have no inad-vertent side effects, but these are of secondary importance. For example, if the primary objective is to increase manufacturing throughput, you will also monitor defects to ensure that you do not increase defects when you use MVT to test dozens of alternatives for changing the process. If you are working to increase sales, you will monitor profit margins to make sure that they do not suffer.

Now study the proposed measurement-gathering systems to ensure that the measurements are valid. We have learned to assume that mea-surements are bad until they are proven otherwise. You have to ensure that measurements are accurate, not biased high or low, and that they are precise and can recognize small changes.

Step 3: Use Control Charts to Hunt for Good Ideas to Test

The next step is to use statistical process control charts to examine the historical data from a business process. Here you are looking for any possible direct causes of uncontrolled variation (for example, factors that cause sales to shoot up or plummet, or factors in a production process that cause output to significantly increase or decrease). In many cases, studying control charts helps us identify the most important fac-tors to test using MVT—the factors that prove to play the biggest role in dramatically improving a process.

Step 4: Use Data Mining and Other Statistical Techniques to Find Good Ideas to Test

The MVT process also uses data mining techniques and other multiple variable analysis techniques to analyze historical data before performing the MVT experiments. Once again, the question being answered here is: Are there conditions in the past which may have led to good or bad results? As in Step 3, the objective is to identify high potential factors for MVT experimentation. (By the way, it is important not to jump to the conclusion that the possible improvement factors identified in Steps 3 and 4 are "the answer.") The MVT Process requires that these improvement factors be tested to see if they really work under real-world conditions, in combination with other factors.

Step 5: Brainstorm for Improvement Ideas with Everyone Who Could Have Worthwhile Suggestions

The MVT process is unusual in that it includes "everyone who might have a worthwhile idea." We conduct brainstorming sessions with everyone in the organization who touches the processes involved and who possibly could have worthwhile suggestions for improvement. It is important to involve every level in the organization, from executives to front-line workers. In addition, we include suppliers in the process—sometimes even customers. All are invited to submit ideas for improving something. The objective is to generate many ideas for improvement (at least 50). We use a structured process (more details on this in Part II) to ensure that everyone participates but no one dominates.

Step 6: Select Improvement Ideas That Are Practical, Fast, and Cost Free

We take all the ideas generated in Steps 3, 4, and 5 and categorize them to determine exactly which ideas will be tested in the MVT screening experiment. We separate the ideas that are practical, fast, and cost free from those that are not. (During the previous brain-storming step, we set the expectation with all participants that only practical, fast, and cost-free ideas will be tested in the initial screening MVT, and that the remaining ideas will be shelved for later consideration.) The only ideas that we take forward are those that are practical, fast, *and* cost free, and we test every idea that meets these three criteria. This results in ideas that are easy to test and, if appropriate, easy to implement. We want only solutions that can be implemented immediately, with no capital investment.

The terms are defined as follows:

- *Practical:* We define an idea as practical if the people who do the work indicate that the idea can be done with no more effort than what they have been expending. If they say that it would take more effort and be harder to do than what they have been doing, we say it is not practical.
- *Fast:* The focus is on immediate results. An idea is considered fast if it is quick to test and implement (that is, it can be implemented in the short term, such as next Monday or the first of the month). If it cannot be implemented in a timely manner, we define it as not fast. If you can make things happen quickly and the results are significant, you can find the time to explore more incremental changes that help to sustain long-term success.
- *Cost free:* An idea is considered cost free if it can be implemented without raising costs. This means that it would cost no more than what the organization is currently doing—not one dime more! If it will require any capital or increased operating expense, the idea is disqualified.

If an idea does not meet the criteria to be deemed practical, fast, and cost free, it is shelved. We may consider the idea later if we do not get enough improvement with the first batch of improvement ideas that we test. However, MVT results over the past 22 years indicate that, of all the improvement ideas that worked, four-fifths of them are methods changes that require no capital expenditure and no increase in operating expenses.

Step 7: Design an MVT Screening Experiment to Test Many Ideas with Only a Few Tests

The heart of the MVT process is the MVT screening experiment. The screening MVT is designed to test, very efficiently, all the practical, fast, and cost-free potential changes in the process to determine which ones help, hurt, or do not make a difference. The MVT screening design is a series of tests that "activates" or "turns on" about half of the ideas, while leaving the others "turned off" or in their status quo condition. Each test is a different, statistically engineered combination of ideas. Using very advanced statistical and mathematical concepts (for example, matrix algebra), only a small portion of the many potential combinations of ideas are selected for testing. For example, if you were to test all combinations of 30 ideas, over a billion tests would be necessary. Fortunately, with MVT only 32 tests are necessary to calculate the specific impact of each idea, individually and in combination with other ideas, on each measure.

The MVT design also determines the right size and duration of the experiment, whether some tests are to be repeated, and the logistics of running the tests.

Step 8: Execute the MVT Screening Experiment and Measure Test Results

Screening MVT tests are put in place for short periods of time, and the real-world results of each test are measured. Careful monitoring is necessary to ensure conformance with the conditions defined by each test (some ideas "turned on" and others "off").

Step 9: Analyze Screening Test Results to Determine Which Ideas Help, Hurt, or Have No Impact on Performance (Prepare to Be Surprised)

We use a sophisticated (proprietary) procedure to calculate the impact of each tested idea, independent of the others, for each important measure. We also uncover evidence of synergies between ideas. Qual-Pro experience indicates that about 70 percent of the total improvement achieved by the MVT process is revealed by the screening MVT experiment. Very often, the ideas that our clients are most convinced will impact business performance prove to have no impact or actually hurt performance. Small, simple changes to any process, especially in combination with other small changes, very often have a huge impact on performance.

Step 10: Design and Execute an MVT Refining Experiment to Optimize Results

The refining MVT experiment takes what we know and/or suspect from the screening experiment and further investigates to determine more optimum conditions. From the design standpoint, most of the techniques that are used here can be described as classical design of experiments (DOE) that many engineers are familiar with. Classical DOE typically tests all combinations of five or fewer potential process changes. The major difference here is that the refining MVT experiment is DOE with the "right" test ideas. They are the right ideas because the screening MVT experiment has quantifiably shown that they improve results. In contrast, DOE ideas come from the opinions of the experimenter or other experts. As we mentioned earlier, our data from thousands of experiments show that improvement ideas generated by experimenters or experts either have no impact or actually hurt the process 75 percent of the time.

About 30 percent of the total improvement achieved by the MVT process is typically obtained through the findings of MVT refining experiments.

Step 11: Analyze the Results and Decide Which Ideas Will Make the Biggest Impact on Your Business

We review the implementation options with key managers and determine exactly what actions will be taken. Although MVT evaluates the impact of each improvement idea on every measure that matters to the business, a "what-if" process allows management to balance the trade-offs involved in implementing ideas or combinations of ideas to decide which will have the most powerful overall business impact.

Step 12: Carefully Implement the Most Powerful Ideas, Calculate the Bottom-Line Impact, and Take the Money to the Bank!

MVT experimentation typically is performed on only one process or one part of an operation or organization. After management decides which ideas will be implemented, the ideas must be rolled out across the entire operation or organization. It is critical that a monitoring system be established to ensure compliance with the new procedure. This ensures that the organization realizes the same dramatic benefits that were achieved during testing.

FINANCIAL IMPACT

Figures 2.3 and 2.4 are two examples of the type of improvement achievable through the MVT process. As the figures illustrate, the payoff often begins during the MVT experiments, even before the final MVT findings are determined.

As Figure 2.3 shows, a major chemical manufacturing client of QualPro used the MVT process to increase output. Output increased $10 million per year while costs were reduced $3 million per year— a total bottom-line impact of $13 million per year.

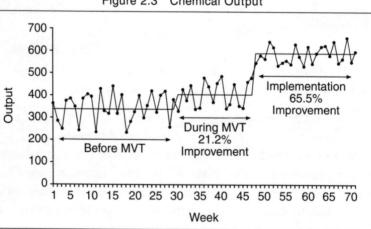

Figure 2.3   Chemical Output

Figure 2.4   Retail Sales

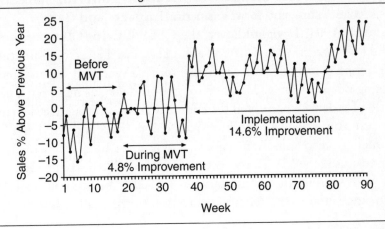

Figure 2.4 shows a nationwide retailing client of QualPro who used the MVT process to raise sales by 14.6 percent. (Within a year, the stock price increased more than elevenfold.)

MVT AS SCIENCE

The MVT methodology works because it is good science. MVT determines what to test, how to test it, and how to measure the results; and it manages the experiments to ensure that the results are reliable. When you implement a change that is verified by MVT analysis, you know that the change will produce results and exactly how much the change will affect your results. There is no substitute for reliable, understandable data when making important business decisions.

The Evans Clay Story

Executives are rewarded for making slow, steady, incremental progress in their organizations. They are called "good stewards" and "steady leaders." But when an executive achieves breakthrough results, everyone in the organization, from the boardroom to the client/customer interface, gets excited about the organization and its future.

MVT produces breakthrough results more often than not. Sometimes MVT saves a company from extinction.

In early 1994, Dwight Glover, the CEO of Evans Clay, one of the leading producers of air-floated kaolin clay, faced a terrible situation. The company had not been profitable for five years and was in danger of going out of business. Demand for the product was high, but a production bottleneck prevented the company from meeting that demand. The company was forced to buy from competitors and resell at a loss in order to keep important clients. Dwight set up a seven-member team that used the MVT process to solve this problem, saving the company and winning the prestigious *USA Today* Quality Cup in 1996. Following is the *USA Today*'s description of the challenge:

> Evans Clay operates a plant in McIntyre, Georgia, that dries and grinds clay trucked in from nearby mines. The processed clay is used to strengthen fiberglass used in boats and auto parts, and paper manufacturers use the clay as a low-cost filler and extender.
>
> The problem: One of the plant's two mills consistently produced fewer tons of finished product than the other. "We had two machines, which should have been identical, and one was behaving very differently, and it was the newer of the two," says Camp Bacon, vice president of operations.
>
> The team met once a week. The first few meetings were devoted to brainstorming. Every member, from the shift foreman to production superintendent, offered ideas. Some suggested changing the size of the grinding hammers. Others said the amount of air pressure should be changed. And several believed that the bottleneck had something to do with the mill's dust collectors, which capture dust created during the grinding process and release clean air into the atmosphere.
>
> Suggestions that cost money were discarded. By the end of the sessions, the team had 11 ideas to test.
>
> The next step was more complicated than simply adjusting a few air-pressure nozzles. The team had to test different combinations, such as testing a new hammer configuration while increasing air pressure. After numerous trials, the team narrowed the experiment down to two related variables: the dust-collector bags and the "horn," an instrument used to shoot sonic blasts into the bags, dislodging dust and increasing air flow.

That led the team to replace Polydacron dust-collector bags with bags made from GORE-TEX®. GORE-TEX lets more air flow through the dust collectors, resulting in fewer clogged bags. The team also changed the frequency of the horn blasts, which helped increase the amount of air flowing through the system.

Average daily production from the mill rose to 150 tons, up from 96 tons before the experiment . . . and the company . . . turned a profit for the first time in five years. . . . (*USA Today,* 1996)

Dwight Glover believes that this MVT project saved the workers' jobs and the company.

WHY MVT IS MUCH MORE EFFECTIVE THAN OTHER METHODS

The MVT methodology is different in several key ways:

- *MVT is fast.* The MVT process itself is very fast; people routinely move from analysis to experiment to implementation in a matter of days or weeks, and frequently see positive results before implementation is complete. Also, the MVT produces very large results at amazing speed. By stacking up the numerous ideas that work, you make big results possible. By avoiding those results that hurt, you can make the results even larger. When you take the combination of these two actions, implementing only those results that help and actively avoiding those results that hurt, the impact can be enormous.

- *MVT makes the organization more efficient.* The MVT process identifies solutions that are practical, fast, and cost free to execute. It eliminates ideas that are difficult, expensive, or time consuming to test. If an idea would increase operating costs or entail capital expenditures, it is not even tested. MVT projects seek out improvements that the organization can make right away, using its same equipment and people.

- *MVT eliminates wasted effort.* Because 75 percent of the ideas to improve a company's results do not help, 75 percent of improvement efforts are wasted. They are wasted on the 53 percent of ideas that do not matter and on the 22 percent of ideas that actually hurt the result. Eliminating wasted effort improves business results with less energy and money expended.

- *MVT is better science.* The MVT methodology tests many factors simultaneously; with time-to-market and competitive pressures, an organization will never have enough time, resources, or discipline to do enough one-factor testing to answer the really important questions. The MVT method allows you to test far more factors in a fraction of the time to obtain accurate, verifiable results.

- *MVT boosts organizational morale.* The improvement ideas come from the people involved in the process or problem, as well as many others, and employees at all levels feel great about being involved in successful projects. There is no better team building event than a successful MVT project.

- *MVT provides organizational focus.* We sometimes hear from prospective clients that they are too busy to use MVT—that things are too chaotic or they have too much on their plate to embark on an improvement process. We have found that MVT provides focus for chaotic organizations by scientifically narrowing the range of business options to the few best ideas on which management needs to focus. Management can stop directing resources, organizational energy, and time to other issues. The overall focus becomes (1) implementing those 25 percent of the ideas that help and (2) avoiding those 22 percent of the ideas that hurt. (Some organizational energy does need to be focused on the ideas that were tested and proved damaging, because these ideas are probably being used in some part of the organization.)

The CEO of a provider of healthcare products and services learned this lesson from MVT and, as a result, began focusing his time on initiatives that MVT proved would make a bigger impact on his company. Like Bill McBee in the earlier example, the CEO believed that, to get his salespeople to sell a new product, the key component would be his personal intervention. He wrote personal notes to each salesperson, telling him or her how important the new product was going to be to the success of the company, and explaining the benefits customers would receive. Through MVT experimentation, the CEO found that his personal intervention actually hurt rather than helped. MVT identified a number of key tactics for successfully introducing new products (for example, providing family vacations for successful salespersons as a sales incentive). Taking time and energy to communicate with salespeople was not the best use of the CEO's time and, in fact, was counterproductive.

In summary, MVT experiments show that decision making the old-fashioned way is not good enough in today's business environment. Businesses cannot afford to be wrong 75 percent of the time. They cannot afford to spend 22 percent of their improvement energies on ideas that hurt results. The competitive advantage that is provided by fact-based decision making and by focusing on ideas that are known winners is immense. No organization should let mere judgment calls, opinions, instincts, clichés, or best guesses influence its future. The only reliable way to avoid these kinds of all-too-human tendencies is to use the MVT process to identify and implement your organization's most powerful business ideas.

CHAPTER 3

USING MVT TO INCREASE SALES, CUT COSTS, AND IMPROVE CUSTOMER SATISFACTION

Stories from Citibank, DuPont, Williams-Sonoma, and Others

Companies often become consumed by issues that are urgent and that need to be addressed in the short term. These issues may not, however, be truly high priorities from a financial or a strategic standpoint. MVT probably should not be utilized to address such issues. MVT is a very powerful tool that works best when directed toward large, important business problems that have a significant financial impact.★

MVT is able to improve the financial performance of an organization in three major ways: (1) increased sales, (2) reduced costs, and (3) improved customer satisfaction.

★ QualPro places such a strong importance on the financial impact of MVT projects that we have built it into our internal bonus system. To earn a bonus for a successful project, QualPro consultants must ensure that a project achieves at least a fivefold return for the client in the first year and each year thereafter. That is our standard of success. Anything less than a fivefold return on investment for the client results in no bonus for our consultants.

INCREASED SALES

MVT has a long history of helping companies increase sales by improving retail store sales or salesforce effectiveness. It has been used to increase call-center effectiveness, both on inbound and outbound telephone calls. It has been used to improve direct-mail results and advertising effectiveness in television, radio, and print media. Even in manufacturing operations, sales may be improved by increasing the output of a manufacturing process. Increasing production automatically increases sales when there is a market for the additional product.

CarMax, a nationwide superstore for used cars, began as a subsidiary of Circuit City. When QualPro began working with Circuit City, CarMax's performance was very poor. Its stock had gone public in an initial public offering several years previously and, with CarMax's poor financial performance, the stock had languished, dropping to very low levels. When Circuit City began to use MVT, the chairman, Richard Sharp, recognized the potential of MVT to help turn around the sales of the CarMax operation. An MVT project was launched, two rounds of MVT experimentation were performed, and the findings were implemented. Sales rose immediately and dramatically. CarMax's stock price rose elevenfold after two quarters of improved performance. (It was also the best performing stock on the New York Stock Exchange during the following year.)

Williams-Sonoma also uses MVT to improve financial performance. They increased the effectiveness of their catalogs by testing ideas such as cover design changes, blow-in cards, new graphics, "lifestyle" illustrations, more/less density on pages, and order form enhancements. Williams-Sonoma also improved call center sales with MVT. More detailed examples of the use of MVT to improve sales follow.

Southwestern Bell Telephone has used MVT to improve many of its sales processes. One example is in its sales operations, selling telephone switches in business-to-business sales situations. This story was described in *Sales and Marketing Management* magazine. It started with a state sales manager attending a QualPro seminar. He recognized the potential for MVT to help him improve his organization's sales results and knew that this was very important to his career. His sales quota had been increased 40 percent over the previous year, and he needed to achieve that objective with no new sales resources. In about three months of MVT experimentation, he was able to identify critical actions for immediate implementation. Keys to raising sales included the involvement of a design consultant in sales calls, the use of demos in certain situations, a specially targeted calling plan, and a scripted contact outline. Surprisingly, many ideas that he thought were most likely to improve results including more sales calls per day, flexible pricing, extended office hours, special mailings, and a number of other "good ideas," actually added no value at all or even hurt. Before the end of the year, his group's sales had more than tripled.

Other state sales managers questioned the accomplishment saying that, given the previous poor performance of that state, achieving substantial improvement was no surprise. Executives of Southwestern Bell decided to test that theory and used MVT in their best state. The results were amazing; even in the best sales operation, MVT improved sales by 58 percent. Several of the solutions implemented were the same in the two different sales operations, but some things that worked in the first state did not translate successfully to the second. Conversely, several new actions were identified that worked in the second state but not the first.

In a 2004 QualPro Symposium, Citibank executives described how they used MVT to improve call center effectiveness. They had hoped MVT would help them achieve a stretch goal of a 50- to-75-basis-point increase in net sales. They actually achieved a 205-basis-point increase that translated into millions of dollars per year. Actions identified by the MVT process showed Citibank how they could significantly increase their net sales rate . . . and at the same time reduce call-handling time and increase employee satisfaction.

Ten improvement ideas, generated in part by call center representatives themselves, were tested across several sites:

1. Sales coach availability.
2. Unit managers monitoring calls.
3. Use of lead associates as coaches.
4. Operations manager availability.
5. Use of unit managers as coaches.
6. Increased time off the phone for call center representatives.

7. Unit manager availability.
8. New hire coaching.
9. Self-paced training for call center representatives (via taped calls).
10. Self-paced training for call center representatives (via Web).

The MVT tests showed that the most powerful factors leading to increased sales were: monitoring by unit managers, increased availability of operations managers, use of lead associates as coaches, and self-paced training (items 2, 3, 4, 9, and 10).

Kamran Jahanshahi, senior vice president and director of quality for CitiCards, also described the value of MVT as a catalyst for culture change, saying,

> One of the nicest surprises was the impact of MVT on the environment and the culture of the organization. . . . We heard a lot from our associates across all the sites that were participating in the MVT process that the value they gained was, not only from the fact that they were heard or their ideas were taken into account, but also the time we took to develop them and to nurture them and coach them.

Numerous manufacturers have used MVT to increase the output of their manufacturing facilities to satisfy market needs. This increased output directly results in increased sales revenues. One example is DuPont's Parkersburg, West Virginia, operation. Its MVT effort allowed DuPont, with no increase in operating expenses or capital costs, to double the run life of the polymerizers that produce Delrin, a major DuPont product. By testing the ideas of DuPont operators and implementing the best ones through the MVT, production was increased by 15 percent, while production expenses decreased by $8 million, which translated to over $26 million annually. The Parkersburg story is told in detail in Part III.

REDUCED COSTS

The second way in which MVT helps organizations to improve their financial performance is by reducing costs. MVT frequently has been used to improve the efficiency of things ranging from advertising to chemical processes to paper machines to labor. It also has been used frequently to reduce waste, to decrease defects, and to reduce rework. In a 2004 QualPro Symposium, the head of the Hexacomb division of Pactiv Corporation, Bill McBee, described his organization's use of MVT to reduce waste by half in its Trenton, Illinois, manufacturing facility for honeycomb packing materials while cutting setup time by 35 percent. By varying the number of tension lines, the tension on the lines, the core line speed, and the steam pressure, the company not only reduced waste but also increased uptime and lowered setup times.

In another example, a spokesperson for Deluxe Corporation described Deluxe Corporation's reduction of wasted capacity in the printing of checks. Deluxe is one of the largest check printers in the world; using MVT, it was able to reduce waste by $11 million as a result of changes in its production scheduling, staffing strategies, and the type of paper stock it used. The drop in waste was so dramatic that the recycler, who hauled off the wasted paper, suggested Deluxe was funneling wasted paper to another recycler!

Scott Gray, plant manager of DuPont's LaPorte, Texas, agricultural chemicals operation, described his use of MVT to reduce costs. He told us that continual use of MVT techniques over an eight-year period enabled him to reduce his costs to the point that he was successfully competing in China, against Chinese-made products, and beating the competitors on price. This accomplishment was achieved through dozens of MVT projects that increased manufacturing yields, improved product quality, improved performance of the waste-treatment facility (to prevent a $30 million capital investment), decreased maintenance costs, and reduced equipment failures. Scott also stated that he had never budgeted for MVT expenditures, training, or consulting. He said that he had received a 20- to 25-fold return on his MVT investments, within the same fiscal year, throughout his eight years of using MVT.

IMPROVED CUSTOMER SATISFACTION

The third way that MVT can help increase an organization's financial performance is by improving customer satisfaction. Improving customer satisfaction drives long-term sales and builds revenue volume by increasing penetration in the marketplace. MVT improves customer satisfaction by enhancing product design and improving the quality of products. Additionally, MVT frequently has been used to optimize service levels and even to improve the ability of companies to react to service failures.

For example, MVT was used by a Midwestern hospital to improve patient satisfaction with emergency room care. MVT proved that separating the children's waiting area from the adults' (providing separate but appropriate settings for both adults and youngsters) and using a "fast track" check-in process for nonemergency patients made a big difference in customer satisfaction.

A second example involved a manufacturer of plastic containers that held syrup for fountain soft drinks. The problem was that these containers were chronically leaking and creating serious messes. The manufacturers of the soft-drink syrup were very unhappy and were threatening to withdraw their orders. This would have been a disaster for the container-manufacturing firm that would have lost over $100 million in revenue. There were two sources of leaks: weld failures and poorly sealing spigots. As the result of several MVT experiments over a period of a few weeks, the manufacturer was able to identify two very subtle changes in its welding process (increased electrode pressure and an alternative fitting) that dramatically strengthened the plastic welds that were the sources of the leaks. In separate MVT experiments, the company developed an improved spigot that virtually eliminated sealing problems. The spigot improvements resulted from a combination of three actions: a 1 percent change in the size of one component, changing the corner angle of one part, and the addition of a chemical additive to the source material of the spigot cover. Immediately after implementation of the MVT findings, the company's customer complaints about leaks went to zero. Not a single leak complaint was received during the next two years.

Another customer-satisfaction example came from SBC-Ameritech, the "Baby Bell" telephone company for the midwestern United States. Ameritech's ability to install and repair telephones on a timely basis had deteriorated because of weather problems and other operational circumstances. Its backlog of installation and repair orders had grown to a point that it was receiving very negative publicity because of the long delays that customers were experiencing in getting service. A very large MVT process, involving several states and over 10,000 Ameritech employees, discovered the right combination of actions to be taken including: (1) resetting the time interval for truck dispatches for new service and repairs of "affected" service and (2) using job aids in service centers to reduce unnecessary dispatches. Ameritech implemented the solutions and was able to rapidly reduce the backlog by half, to the best level ever. This level, which previously was believed to be impossibly low, has been maintained for several years.

American Express used MVT to improve its process for preventing customer attrition. Like many credit-card operations, American Express evaluates customer usage of cards in order to identify customers who may be on the verge of canceling services and/or moving to another credit-card company. It then calls customers in an effort to prevent the cancellations. Using MVT, American Express tested potential solutions, including using different call scripting, using sales goals, changing the type of questioning during calls, implementing different card offers, and changing the nature of follow-up communications. Four helpful actions were identified that dealt with call flow, communications during the call and after the call, and some competitive positioning during the call. The changes to the process resulted in an 18 percent reduction in customer attrition, a 7 percent increase in credit card spending, a 12 percent increase in transaction volume, and a 5 percent increase in loyalty program participation.

IMPROVED ORGANIZATIONAL CULTURE

MVT improves organizational culture by raising morale, increasing innovation, and building a can-do attitude.

MVT raises morale because it involves the entire workforce in finding solutions to important problems. Everyone has a chance to suggest possible solutions. The criteria for categorizing ideas are explained to all at the beginning of the process, so everyone knows why certain ideas are selected for testing—management gets no special treatment. Then, when the MVT is completed and the best suggestions are implemented, results are improved. It works every time, and success breeds success. Broad involvement, accompanied by large, timely successes, improves the satisfaction of the entire workforce.

At the Calvert City, Kentucky, site of International Specialty Products, MVT helped to build a bridge between management and the union. A long history of poor relations was turned around as both management and the union viewed MVT as a way to work together to improve plant performance. DuPont also had a similar experience. At one site, an hourly employee, making a presentation at a QualPro Symposium, said, "Before MVT, people were viewed as if they could not even think—as if they left their brains outside the fence when they came to work." He went on to say, "Now the workforce feels like they own the process." Another DuPont employee who worked in the environmental compliance area said that his group had always been viewed as a useless overhead expense. He felt that using MVT to improve the problem-solving effectiveness of his group helped turn that image around and said, in colorful language, "If you have never made the trip from the overhead scum to the competitive advantage, you should. . . . It is quite a thrill!"

MVT improves corporate culture by promoting innovation. When MVT is used in an organization, employees learn that there is no such thing as a bad idea. Initially, all ideas that are simple, fast, and cheap to implement are welcomed and treated equally. Also, the testing efficiency of MVT allows "wild" ideas to be included in experiments as long as they meet the three criteria. This results in big surprises and counterintuitive solutions. An environment of innovation also is promoted because MVT tends to build on itself. MVT findings often stimulate a whole new set of ideas to be included in the next MVT experiment. QualPro has learned that organizations sometimes struggle to come up with enough ideas the first time they use MVT. People in the organization may worry that all the good ideas will be exhausted. However, as an organization performs more MVTs, the quantity and quality of improvement ideas brought forward grow rather than decline.

Rick Ray, vice president of BASF's pharmaceutical operations, described another example. As his company embarked on its MVT efforts, BASF employees were concerned whether they could identify enough improvement ideas that met FDA regulations. After going through the MVT brainstorming process, however, they came up with 200 suggestions, all of which met FDA requirements.

Some people have expressed concern that the MVT process attempts to apply science to an art, such as advertising, and might stifle creativity. The experience of those using MVT has been exactly the opposite. Lowe's and many other companies that have performed MVT in the area of advertising found that "creative" advertising people actually embraced MVT. It really allowed them to demonstrate the value of their creativity by measuring the precise impact of their ideas on sales and profitability.

MVT enhances corporate culture by helping to establish a can-do attitude. This is a result of the fact that MVT works on virtually any challenge. The continual successes of MVT build confidence that any problem can be solved. The can-do attitude is reinforced by the involvement of all organizational levels in the process, and a team sense of excitement for improving performance is created. MVT also helps to establish a broader ownership of the process, because everyone's ideas are solicited. The improvement of results does not fall on the shoulders of a small group of employees.

An example of MVT's effectiveness in building a can-do attitude is found in DuPont's pigment operations in De Lisle, Mississippi, that had been working for 20 years to reduce the occurrence of black specks in white pigments. Lack of success over such a long period of time resulted in the belief that the level of black specks was as low as it could be. Using employee suggestions and MVT experiments, DuPont was able, in just a few months, to reduce the incidence of black specks by almost half—a level that no one believed possible. This showed the plant that, with MVT, they could break through their old thinking about what was and was not possible.

CHAPTER 4

MVT COMPARED TO SIX SIGMA AND OTHER POPULAR IMPROVEMENT APPROACHES

Business executives often must consider a variety of options when implementing a business improvement approach. The MVT process typically yields much more powerful results than any of the other improvement approaches that are popular today. Following are brief descriptions of several currently popular approaches and a comparison of each to the MVT process.

SIX SIGMA

The objective of the approach known as Six Sigma is to reduce direct cost by decreasing defects and errors to six sigma frequency (3.4 per million). This objective is accomplished by getting large numbers of employees to use statistical tools based on a four-step framework (measure, analyze, improve, and control) in order to improve the processes with which they work. Typically, employees are trained in the use of a wide array of statistical tools by means of a cascading teaching approach. An external Six Sigma expert trains "master black belts." The master black belts then train black, green, and yellow belts. After several weeks of classroom training and, possibly, a practice project (depending on the level of belt), employees launch their process improvement efforts. The objective is for the methodology and systems thinking to become a part of the company culture, and processes to be continually and perpetually improved.

Like many other business improvement approaches, Six Sigma has some fundamental weaknesses that may not be obvious.

- Six Sigma typically underestimates the amount of training required to become an effective Six Sigma black belt or process improvement expert. Internal training is often performed by black belts who themselves have only been exposed to four to five weeks of classroom training and a practice project. If any guidance is provided to newly trained persons attempting projects, it is provided by these process-improvement novices. The reality is that process improvement competence cannot be developed in only a few weeks or even a few months of Six Sigma training. Six Sigma black belt process improvement novices may get the low-hanging fruit (that is, the obvious successes), but they will not be able to take the company to a whole new level of performance. Just as learning to use a hammer and saw does not make a master carpenter, learning to create flow charts and control charts or to perform t-tests and F-tests does not make a process improvement expert. In contrast, an MVT improvement project can be implemented in an organization with very little employee and management training, provided the organization has the assistance of a seasoned process improvement expert with advanced statistical training in MVT. This competence can also be developed internally but the training process may take several years.
- There is no assurance of a high success rate. The Six Sigma methodology lays out a very loosely structured path. Black belts are taught a wide variety of statistical tools and are given great latitude in deciding when to use each tool. This loosely organized methodology and the limited training experience provided combine to create a questionable success rate.
- The tools used in Six Sigma are not powerful. A look at the American Society for Quality (ASQ) black belt curriculum reveals that the topics taught are simple statistical methods and statistical process-control techniques. In our experience, these methods yield about 10 percent of the total process improvement in a project, with MVT accounting for 90 percent.
- A tremendous upfront outlay of time and money is required. In a large organization, thousands of people are trained, tens of

thousands of hours of organizational time and energy are absorbed, and millions of dollars of direct and indirect costs are incurred.

- With the organizational pressure on managers to do Six Sigma, they often feel compelled to undertake improvement projects that do not have a high potential payoff just so they can say they are doing something. A lot of activity is often wasted on projects with low potential.

Despite these concerns, Six Sigma has helped many companies. I do not mean to discourage the use of statistical methods in organizations. Their use can enhance communication within a company and result in some improvement in operations. However, most top managers I have talked to are not overwhelmed by their Six Sigma results. Let me quote one manager who is well acquainted with both approaches.

This vice president, in charge of manufacturing for one of Qual-Pro's chemical clients, had worked for General Electric for 19 years. He became very familiar with GE's Six Sigma program. At the 2004 QualPro Symposium in Orlando, Florida, he said:

Let me talk a little bit about the QualPro MVT process and Six Sigma. QualPro's MVT process delivers results, and I would say Six Sigma does, too. It's been successful. . . . Motorola and GE wouldn't do it if it didn't deliver results. So there is no argument there. The QualPro MVT process requires discipline, and Six Sigma requires discipline to a fault, as I will talk about later. It's all about discipline there. Here is where we start to get different. The QualPro MVT process is fast. We had results in three months without pushing hard. Six Sigma, in three months, you might have gotten your organization identified, and maybe not even named your black belts or your green belts, or talked about the process. It is just very slow. It is extremely slow, in my opinion. I have been there. I know once it gets going it delivers results, but it takes too long, and you lose a lot of people in the process of getting it up and running. The QualPro MVT process is very practical. You just go out and do it. You train the people that need to be trained. You only train them in what they need to know and then you go do the project. You don't have people who get training and then six months later get asked to use it. They are using it right away. So GE is bureaucratic. You go through the three- or four-week training to be a black belt or green belt. You might get involved in a project. When you do, you might have forgotten what you learned. A lot of different sign-offs on each of the twelve steps—the MAIC steps. So it is, I think, extremely bureaucratic, and only companies like GE and Motorola, in my mind, have the infrastructure to be able to drive such a bureaucracy. . . .

It's easy to involve the front-line operators with the QualPro MVT process—extremely easy. In Six Sigma, the statistics just blow some of the operators' minds. It's all about statistics. You can't just engage the people in it. In the time I was in GE, we were not successful in engaging the front-line operators. We had to do it through the engineers, mainly. Focus on the people is what QualPro does, and Six Sigma focuses on statistics. I think we all want to be on the side of focusing on our people, because that's what this is about.

This is interesting, in my mind. I came to realize that, if you want, you can take the QualPro MVT process and use it to culturally change your organization, turn it upside down if you want, and you can do it very effectively. Or if you think you have some good things going, you can take some rifle shots at certain areas of your plant, or single plants, and apply the process narrowly. And you can be effective and not lose anything by doing it. I think that is important. You can tailor this to where you are in your own productivity process. You know, with Six Sigma, it is all or nothing, and they say that. You cannot do it half way.

Finally, I think the QualPro process is done for lower cost than Six Sigma. With all the bureaucracy, Six Sigma is extremely high cost. So this decision, in the end, was really, really easy for this division of our company. There was no doubt in my mind it was the right decision for us. Now that we have done it, it has been perfect. We have gotten great results and we are really anxious to go forward and drive more of these great results.

Table 4.1 summarizes his comparison of the MVT process and Six Sigma.

At the 2002 MVT Symposium another chemical company executive commented on his experiences with the two approaches.

We got together a cross-functional team of engineers, chemists, and plant technicians. We set them a key objective—become experts in applying statistical methods for process improvement and use that

Table 4.1   QualPro Process versus Six Sigma

QualPro Process	Six Sigma
Delivers Results	Delivers Results
Requires Discipline	Requires Discipline
Fast	Slow
Practical	Bureaucratic
Easy to Involve Operators	More Difficult
Focus on People	Focus on Statistics
Can Apply Broadly or Narrowly	All or Nothing
Low Cost	High Cost

knowledge to improve our plant—and it was here we were introduced to MVT. We sent people on this team to various courses to learn about statistics and SPC, primarily how to use them properly. One of those courses was offered by QualPro and in that course, a statement was made that we found very profound. Basically, 10 percent of process improvements come through statistical methods and SPC, and 90 percent comes from breakthroughs uncovered by MVT. This was really incredible. We could actually go out and probe our plant and try to find improvements. We tried it out, and the first two tests worked. We saved, I guess, about $7 million (in the first two tests) . . . the cumulative effort, since we started, is about $47 million. . . .

The QualPro MVT process was a simplified approach that encouraged plant-technician involvement, and, for us, this is very important. We had just started reengineering of our site, and that left us very much team based, so technician involvement was very important to us. The MVT process seemed very logical, and we had proven it worked. It had focused training, which meant we could train managers on what was important for them to know, and we could train technicians on what was important for them to know. We could also train technical experts if we wanted to get more detail and in-depth knowledge within our site, and, of course, coaching was always available as we might need it.

His comparison of the MVT process to Six Sigma, as he presented it, is shown in Table 4.2. When asked specifically to compare his financial results with similar results that he had observed in Six Sigma

Table 4.2   Six Sigma and QualPro MVT Process

Similarities Both:	Differences MVT Process:
• Use a statistical approach	• Is simpler and less complex
• Have a focused methodology	• Is less expensive to implement
• Show proven results	• Does not require a separate structure of Black Belts or site experts
• Offer speed	
• Challenge "sacred cows"	• Offers more team involvement
• Require high degree of commitment from top management	• Requires less training to be highly successful

efforts in other chemical plants in his company, he said, "The savings in their projects were of a much smaller size. I would say that the size of the results that we have gotten so far [with QualPro] have been almost an order of magnitude larger. I feel the speed of implementation is also faster with the QualPro MVT process. There is a tremendous amount of training that has to go on in a Six Sigma effort that we didn't have to go through to achieve very big results [with QualPro]."

However, there are many situations in which MVT has been used in conjunction with a Six Sigma effort. MVT has demonstrated the ability to take Six Sigma results to a whole new level.

Some Six Sigma users have chosen to have QualPro teach the powerful MVT process to their black belts. They have then become able to achieve results beyond the capabilities of the standard four- or five-step Six Sigma framework.

Other Six Sigma organizations use MVT on high value efforts where a large and fast result is necessary. These projects are typically performed by MVT experts. An executive at one of the world's largest chemical companies described the QualPro consultants whom he engaged to attack major opportunities as his "go-to guys."

DATA MINING

Data mining involves the use of various statistical methods, particularly multivariate regression, to analyze existing data. Data mining has been used by many companies in the past few years to analyze historical data, to try to determine conditions to incorporate into their activities to immediately improve results. Used in this manner data mining is unlikely to yield the types of breakthrough improvements achieved by MVT because most of the improvement ideas that are investigated in an MVT experiment have never been in place in the company's history. Without seeking out creative new improvement ideas, it is nearly impossible to discover process conditions that will yield quantum-leap improvements in results.

The 12-step MVT process uses data–mining techniques to analyze historical data prior to performing MVT experiments, but data mining is just a small step in the process. Data mining can be used to identify some factors for MVT experimentation, but it cannot uncover new ideas that would immediately improve a process.

BEING LEAN

The concept of companies being "lean" began decades ago when Toyota developed *Just-in-Time* (JIT) manufacturing and other tools and techniques for reducing waste in a process. The basic idea is to speed up the process, to turn out more, and to reduce waste. We have used the MVT process in many manufacturing companies that have adopted lean manufacturing methods. In every case, we found that we were able to use the MVT process to reduce setup times and increase throughput over and above what the company had accomplished with its lean manufacturing efforts. In addition, the MVT process can be used to dramatically improve quality.

OTHER APPROACHES

Other improvement approaches include Total Quality Control (TQC), Total Quality Management (TQM), SPC, reengineering, ISO, benchmarking, and organizational psychology-based approaches. Several of the approaches have some merit. Some have been very popular in the past and have run their course. None of them have demonstrated over the long term that they have the consistent improvement power of the MVT process.

In Part II, the 12 steps of the MVT process are described in detail.

PART II

IMPLEMENTING AN MVT BUSINESS IMPROVEMENT PROJECT IN YOUR COMPANY

CHAPTER 5

STEP 1

Choose a High-Payoff Goal and Create the Environment

In the MVT process, laying the proper groundwork is critical to ensure that an improvement project will succeed. The following actions are important to take at the beginning of every project:

- Select an important, high-payoff project.
- Get the right people involved.
- Provide training to allow people to execute their roles.
- Ensure that project participants are motivated to succeed.

SELECT AN IMPORTANT, HIGH-PAYOFF PROJECT

The MVT process is a powerful tool that can be used to improve almost anything, but it should not be aimed at trivial objectives. Some criteria for choosing an appropriate project include:

- *Significant profit impact:* The MVT process can be used to improve almost anything. The objective of a project may be to increase sales, increase production, raise service levels, or improve product performance. It may be to decrease labor utilization, reduce defects, lower raw-material costs, or eliminate customer complaints. You may want to reduce employee turnover, increase employee use of generic prescription drugs, or test whether increasing sales commissions increases your sales. Whatever the specific goal, the primary characteristic of every MVT project must be a clear and significant opportunity to improve the company's profitability. If there is not a large profit opportunity, do not use MVT.

- *Timely results:* One of the features of MVT that is valued most often by executives is its ability to provide quick solutions. Careful selection of projects contributes to this speed factor. The best MVT projects have the potential to improve profitability soon.

  An MVT improvement project may have significant financial potential, but if the process operates extremely slowly, it may take years to measure the impact of improvement ideas. MVT will work very well on slow-moving processes (for example, MVT has been used to speed the growth of trees used to produce pulp for paper mills). Sometimes, the use of surrogate measures allows a project's timeline to be shortened. However, if a project is expected to require more than a few months total time (from inception to implementation of findings) and if other projects can be identified that can contribute sooner to the company's bottom line, those other projects should be given priority. Basic economic principles teach us that a profit dollar generated a month from now is of much greater value than a profit dollar generated years later.

- *Challenging objective:* Over the years, some QualPro clients have expressed a desire to use MVT on "easy" projects. Their rationale has been that employees will have more confidence in, and more effectively support, a problem that they know can be solved. Our experience has demonstrated that exactly the opposite is true. Addressing an easily solved problem trivializes the effort, diminishes its importance, and decreases the enthusiasm and pride of those involved. MVT is best suited to the tough problems that a company has been trying unsuccessfully for years to address. Employees become excited about correcting a chronic problem, and, when successful, the project may create legendary support for the MVT process.

GET THE RIGHT PEOPLE INVOLVED

Every project must have an executive sponsor. Top managers must endorse the importance of the project. They must communicate their confidence in the MVT process and monitor progress—or there will not be any. Top managers must be prepared to require someone to do something. Management cannot get away with just providing resources; management must provide the system and the motivation so that people can accomplish their objectives.

Include Representatives of QualPro's Elements of a Process

Every process is made up of methods, materials, machines, people, and measurement. Ensuring that at least one person who represents each of these five areas is involved in the project will maximize project benefits while minimizing unanticipated problems (see Figure 5.1). It also is useful to include representatives from various organizational levels in the project in order to include a wide range of knowledge and to ensure the ability to get things done.

FILL SPECIFIC ROLES

The specific roles of people involved in an MVT project are as follows:

- *Project leader:* A project leader is responsible for developing an action plan, communicating assignments, coordinating activities,

Figure 5.1   QualPro's Elements of a Process

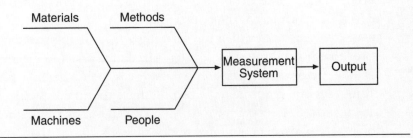

monitoring completion of tasks (timing and quality), and bringing attention/action to bear when weaknesses in execution are discovered. Usually, the best project leader is the line manager directly responsible for the day-to-day operation of the process that MVT is being used to improve.

- *Brainstorming participants:* Participants in the idea-brainstorming phase may invest only a few minutes or an hour or two in the entire project. Although the duration of their involvement may be short, it is enormously important. This is where the improvement ideas are developed. Persons from every element of the process should be involved. All organizational levels should participate. Persons of long tenure should be included as well as new hires. If at all possible, customers and suppliers should be included in brainstorming sessions. Even people who are not knowledgeable about the process can contribute.

   Brainstorming may be done in a group meeting with one to two dozen participants, in small groups of two to five people each, or even in individual discussions. Often, individuals who are reluctant to speak up in groups will contribute worthwhile suggestions in individual discussions.

- *Idea categorization participants:* Idea categorization is the process by which improvement ideas are narrowed to only those that are practical, fast, and cost free. Those involved in the categorization process should be very knowledgeable regarding the process to be tested. Once again, it is critical that representatives from each element of a process be included (materials, machines, methods, people, measurement system). It also is very important that those who are aware of safety issues (for employees, customers, and the process itself) be included.

- *Factor owners:* Execution of the improvement factors tested in an MVT experiment is the responsibility of factor owners. Each factor owner is responsible for defining a specific improvement factor that was brainstormed, categorized, and selected for testing. The factor owner prepares the materials, training, and monitoring system required to execute the experiment while it is being tested. Every improvement factor must have an owner. Some factor owners will be responsible for more than one factor. A factor owner typically is the person who is already responsible for executing the status quo condition of the factor on a day-to-day basis.

- *Data owner:* The data owner is the person responsible for ensuring that data are properly collected during the execution of the experiment. Like the factor owners, this person usually is already responsible for this activity, collecting and distributing data, on a day-to-day basis.

- *MVT consultant:* Each MVT project should have the support and involvement of a person who has extensive MVT training and project experience. The consultant's role is to ensure that the MVT process is followed properly; that practical, fast, cost-free factors are developed; that appropriate MVT designs and tests are created; that preparations and logistics do not inadvertently compromise the design; that data are collected properly and analyzed correctly; that proper conclusions are drawn from MVT findings; and that, when fully implemented, the results of the MVT improvement deliver the results promised by the testing. In short, the consultant is the steward of the process.

MVT is an extremely sophisticated and powerful method of applying advanced statistics to real-world problems and, unfortunately, it is not possible to develop the knowledge and skill to be a competent MVT consultant in a few months or through a few days or weeks of training and/or completion of a single project. Extensive training and experience with many projects is necessary to develop this expertise, which usually must be provided from outside the company until the company can create the appropriate internal expertise.

PROVIDE TRAINING TO ALLOW PEOPLE TO EXECUTE THEIR ROLES

There are several approaches to involving company personnel in the MVT process. Which one is chosen depends on the nature of the problem, the process(es) to be involved, and the personnel to be involved. The training that is appropriate varies substantially, depending on whether the company is interested in learning the MVT process (which takes more time and training) or simply wants a quick solution to a major business problem, relying heavily on outside expert support.

The SWAT Team Approach

The SWAT team approach uses minimal involvement of the personnel within the process; instead the MVT planning, design, and analysis is performed by outside experts. This approach requires no formal training of persons inside the company process. Explanation is provided for the activities that the "inside" people must perform, but there is no attempt to teach anyone the MVT process. Individuals are provided only the information they need to know to assist in the execution of the MVT projects.

Learning the MVT Process

Another approach is to provide customized training for each organizational level, as follows:

- *Top management:* Top management does not necessarily need to learn the details of the MVT process. The members of top management do, however, need to understand the basic concepts. They need to learn enough about the process to ask intelligent questions and to understand the differences between good and bad answers. Training for top management often is provided in a one-day session, but some executives choose to go into more depth with a two- or even three-day session. A few executives become very involved in the MVT process and go through several multiday sessions with their direct reports. Invariably, the improvement efforts are more successful in these organizations.
- *Mid-management, supervisors, professional and technical staffs, and selected local workforce members:* These persons are the core participants of any MVT project. They will serve in key roles— as project leaders, factor owners, and data owners—and they frequently will be members of brainstorming and idea-categorizing groups. Their training typically includes two three-day sessions to learn the fundamentals of the MVT process. This training, along

with project experience over time, eventually minimizes the need for support from an outside MVT consultant.

- *The local workforce:* The local workforce plays an important role in the MVT process. Its members execute MVT tests and often maintain control charts on an ongoing basis. They usually are the most knowledgeable in investigating "special causes" of exceptionally good or bad results, and can provide insight into the process. The training required to prepare them for their role is typically a one-day session.

- *MVT consultant:* The process of becoming an MVT consultant is arduous. A substantial amount of classroom training is required to provide the necessary statistical foundation. But in order to solve the planning, logistics, monitoring, execution, and analysis/interpretation challenges of MVT experiments, several years of experience working with dozens of projects are necessary. A minimum of two or three years' experience, accompanied by a strong quantitative ability and good organizational skills, is typically required for a person to become a qualified MVT consultant.

Just-in-Time Training Only

Training is most effective when provided just before the person will use it. Therefore, training the people to be involved in an MVT project usually occurs at the beginning of their involvement in a live project. Often, the training is actually part of a project. During the training, control charts for the project are constructed from historical data, brainstorming for improvement ideas is begun, and a preliminary MVT design is developed. This immediate, real-life application can make the training far more effective.

ENSURE THAT PROJECT PARTICIPANTS ARE MOTIVATED TO SUCCEED

The executive sponsor typically drives the motivation of those involved in an MVT project. His or her responsibilities include the following:

- *Proof-of-the-need message* The executive sponsor must clearly communicate a proof-of-the-need message to everyone who will be supporting the project. This is a clear articulation of the reasons that the project is important to the business—financially, strategically, and competitively. The message should clearly and simply state why the project is important to the shareholders, to the employees, and to the customers, in both the short-term and the long-term.

- *Timing expectation:* The sponsor also should create a clear expectation of a fast pace for the project. A great deal of inertia exists in most organizations. Unless clear expectations are set for moving rapidly, the effort will unfold at a much slower pace than desired. Specific timing benchmarks should be set aggressively and communicated throughout the organization. The mind-set must be created that "staying on schedule is important, and we will not fall behind!"

- *"We're-serious-about-this!" message:* The executive sponsor must also communicate a sense of accountability to the organization. Everyone must understand that the MVT project is important and that it has the attention and support of the management team. Each person must understand that he or she will have a role and that all involved are expected to fulfill their obligations in a timely and effective manner. The sponsor also should communicate (in a positive way) that individual performance will affect not only the success of the effort but also the performance assessments and even compensation of those involved.

For example, in a high-tech manufacturing company, the CEO made the management-compensation plan dependent on the improvement and success achieved through the MVT effort. The entire top-management team got behind the effort and cut costs while raising production to such an extent that profits more than doubled in a four-year period. A heightened sense of urgency must be established by some means.

SUMMARY

Step 1 of the MVT process, *Create the Environment,* is very different from what most people anticipate. It is not about changing a company's culture to improve results; it is not about changing personal interactions between employees; it is not about making them like or "get along with" one another; it is not even about aligning their values with those of customers and management. These are all aspects of an organization that may be very desirable, but they are not prerequisites for improving the organization's performance. Cultural and broad work-environment improvements are best achieved as the result of improved performance, not the source of it.

One client had an average of 450 union grievances waiting to be resolved. After three years of MVT projects, labor complaints had evaporated. People who previously had found fault with the company now shared in its new pride. The company, which had been stubborn about rules and regulations, was a better, kinder place to work.

If a company begins to produce a dramatically better product or makes astonishing progress in satisfying its customers or makes cost-reduction gains that allow it to improve its competitive position, the company is much more effective at making its employees proud of the company and building a positive culture than it would be by organizing a thousand pep rallies or utilizing "quality" slogans and "flavor-of-the month" training programs.

Case Study: Step 1

A nationwide retailer with over a thousand locations had been experiencing falling sales. The basic retail strategy over several years had been consistent, and customers viewed the retailer as being very successful. Although the stockholders were making lots of money, they were concerned about the falling sales. Competition and market saturation were considered the likely culprits.

Several executives, including the CEO and the vice president of advertising, had friends in other businesses who recommended they consider using MVT to address this challenge. Based on these strong recommendations, the CEO made the decision to launch an MVT project to identify actions which could turn around their sales decline.

The CEO was the executive sponsor of the project, and he assigned the vice president of marketing to serve as the project leader. The CEO held a one-and-a-half hour meeting with his direct reports and explained the critical nature of the effort and discussed the support needed from each

Project Plan for Sales MVT Project

Activity	Mar					Apr				May				Jun					Jul				Aug				Sep				
	3	10	17	24	31	7	14	21	28	5	12	19	26	2	9	16	23	30	7	14	21	28	4	11	18	25	1	8	15	22	29
Determine project team/resources	X	X																													
Define key measures		X																													
Analyze historical data			X	X	X																										
Brainstorm, categorize, and define test ideas			X	X																											
Construct screening MVT				X	X																										
Develop logistics and monitoring plans				X	X																										
Present design to management					X																										
Prepare materials and communication to execute ideas						X	X																								
Distribute screening materials and communications						X	X																								
Execute screening MVT								X	X	X	X	X	X																		
Analyze screening MVT data									X	X	X	X	X																		
Present screening results and agree on refining													X																		
Distribute refining materials and communications														X																	
Execute refining MVT															X	X	X	X	X	X											
Analyze refining MVT data															X	X	X	X	X	X											
Present refining results and agree on implementation																					X										
Distribute implementation materials and communications																							X	X							
Execute implementation																									X	X					
Verify appropriate movement of key measure control chart																											X	X	X	X	X
Present implementation results																											X	X	X	X	X

66

department. The CEO explained in no uncertain terms that this project was a high priority and that he expected full support in a timely manner. He asked one of the QualPro MVT consultants to provide a brief overview of the MVT Process; and, along with the project leader, present the preliminary project plan shown in the table on page 66; and answer questions regarding timing, logistics, and the involvement likely to be needed from each department.

Because the plan was to test factors that included ideas from operations, advertising, merchandising, and human resources, similar meetings were held with each of those departments. The project leader, MVT consultant, and department vice president jointly led each of these meetings. Additionally, they met with the information systems group to discuss data needs, and a data owner was assigned to support the project.

During these meetings, several adjustments to the project plan were made, but the overall schedule and scope of the project were confirmed as doable.

Because there was no intent for the organization to "learn" the MVT process, no formal training classes were held.

CHAPTER 6

STEP 2

*Define How You Will Measure
Success and Validate Your
Measurement System*

Step 2 of the MVT process is to identify the key measure(s) of success and to ensure that a valid measurement system is being used to generate the measure(s).

IDENTIFY KEY MEASURES OF SUCCESS

Each MVT project has an objective. The objective might be higher plant output or faster collections or increased advertising effectiveness. Many project objectives, such as these, do not translate directly into numbers that can be measured. Step 2 of the MVT process begins with the identification of the key measure(s) that will reflect the successful achievement of the project objective.

A project objective, which usually is a business objective, needs to be translated into a "key measure," which is a specific number or numbers whose movement will represent the success (the numbers are moving in the desired direction) or lack of success (the numbers fail to move in the desired direction) of the project effort. A key measure is a numerical output. For the project objectives described, key measures might be as follows:

- Higher plant output might be measured by tracking first-quality throughput (the pounds of first-quality product that are created by the plant in a particular time frame).
- A key measure of faster collections might be the number of days of outstanding sales invoices.
- Increased advertising effectiveness might translate to the number of profit dollars that are created by the advertising.

There should never be more than one or two key measures, and usually it is best to have just one.

SECONDARY MEASURES MAY BE APPROPRIATE

Sometimes secondary measures are appropriate in addition to the key measure(s). Secondary measures may be necessary to ensure that you avoid hurting an important outcome at the same time that you are achieving the primary project objective. Examples of this are:

- With first-quality throughput as a primary key measure, we may also measure cost per pound as a secondary measure. We would not necessarily want to accept an increase in cost per pound in order to achieve an increase in throughput.
- The number of days that sales invoices are outstanding might be the primary key measure, but we probably would want to measure write-offs to ensure that the outstanding invoices were not reduced by writing off receivables.
- With profit dollars as the primary key measure, we might also measure market share, because a short-term improvement in profit may not be desirable if it is accompanied by a shrinking of the company's market share.

Secondary measures might also be appropriate to help us understand the impact of improvement ideas on a process. For example, if first-quality throughput in a chemical process were the primary key measure, we might also be interested in catalyst life, because increasing catalyst life could enable us to save money. If the primary key measure were profit dollars, we might also be interested in traffic patterns. Understanding the pattern of consumer traffic coming into a store might have a big impact on the staffing schedule. We also might have an interest in measuring sales mix—what categories of products were being sold and whether that had changed. This sales mix could have an impact on inventory decisions.

Secondary measures may be very valuable to our improvement effort. However, be careful not to lose sight of the primary key measure(s). An excessive number of secondary measures can distract attention from the real objective and potentially interfere with achievement of a large, fast improvement.

USE "REAL-WORLD" MEASURES

It is very important to use measures of "real-world" results, not measurements that rely on focus groups or laboratory scale processes or pilot plants that often do not translate well to the real world. Focus groups, for example, can be very useful in generating ideas, but relying on the opinions of consumers who participate in focus groups can be very dangerous if you are going to act on those opinions. MVT experiments have shown that consumers often are no better at predicting their own behavior than we are. They are not intentionally being misleading; but when in an artificial environment, they cannot predict what they will do in real life. We found that it is important in sales experiments to allow consumers to vote with their money, not with their mouths. In a manufacturing environment, an R&D facility may be able to successfully manufacture a beaker of quality product. However, that does not mean that the process that created the beaker of product will also create tons of products successfully in a plant environment.

The bottom line is that measurements should always be taken in the real world if at all possible. Only then can the real process be reliably improved.

EACH MEASURE SHOULD BE OPERATIONALLY DEFINED

After key measures and secondary measures are identified, it is very important that they be operationally defined—that is, very carefully described in terms that everyone can agree on. When you talk to members of any organization, their answers about how a particular measure will be calculated and where it will come from will differ when you go from department to department, or from person to person, or even with the same person from time to time. Therefore, it is critical to carefully describe how each measure will be calculated and what its source will be. If the measures are not operationally defined well, misunderstandings can be expected.

For example, a large retailer's interest was "to improve sales." The primary key measure was to be "comparable sales." The MVT consultant asked, "What is the definition of comparable sales?" One person said, "It is very simple; comp sales are this year's sales for a time frame divided by last year's sales for the same time frame." A second person said, "That is not quite right, because sales in total for our organization divided by last year's total would represent some stores that were either opened last year but not this year, or opened this year but not last year. And those should be excluded." He thought the calculation should be dollar amounts of sales this year versus last year but only for stores that were open both years. A third person said, "That still does not account for how we actually calculate comparable sales in our organization, because total sales includes some leased property and some advertising contributions by our venders, and that should be excluded when calculating comparable sales." As is true in many cases, it was critical to the success of the effort that one of these definitions be agreed on and that everyone understand exactly what the measure of success was.

In another example, a large paper manufacturer used premium and nonpremium logs to manufacture high-quality paper. It was important to measure the amount of premium logs because they made a large contribution to the cost structure. As a part of the MVT project, we laid out 50 logs and asked each of the company's 20 inspectors to assess each log as premium or nonpremium. Every log was classified as a premium log by at least one inspector, and every log also was classified as a nonpremium log by at least one inspector! In order to understand how this happened, we went log by log and asked each inspector to describe what made it premium or nonpremium. The company had very precise criteria for classifying the logs. One criterion was the diameter of the log; a log had to be between 8 and 12 inches in diameter to be rated premium. However, the company had never operationally defined the diameter adequately. Some of the inspectors applied the diameter criterion to the top of the log, others to the bottom of the log, and some to the center of the log. A very simple lack of clarification was costing the company a lot of money and interfering with the quality of its product.

EVALUATE THE MEASUREMENT SYSTEM

Every key measure or secondary measure is generated by some kind of process. Cash register receipts are totaled by a computer to generate a sales report. Manufacturing defects are identified, classified, and counted by an inspector, resulting in a defect report. Chemical assay is determined by a technician and a piece of equipment, such as a spectrophotometer, that generates the chemical-assay measurement. Like any other process, the output of a measurement process will have some amount of variation, and the average of that varying output may be an accurate number or a number that is too high or too low.

The components of a measurement system typically are (1) samples to be measured, (2) instruments or equipment to make the measurement, (3) a method of measuring, and (4) people who measure. All these components contribute to the accuracy and amount of variation of the measurement process.

EVERY MEASUREMENT SYSTEM SHOULD BE VIEWED AS GUILTY UNTIL PROVEN INNOCENT

Most measurements are inadequate at first. Even measurement systems that seem as if they should be infallible often have errors. For example, we have found instances in grocery stores in which the totaled receipts did not equal the total sales for the day as reported in computer-generated reports. In another instance, a telephone company was tracking dispatches (repairs that require a truck to visit the site) and discovered that a computer program totaled the dispatches for Monday, Tuesday, Wednesday, Friday, Saturday, and Sunday and reached a weekly total, omitting Thursday from the calculation! In a manufacturing firm, the objective of a project was to reduce downtime. The equipment supposedly tracked downtime automatically, but when a stopwatch tracking was done, it was found that downtime for the machine was dramatically understated.

Measurement systems that involve human judgments are especially problematic. Subjective measures, such as visual defects, taste tests, and aroma quality and intensity can have tremendous amounts of variation and may be far off target.

The quality of a measurement system is critically important for two reasons. First, a poor measurement system may cloud one's view of the process to the point that it is difficult to distinguish a good result from a bad one. We have seen many instances in which lab results were used to separate good product from bad, but the lab measurements varied so much that the sample would be judged bad one time and, if it were sent to the lab again, it might be determined to be good. If it were analyzed again, it might be judged bad. In some organizations, this sort of measurement error has led to a "sample-until-you-win" strategy for quality control. A manufacturing organization will manufacture a batch of product and send in a sample. If it is judged to be bad, the company sends in another sample. Eventually, one will be found to be good. Neither the manufacturer nor its customers win with that kind of process.

Second, an inaccurate measurement system may cause poor business results. An example is a large chemical plant that makes intermediate products used in the manufacturing of agricultural chemicals. The chemical plant sold the intermediate product by "pounds of active ingredient." Its laboratory assay had established that the active ingredient was consistently 97 percent of the product. As part of an MVT process, evaluation of the measurement system showed that the laboratory results were consistently low. The material was actually 98.5 percent pure. This was good news for the plant, as it was able to pick up a 1.5 percent improvement in revenue just by changing the label to read "98.5 percent pure" and raising the price accordingly.

Several months later, a key customer (an agricultural chemicals plant) called the intermediate-products plant and congratulated it on the improvements made to the product. The customer plant personnel said that its process was running much more smoothly with the improved product that was now being shipped to it. At first, the intermediate's manufacturer was puzzled. The product had not been changed, only the label. After a little bit of detective work, both parties realized what had happened. The agricultural chemicals plant dosed its chemical reactions based on the analysis that was reported by the intermediate manufacturer. When the product was reported as 97 percent pure, the agricultural chemicals manufacturer was overdosing its reaction. The result was the creation of solids in its process that were plugging screens and causing pump inefficiencies and a variety of other problems. So the discovery of a measurement inaccuracy resulted in increased revenue for the intermediate manufacturer as well as a better quality process for its customer.

PERFORM MEASUREMENT STUDIES TO EVALUATE MEASUREMENT SYSTEMS

Because an understanding of the capabilities of the measurement system and the quality of the numbers it produces is so important, measurement studies are part of every MVT project. There are two criteria regarding the outputs of the measurement system.

First, it must be determined if the measurement is accurate. Accuracy is whether the numbers on average are high, low, or correct. The accuracy of a measurement system typically is determined by comparing its results to those of a standard. For example, if one were measuring chemical assay, a sample that was known to be 90 percent pure would be run through the measurement system to see whether the measurement system determined that it was 90 percent pure. If the average result were 92 percent, the measurement system would be biased high. If the average result were 88 percent, the system would be biased low.

Often, a standard is not easily available. With subjective measurements, the standard against which a result is compared may be created by a group of experts who evaluate the visual defects, taste, and so on, and define a "standard" that is then compared to the measurement system's result. In some situations, an expert panel is not an option. For example, in measuring sales reported by a computer, the standard against which the report may be compared could be the manually added cash register receipts for the day.

The second criterion for a measurement system is precision. Precision has to do with the repeatability of the measurement. Does it have the ability to reliably recognize a small enough measurement increment to be meaningful in the improvement effort? Usually, precision is determined by measuring the same thing more than once and analyzing the differences between the multiple measurements. For example, the same part might be sent multiple times through the inspection system. If the part is found to be defective every time or not defective every time, the measurement is precise and repeatable. If it sometimes is found to be defective and sometimes is found to be not defective, the measurement is not very repeatable. If one were measuring the physical size of a part, it could be sent through the measurement system multiple times. Comparison of multiple measurements would provide an understanding of how small an increment could be meaningfully measured.

Use Measurement Study Information

Once you have an understanding of the accuracy and precision (or lack thereof) in your measurement system, you have two options.

The first option is to improve the measurement system. Sometimes, this can be as simple as recalibrating a measurement device. The solution might be better training for inspectors or repairing poorly operating measurement devices. Often, the improvement of a measurement system may be more complex. In that case, the entire MVT process may be used on the measurement system itself. A thorough evaluation of potential improvement actions to be taken on the measurement system through MVT testing can make fast and dramatic improvements in the quality of the numbers that are produced.

The second option is to accommodate the inadequate measurement system. For example, if a bias is determined in the result, that bias might be added or subtracted from the output of the measurement. A measurement system with an inadequate level of precision may be accommodated by taking more samples and averaging them in order to reduce the variation in the result. This averaging allows an imprecise measurement system to successfully identify a small improvement.

EVALUATION OF THE MEASUREMENT SYSTEM SHOULD NOT BE A ONE-TIME EVENT

Given the importance of measurement in the control and improvement of business results, measurement studies should be performed routinely. Control charts should be established on both the precision and the accuracy of the measurement system, and the control charts should be monitored over time. As every measurement process has human and equipment components, there is no assurance that a measurement system that is adequate today will continue to be adequate next week, next month, or next year.

THE USE OF SURROGATE MEASURES

Sometimes the best measure of a project objective is available so rarely or slowly that it is not practical for use in the short term. In such a case, a surrogate measure may be developed, if data indicate that an improvement in the surrogate will be accompanied by an improvement in the key measure. For example, an MVT project was initiated to reduce customer complaints about the quality of a manufactured product. Examination of the customer-complaint data showed that the complaints were not very frequent—only a handful each month. But several large accounts were about to be lost as a result of the dissatisfaction. Evaluation of the customer complaints and the reasons for them showed that a particular defect in the strength of the product was the most frequent problem. If customer complaints were used to measure improvement, many months would have been required to gather enough data to indicate whether the problem was getting better or not. In this instance, a surrogate measure, which was the strength component of the product, could be measured in the short term. The strength component was dramatically improved within a matter of weeks, and customer complaints (as measured over the next year) were virtually eliminated.

In another example, a manufacturer of molded parts had a problem with holes or voids appearing in its parts. The voids were not visible but appeared when the parts were machined. In order to speed up the ability to evaluate voids during the MVT experiment, a different measurement system was used in which the molded parts were sliced thinly and the voids were counted. This change provided a much greater amount of data from each part and dramatically shortened the experimentation process.

In a third example, an MVT project focused on improving sales in a sales process with a long, 18-month cycle time. If the experiment were to run throughout the sales cycle, an experiment of two years or longer would have been necessary. The company had no intention of waiting two years to take action on its inadequate sales process. The surrogate measure was tracking progress through the sales cycle. The actual measurement was the time that was required to get from step one to two, or two to three, or three to four in the sales cycle. This surrogate measure allowed a two-month experiment to identify actions that resulted in dramatic sales improvements.

SUMMARY

Choosing correct measurements, defining them properly, and assuring that the numbers are precisely accurate are critically important steps to improving results. Never underestimate their importance. Every measurement is guilty until proven innocent.

Case Study: Step 2 (Continued from Chapter 5)

The objective of the retail sales MVT project outlined by the CEO was to increase sales. After discussion with the entire executive team, however, it became clear that there was actually another important objective—increasing profitability. To be considered a clear success, the project needed to achieve an increase in sales . . . but that sales increase needed to result in a substantial increase in profits. The CEO did not want unprofitable sales growth.

Management recognized that sales and profits from store to store varied due to market differences, store size, and so on. Therefore, direct comparisons of sales and profit dollars from one store to the next could be quite misleading. A small, but very profitable, store might have lower sales than a large but poorly performing store. To allow a valid comparison between stores, "comp" sales and profits were used as the measures of success.

Comp sales and profits were operationally defined as the difference between this year's sales or profit dollars and the sales or profit dollars for the same store for the same time period during the previous year.

A long discussion was held to consider the need for secondary measures such as traffic, number of transactions, and average purchase amount. Some people felt that understanding these diagnostic measures would have value. The CEO ended the "discussion" abruptly when he stated that all he really cared about was improving sales and profits and he did not want to take any risk that the evaluation of measures of secondary importance would distract them from their real objectives.

While sales and profit data resided in several databases, the CEO decided that sales and profit information for the project would be taken directly from the database that generated corporate P&Ls. These are the numbers that the CEO and the shareholders saw. A measurement study was performed by running pro forma reports using the queries created for the project and retrospectively comparing the reports to actual data reported on P&Ls.

CHAPTER 7

STEP 3

Use Control Charts to
Hunt for Good Ideas to Test

STEPS IN STATISTICAL PROCESS CONTROL

Statistical process control (SPC) charts are used throughout the United States, especially in manufacturing, to identify instances in which a process goes out of control. An even more valuable use of SPC charts is to identify potential changes in a process that can be tested. MVT process improvement factors developed using SPC charts have a significantly higher probability of helping results than do test factors developed through brainstorming. In our experience, only about 25 percent of all improvement ideas actually help to improve a process, but improvement ideas (i.e., "test factors") that are identified using SPC charts are helpful about 50 percent of the time.

We have been very successful in using SPC charts in both manufacturing and service industries to identify uncontrolled variation in historical data and to identify special causes for these instances of uncontrolled variation—or, at least, suspected special causes. The rest of this chapter summarizes our basic approach.

CONSTRUCT THE APPROPRIATE
STATISTICAL PROCESS CONTROL CHART

First, you must construct the appropriate SPC chart for each key measure of success. The basic purpose of a SPC chart is to separate common cause variation (normal variation in a process) from special cause variation (unusual variation in a process). A process that exhibits no special cause variation is a *stable process.*

There are two basic types of SPC charts. One is for variables data. Variables data involve the measurement of units on a continuous scale in which a fractional or partial unit is possible. For example:

- *Time:* Cycle time, down time, response time, wait time.
- *Dollars:* Invoice errors for the week, weekly or monthly revenue, monthly unbudgeted expenses.
- *Amount:* Tons of product produced per week, barrels of liquid produced per shift.
- *Physical and dimensional measurements:* height, width, weight, viscosity.

X-bar and range charts are the most commonly used SPC charts for variables data. However, sometimes X-charts or individual charts and moving range charts are used. In instances in which measurements occur slowly (for example, monthly or less often), moving average and moving range charts are used.

The other main type of data is *attribute data,* involving the classification or counting of events or items based on their characteristics. Classification often is by yes/no data or good/bad data. The term *count data* means that we count occurrences of events or items that have a particular characteristic. Typically, the chance of occurrence is small relative to the potential number of such events that could occur.

For classification data, the statistic of interest usually is the proportion—occasionally the number—of events or items that fall into each of two groups, yes/no or good/bad. For example:

- The proportion of product produced that is defective.
- The proportion of invoices not paid within 60 days.
- The number of the 600 business-service representatives who are on sick leave each day.

Typical key measures for count data are:

- The number of defects per unit of production.
- The number of inquiries per day about a new service.
- The number of accidents per month.
- The number of invoice errors per week.

Proportion-defective charts (*p* charts) and number-defective charts (*np* charts) are used for the classification data (yes/no or good/bad). Number-of-count charts (*c* charts) and rate-of-occurrence charts (*u* charts) are used for count data. (It is beyond the scope of this book to explain which control chart ought to be used for every conceivable measure of success.)

Whenever measures of variables are possible, they usually provide better statistical information than measures of attributes.

IDENTIFY EACH INSTANCE OF UNCONTROLLED VARIATION IN THE HISTORICAL DATA

We use the SPC charts that we have constructed to identify instances of uncontrolled variation in historical data. We usually look at one to five years' worth of historical data. Sometimes, we have monthly measures of success, such as sales revenue. Other times, we have more frequent measures of success, such as the number of customers per hour. In the latter case, we will be looking at massive amounts of data.

The instances of uncontrolled variation that we are looking for are of several types:

- Individual instances of unusual results (points outside the control limits).
- Shifts in average results (at least eight points in succession above or below the central line).
- Significant trends in results, upward or downward.

Figure 7.1 is the control chart for percentage yield for a chemical process. There are three instances of points outside the control limits

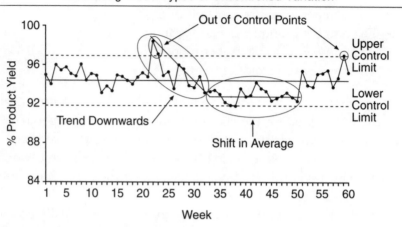

Figure 7.1   Percentage Yield for a Chemical Process
Illustrating Three Types of Uncontrolled Variation

on the X-bar chart. This is the most common type of uncontrolled variation for most processes.

There is one instance of shift in process average—eight or more points in succession below the central line of the control chart. This indicates that, during this time period, there was a shift in the process itself. This is another type of uncontrolled variation that we want to test for on the historical data control charts.

Notice that there is an instance of a significant trend downward. This is another type of uncontrolled variation that we will routinely test for in the historical key-measure results.

Each of these instances of uncontrolled variation, or unusual results, was caused by something special, or outside the regular fluctuation of the process. Our goal is to identify these special causes.

INVESTIGATE EACH SPECIAL CAUSE TO IDENTIFY ITS SOURCE

If you are keeping SPC charts on an ongoing basis, and if the people working in the process are working diligently to identify special causes (and have been properly trained), you can successfully identify special

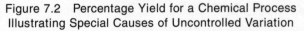

Figure 7.2   Percentage Yield for a Chemical Process
Illustrating Special Causes of Uncontrolled Variation

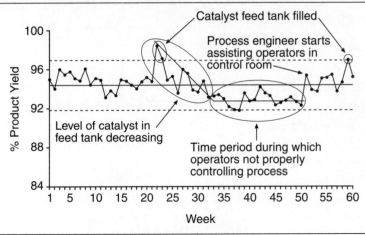

causes about 75 percent of the time. The success rate usually is a little higher for manufacturing processes than for service processes.
However, when analyzing historical data, we find that, even with the
help of an expert, we rarely can identify the special causes of uncontrolled variation with certainty. Usually, there is uncertainty about
the special cause. But if you get input from everyone familiar with the
process, you usually will be able to identify a few suspected special
causes. These suspected special causes are ideal potential factors for
MVT experimentation.

Figure 7.1 showed instances of uncontrolled variation in chemical
yield. In Figure 7.2, the suspected special causes of those instances of
uncontrolled variation have been identified:

- The high-yield results that were above the control limits were
  believed by the process operators to have occurred just after the
  feed tank was refilled with catalyst.
- The downward trend in yield was believed to have resulted from
  the gradual emptying of the feed tank.
- The upward shift in process average occurred when the process
  engineer started assisting in the running of the process from the

control room. Investigation revealed that he controlled certain process variables within tighter limits than the operators had been taught.

USE SUSPECTED SPECIAL CAUSES AS A BASIS FOR MVT TEST FACTORS

Suspected special causes are excellent sources of high-potential MVT test factors. Each controllable special cause can be tested in an MVT screening experiment.

In the instance illustrated in Figure 7.2, the amount of catalyst in the feed tank was thought by the operators to have a strong impact on yield. Therefore, it was included as a test factor in an MVT experiment. The R&D engineers believed that this was a waste of time and effort, but it was included in the MVT because it was practical, fast, and cost free. It turned out that this was the most important of 17 factors that were tested. The result of implementing the MVT findings was a dramatic and consistent increase in yield beyond what the experts thought could be achieved. As mentioned earlier, six months later the R&D engineers gave a presentation describing the theoretical reasons that the increased catalyst in the feed tank had such a dramatic effect.

SPECIAL CAUSES KNOWN WITH CERTAINTY ARE A "GIMME"

In the rare instances in which there is certainty about the special cause of the uncontrolled variation, that special cause may be acted on immediately. We refer to a change that obviously needs to be made and that will definitely improve results as a "gimme."

An example is the third special cause in the previous example. The cause of the improved yield when the engineer assisted was known with certainty. After the operators were retrained and provided with better written instructions, the effect of this action was an increase in yield of almost 2 percent.

Some uncontrolled variation may be caused by uncontrollable events, and there is nothing to be gained from identifying these special causes, because you will not be able to test those events.

Case Study: Step 3 (Continued from Chapter 6)

To gather sales and profit improvement ideas that could be tested in MVT experiments, several sources of ideas were considered, starting with SPC charts.

Sales and profit data going back almost four years were SPC charted. A meeting was held that included the project leader; the MVT consultant; and representatives from marketing, operations, merchandising, and human resources. All of the department representatives were long-term employees who were knowledgeable about the company and their department's activities over the past five years.

The MVT consultant brought the historical SPC charts. He had marked the instances of uncontrolled variation that were evident.

The group then studied each of the instances of uncontrolled variation and theorized as to what special causes might have resulted in each of the outside-the-control-limits, trend, or shifts-in-average situations.

The following figure shows the sales control chart and the instances of uncontrolled variation:

Sales Control Chart Showing Instances of Uncontrolled Variation

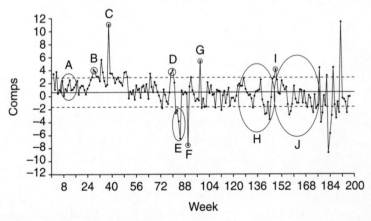

The following table shows the special causes that the group suspected for each instance of uncontrolled variation:

Instance of Uncontrolled Variation	Suspected Special Cause(s)
A	New signage, special sales training program for associates
B	Temporary price promotion, special sports promotion
C	Back to school promotion—heavy radio
D	Telemarketing campaign to best customers
E	New radio strategy—changed time-of-day and day-of-week mix
F	National sales meeting—store managers all off site
G	Christmas week nonaligned with previous year for comps
H	Changed newspaper ads to smaller size and spent the additional money on staffing
I	Special product demo by greeter at store entrance, new window signage
J	Changed TV mix to emphasize cable, decreased size of circulars and increased distribution via direct mail

The group's efforts to identify special causes provided direct insights into possible ideas for improvement. Their output was subsequently shared in brainstorming sessions with others. It inspired some as to the degree of change that could be detected and measured. It gave some people confidence in their convictions to test new things. It gave others a new curiosity.

CHAPTER 8

STEP 4

*Use Data Mining and Other
Statistical Techniques to Find
Good Ideas to Test*

THE PROS AND CONS OF
HISTORICAL-DATA ANALYSIS

The analysis of historical data with data-mining techniques has become very popular in the United States in the past decade. The basic idea sounds good. Every company has computers full of data. Surely, with all the data and with our ability to do sophisticated data analysis, we must be able to extract some clues to improving the company's operations. Our experience doing this with hundreds of companies indicates that data mining can play an important role in the MVT process. By itself, however, it is not the silver bullet that some have claimed.

For a decade and a half, QualPro has taught courses in the use of simple linear regression, multiple linear regression, multivariate regression, cluster analysis, principal component analysis, discriminant analysis, factor analysis, and other multivariate methods by which to analyze historical data. We have written books on the use of these methods, and we believe that analyzing historical data can be very useful in identifying high-potential improvement ideas for MVT experimentation. Improvement ideas discovered via these data-mining methods have a better probability (about 50 percent) of being helpful than do brainstormed ideas, which have a 25 percent success rate.

In our experience, a handful of ideas (two to five) generally surfaces. However, these ideas play a relatively minor role in the improvement provided by the MVT process. What you should expect is high-potential ideas that can be tested in an MVT screening experiment.

PITFALLS OF HISTORICAL DATA ANALYSIS

Reliance on data mining or other forms of historical data analysis for immediate implementation will rarely, if ever, provide breakthrough results. Unfortunately, many companies today are obtaining data-mining "findings," implementing them, and suffering the consequences of a faulty strategy. The problem with relying solely on historical data to make process changes is that no matter how much historical data you have, the best improvement ideas cannot be found among the historical data. We find that the ideas that result in the most significant improvements typically have never been used by the company.

A second pitfall of using historical data analysis to make process changes is that it is easy to be fooled by correlated data. A variable that is analyzed may have been at a particular level when good results happened, but that level of that variable may not have been the cause of the good results. We have seen many instances in which an apparent change in the level of a variable in the process appeared to improve results, but when that variable was tested in a screening MVT, we learned that it did not improve results. For example, when we used multiple linear regression to analyze the historical data of a major retailer, the findings indicated that there was a strong negative relationship between the salaries of the store managers and the improvement in comp sales. Did this mean that sales could be improved by cutting management salaries? Of course not. The reality was that the higher paid, more experienced managers had been sent to the larger, slower growing markets. A correlation existed between higher salaries and lower comp sales, but this was not a cause-and-effect relationship.

A third problem is the fact that historical data analysis is focused on relationships that existed in the past. Even if the relationships were valid then, they probably no longer exist. There are likely to have been many process changes since then that could invalidate the findings.

Another issue is that measurement errors are rampant in historical data. If the data are not accurate, it is very easy to draw erroneous conclusions, which could lead to the implementation of hurtful or wasteful changes. Unfortunately, it is impossible to perform a retrospective measurement study to surface these measurement problems.

Finally, it is very difficult to gain support for implementing the findings of historical-data analysis. The results are very complex and difficult to present effectively. Line managers, whose careers rest on process results, often are unwilling to take action based on complex analyses in which they did not participate and which they do not understand.

METHODS USED IN HISTORICAL DATA ANALYSIS

A number of data-mining methods are used to surface high-potential ideas for improvement to be included in MVT screening experiments. The first two techniques applied to the data are simple linear regression and multiple linear regression. These two techniques are straightforward, reasonably easy to understand and interpret, and adequate for identifying high-potential MVT test ideas about 80 percent of the time.

Simple Linear Regression

Simple linear regression looks at the relationship between a single improvement factor (e.g., the number of postcards sent out) and one key measure (e.g., sales growth). It results in a formula in which y is the value of the key measure, x_1 is the number of units of factor x_1, b_1 is the impact that each unit of factor x_1 has on the key measure, and b_0 is the value of the key measure when x_1 is equal to zero.

$$y = b_0 + b_1 x_1$$

Figure 8.1 (on page 90) provides a graphic representation of this formula.

Multiple Linear Regression

Multiple linear regression is used to evaluate relationships between more than one improvement factor and a single key measure of

Figure 8.1   A Simple Linear Regression

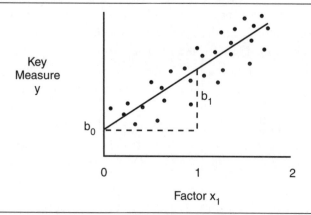

success. It is common to find through simple linear regression that more than one improvement factor can have a relationship with the key success measure. Each factor explains a portion of the variation in the key measure, but simple linear regression cannot weigh their respective impact and does not attempt to untangle any correlations that may exist between factors. Multiple linear regression addresses these shortcomings by creating a model that includes the impact of all statistically significant factors. The output is the equation shown next:

$$y = b_0 + b_1 x_1 + b_2 x_2 + b_3 x_3 + b_4 x_4 \ldots$$

This output can be used to create MVT improvement factors in two ways:

1. Each significant improvement factor in the model that is controllable is a good candidate to be an MVT test factor.
2. The model can be used in a "what if" exercise to identify potential trade-offs that might improve results. For example, if two of the factors associated with sales dollars were the amount of television ads and the amount of radio spots, asking "what if" (using the equation) might identify a combination of more TV and less radio, or vice versa, that would appear to have the potential to increase sales with no increase in cost. This action could then be tested as an MVT improvement factor. The fac-

tor might be TV and radio ads at their status quo levels versus taking money from radio and spending it on TV exposure at the change level. This type of factor allows you to test changing the media mix in a cost-free manner.

ADVANCED METHODS

About 20 percent of the time, simple linear regression and multiple linear regression do not yield useful or interesting findings. In these instances several advanced methods may be used. These methods are discussed next.

Principal Component Analysis

Principal component analysis (PCA) reduces large data sets involving many improvement factors to just a few underlying factors (Figure 8.2). PCA attempts to maximize the amount of improvement in the key measure that is explained by just a few improvement factors.

Figure 8.2 Principal Component Analysis on Retail Factors

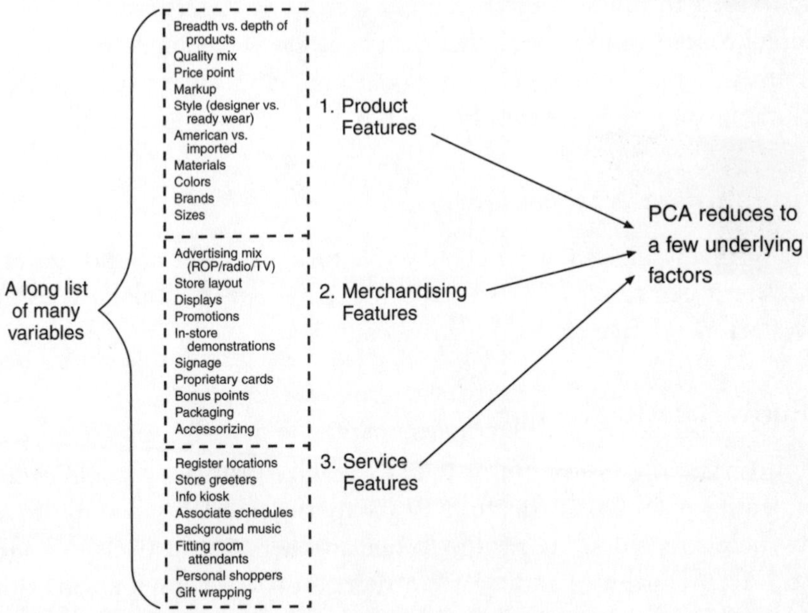

Figure 8.3   Two-Response Cluster Analysis of Lost Accounts

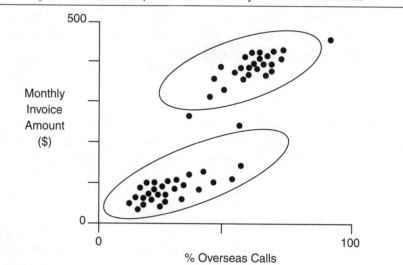

Cluster Analysis

Cluster analysis is similar to PCA in that it is an exploratory technique used to uncover improvement factors. It differs from PCA in that it groups by outcomes rather than by improvement factors. For example, in a study of lost accounts, a cluster analysis identified the two distinct groupings shown in Figure 8.3.

Discriminant Analysis

Discriminant analysis attempts to explain the special causes of differences between groups. Figure 8.4 shows a discriminant analysis using two factors relative to delinquent accounts.

Multivariate Regression

Multivariate regression can be used to analyze historical data in order to identify potential factors for MVT experimentation when multiple key success measures are related to one another. The analysis, output, and interpretation of multivariate regression are complex, but this method is useful when performed by a properly trained statistician.

Figure 8.4   Discriminant Analysis for Delinquent Accounts

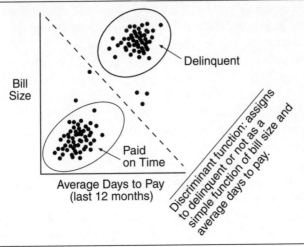

DATA-MINING TRAPS

We have encountered many situations in which novices in data mining have employed analysis tactics that skewed the results and created incorrect or misleading findings. For instance, throwing out unusual measurements, often called *outliers,* is a relatively common practice. Unfortunately, most of the clues for improvement lie in the unusual measurements. We strongly recommend further investigation of unusual measurements. Never remove any data without investigation.

We also have seen cases in which missing data were replaced by averages. This is a dangerous practice. One can very easily conclude that effects are present when, in fact, they are not, or that effects are not present when they are.

Case Study—Step 4 (Continued from Chapter 7)

The retailer conducting the MVT had years of very detailed customer information since every purchase provided updated customer information. Customer loyalty was high, and customers visited the retailer's locations an average of once per week.

Data on retail sales activity were combined with advertising information over a period of several years at the weekly geocode (smaller than zip code) level for both advertising and retail information. Seasonality and store sales events were taken into consideration.

During the time span of the historical data, variation was obvious in advertising campaigns due to seasonality, changing advertising themes, changing corporate strategies, local and national retail performance variation, and budget challenges. Direct mail penetration levels had varied both locally and nationally. Broadcast expenditures and total rating points (TRP) had varied. Flights for broadcast television and radio had varied. Information was also available regarding staffing levels, management tenure, performance reviews, special operations programs, and operations policy changes. While none of these changes were made on any basis that could be considered "designed" from a data-mining standpoint, the variations were large, ranging from totally turned off in some weeks to high levels in others.

QualPro analyzed these data using multiple linear regression and identified some startling insights. Much of the expenditure on advertising appeared to have no effect on sales or bringing in new customers. In fact, some advertising expenditures actually reduced sales. Postcards that were mailed to credit card customers showed a negative relationship with sales. Direct mail appeared to have a positive impact on sales but a negative return on investment. Television was even worse. If television advertising were free, it would still have produced negative returns. None of the broadcast venues—national, local, cable, Hispanic, or sports—appeared to have potential for positive returns.

Analysis of the data indicated that signage programs usually seemed to impact sales, although not always positively. There were no clear indications as to what aspects of the signage were important, but it appeared to be an important factor. Training programs presented the opposite situation. There was little evidence of any sales/profit impact by corporate training, whether positive or negative.

Increasing overall staffing level (at least within the ranges that existed in the data) showed no indication of helping sales, but there were indications that changes in policies in the use of staffing could be important. For example, special programs to provide improved fitting room service appeared to have the potential to be helpful.

The analysis opened many executives' eyes to the need to challenge preconceived ideas and "sacred cows" on a wider and more in-depth basis. It helped the company implement a wider range of testing than would have otherwise been tolerated.

This historical data analysis provided immediate input for potential MVT test ideas. It also gave the company a clear indication that its MVT testing should be broad and should include operational and merchandising factors in the stores, not just advertising.

CHAPTER 9

STEP 5

*Brainstorm for Improvement Ideas
with Everyone Who Could Have
Worthwhile Suggestions*

B ecause the success of the MVT process relies on experimenting with many ideas, the objective of the brainstorming process is to generate many options and many ideas for improvement. This large pool of ideas is then narrowed down to a smaller number that are tested. In Steps 4 and 5, ideas are generated for improvement by using statistical process control (SPC) charts and data-mining techniques. These techniques typically identify potential conditions for improvement that existed at least once in the history of the process and were documented previously.

Brainstorming, however, is valuable because it can generate ideas that have not been implemented previously or that have been implemented but do not show up in historical data analysis. Brainstormed ideas come from the knowledge and imaginations of people.

WHO IS INVOLVED

When brainstorming for improvement ideas, it is very important to include people well beyond the experts. If you merely assemble the usual suspects for a brainstorming session, you wind up with the same old results. In the MVT process, we want to involve a broad range of people in order to extract all possible ideas from the organization. The people whom we usually want to include are:

- *The local, front-line workforce:* These personnel often generate many ideas based on what they have experienced in their jobs. It is important that we listen to their views. If they say that the process they work on every day functions better when the weather is bad, they are probably right.
- *Management:* In the MVT process, it is important that the managers contribute, that they learn the experimental process along with everybody else, that they provide resources, and that they become actively involved. By demonstrating their involvement, they can help the MVT process and its results to be broadly accepted in the organization. Just as important, they are likely to have some good ideas.
- *Technical personnel:* Design, engineering, laboratory, maintenance, quality control, and information systems personnel, because of their technical skills and knowledge, may be able to contribute significantly to the brainstorming process. Although the brainstorming process should include nontechnical personnel in addition to the experts, it certainly should include technical personnel.
- *Customers or those who interact with customers:* Customers' perspectives and input can be very important in the MVT process. If customers cannot participate directly, it is very important that people who interact with them regularly, such as sales and customer service personnel, be included.
- *Suppliers or those who interact with suppliers:* Like customers, suppliers may have a unique perspective and be able to offer ideas for improvement not thought of by others. They also may have ideas about how they can adjust their own processes or products in order to impact the results positively. If suppliers cannot participate directly, it is important to include those who interact with them regularly, such as purchasing agents.
- *Naive observers:* A naive observer does not have specific knowledge of the process. However, he or she may make very creative suggestions for improving the process simply because he or she is

not too close to the problem. Sometimes people can offer brilliant suggestions because they did not know that their suggestions were "impossible."

HOW BRAINSTORMING WORKS

The standardized process for brainstorming has five steps:

1. *Display a clear statement of the objective that the group is considering.* An example is "What are specific actions which we might take that could improve our sales and profit margins?" Next, explain that all ideas should be practical, fast, and cost free. You are not looking for improvement ideas that would be cumbersome, complex, time-consuming, or expensive to test or implement. The best ideas often involve simple changes to existing processes.

2. *Allow a few minutes for silent writing.* During this time, no one should speak. Paper and pencils are provided, and each person is asked to consider the statement of the objective and to write down as many ideas as he or she can identify.

3. *Each member of the group, in turn, offers one idea at a time.* No discussion, questions, or comments are allowed. No one is allowed to criticize someone else's ideas or to interrupt someone else. If someone does not have an additional idea when his or her turn arrives, the person can pass. The group members are encouraged to continue the creative process; if someone else's idea suggests a new idea to another member, he or she should write the new idea down and submit it when his or her turn comes. This is called *piggybacking*; it is a valuable part of the brainstorming process.

4. *The ideas are recorded exactly as they are stated.* All ideas are posted in a place that is visible to everyone. This usually means capturing the ideas on a flip chart and then posting the flip chart on the wall. The moderator should continue to encourage people to look at the list on the wall and continue to come up with new ideas.

5. *When all members pass on the same turn, discussion of the ideas begins.* Some of the ideas may be very similar and can be combined. Identifying common themes or categories of ideas may also be useful. If new ideas surface during the discussion, they are written down and the brainstorming continues.

ENSURING AN ADEQUATE QUANTITY AND QUALITY OF IDEAS

At least 75 ideas must usually be generated in order to end up with an optimally sized MVT. Often, hundreds of ideas are generated. To ensure that there is an adequate quantity of ideas, multiple brainstorming sessions are often necessary. You may conduct a one-hour brainstorming session with a group and come back later on for another 15 or 30 minutes that will yield additional ideas. A single brainstorming session usually should not go beyond an hour—an hour and a half at the most. With a longer duration, people tend to lose interest. Depending on the organization and the attention span of the group, less than an hour may be appropriate.

Although we have said that as many people as is practical should be included in the brainstorming effort, including people from all levels and job responsibilities, they do not all have to be included in the same brainstorming session. In fact, small groups of 5 to 10 members each are usually much more effective than larger groups. Sometimes it helps to combine groups of people differently between one brainstorming session and another. For example, you can conduct one session that includes only operators and then conduct another session that includes some of the same people but people from various other levels, too.

Finally, actually walking through the process to be improved before beginning a brainstorming session on ways to improve it is often very helpful. If it is a manufacturing process, you can stimulate ideas by physically taking the brainstorming group to look at the process being done. If it is a process like a direct mail process, pull out the direct mail advertising pieces and have the group look at them. The more real materials, equipment, and so on that people see to stimulate their thinking, the better their ideas will be.

To ensure that the ideas generated are meaty, two particular techniques can be used during the brainstorming process. These are as follows:

1. Use QualPro's elements of a process (methods, materials, machines, people, and measurement) to organize the brainstormed ideas. If ideas are organized under the various elements of the process, the weaker elements of the process will be exposed.
2. Break up the brainstorming into "chunks of the process." For a sales process, that might mean initially brainstorming for ideas to improve the generation of leads; then brainstorming for ideas to improve the qualification process; and then sequentially looking for ideas to improve the sales visit, the follow up, the proposal, and the close. In a manufacturing process, brainstorming chunks of the process might mean first generating ideas to improve order entry, then scheduling, procurement, production, quality control, and shipping.

Overall, the best way to ensure that good-quality ideas are surfaced is to ensure that there is a long list of ideas. The more ideas there are to choose from, the better the chances that good ideas will be included in the final MVT tests.

SUMMARY

Brainstorming is a critical element of the MVT process. Generating large numbers of ideas that are creative and have the potential to make a great impact goes a long way toward ensuring a successful MVT project. The winning ideas do not come from any one part of the organization. No one has a monopoly on the good ideas. Often, the people closest to the customers may come up with the most counterintuitive and insightful ideas; but the technical experts, managers, naive observers, customers, and suppliers all can make important contributions.

Case Study: Step 5 (Continued from Chapter 8)

One-hour brainstorming sessions were held with the corporate staffs from operations, marketing, and merchandising. Brainstorming sessions were then held with regional, market, and store level management to get detailed ideas for testing. An individual session was held with the CEO.

Stores were visited where all levels of associates (employees) could contribute their ideas for improving advertising, merchandising, and operations effectiveness. Group sessions were held briefly before the stores opened, and individual brainstorming discussions were held with employees unable to attend the group session.

Every brainstorming session was facilitated by the MVT consultant and had the same basic agenda:

- Overview the project and its objectives.
- Describe briefly the MVT process and its reliance on brainstormed ideas from the attendees.
- State the objective of the session: "Identify practical, fast, and cost-free actions that might be taken to increase sales and raise profits."
- Spend five minutes of thinking time.
- Explain the brainstorming rules (for example, one idea at a time, no commenting on the ideas of others, and so on).
- Capture ideas on a flip chart for about 45 minutes.
- Thank the participants and adjourn after an hour.

After all the brainstorming sessions were completed, the MVT consultant consolidated the brainstormed ideas with the ideas generated from Step 3, "Special Cause Search," and the ideas generated from the historical data analysis. The list of over 100 potential MVT improvement factors that remained after redundancies were eliminated is shown in the table on pages 102–103.

Brainstormed Ideas to Improve Retail Sales and Profits

Brainstorming List
1   Increase in-store special sales events.
2   Redesign stores according to adjacencies.
3   Highlight signage using lighting.
4   Use more newspaper (ROP) advertising.
5   Conduct ongoing sales training in each weekly associate meeting.
6   Provide customer visit living room.
7   Award bonus incentives for shoe department managers for sales.
8   Improve visual impact of displays using enhanced lighting.
9   Award associates incentives by department rather than by individual.
10   Call for help if more than one customer in queue.
11   Increase staffing in merchandise intensification areas.
12   Emphasize cosmetics staffing.
13   Have incentives (prize or dinner) for support associates.
14   Play more upbeat background music.
15   Increase density of sales associates.
16   Emphasize product "themes" in window signage rather than "items."
17   Increase number of managers on duty.
18   Use more stylistic ROP advertising.
19   Emphasize accessories in displays to increase cross selling.
20   Provide motivation training to all levels of staff.
21   Sponsor more community outreach programs.
22   Assist customers to other departments.
23   Increase communications to customer.
24   Expand store hours.
25   Relocate stores from declining areas to more upscale areas.
26   Move directional signs into department locations, not central location.
27   Train associates to sell during catalog calls.
28   Increase level of support staff.
29   Use broader play time for radio (not just drive time).
30   Intensify top selling merchandise, capitalizing on success for short term.
31   Use more television and radio advertising.
32   Implement better merchandise locator process across company.
33   Use smaller sized ROP ads.
34   Institute new account rewards for associates.
35   Improve product placement and merchandising in shoe department.
36   Use billboards to advertise.
37   Add runner from floor to assist in fitting rooms (during peak times).
38   Consolidate pricing signage whenever possible.
39   Require professional associate attire.
40   Increase incentives for top 10% of managers (and lower for others).
41   Execute double/triple point loyalty events for card holders.
42   Increase cadence of markdowns.
43   Implement "no holds" policy.
44   Increase direct mail to include non-proprietary customers.
45   Have dedicated cashiers rather than sales associates.
46   Schedule daily demos in kitchenware.
47   Increase vendor-specific mailings frequencies.
48   Use first-class mail for all mailings.
49   Implement week-long pre-sales for sales events for loyal customers.
50   Institute broader return policy.
51   Use four-page circulars instead of two pages.
52   Implement monthly fashion shows.

(continued)

53 Tier commission structure for selling additional items.
54 Market proprietary customers using phone calls, not post cards.
55 Increase quantity and display of jeans.
56 Increase staff ratio of part-time / full-time.
57 Discount multiple in-store purchases.
58 Increase revenue by creating "focus" stores.
59 Use bolder, brighter colors in circulars.
60 Provide on-the-floor training for new associates.
61 Increase frequency of ROP ads.
62 Conduct food and wine tastings in store.
63 Install call buttons in fitting rooms.
64 Optimize adjacencies of merchandise in catalog.
65 Make business adjacencies at key entrances uniform for all stores.
66 Provide incentives for all credit card purchases (not just proprietary).
67 Connect sales associates incentives to high-ticket items.
68 Use store announcements to advertise specials/events to customers.
69 Provide better incentives for credit card acquisition.
70 Have broader customer incentive base.
71 Associates emphasize customer service and assign greeter at entrance.
72 Shift staffing emphasis to base staffing focus on sales per square foot.
73 Implement men's loyalty program.
74 Use stylized mannequins throughout stores.
75 Use electronic video banks in contemporary department.
76 Place impulse items at cashier terminals.
77 Display more folded merchandise.
78 Use fragrance blow-ins.
79 Implement deferred billing.
80 Schedule more associates on the floor during peak traffic periods.
81 Allow returns to any location.
82 Keep fitting rooms unlocked.
83 Redesign cashier stations to face customers.
84 Adopt common marketing theme across all media.
85 Allow associates to wear company apparel while on the job.
86 Allow local discretion in setting salaries for new hires.
87 Locate promotional displays near appropriate department entrance.
88 Hire only full-time associates and part-time support employees.
89 Improve stop-loss program by increasing in-store security force.
90 Offer free gift wrapping.
91 Provide shopping carts.
92 Provide personal shopper in store.
93 Provide extra services to customer (alterations, package carryout, etc.).
94 Implement lenient check acceptance, credit applications, etc.
95 Use less expensive paper stock for circulars.
96 Offer everyday discount program.
97 Provide sales associates out-of-store activity (follow-up).
98 Offer pay incentives for support associates.
99 Change from showcase to open sale display (e.g., handbags).
100 Redesign web site.
101 Improve number of pages and merchandise selection in catalogs.
102 Upgrade fixtures in stores.
103 Improve lighting/security in parking areas.
104 Offer a place for customer to park packages.

CHAPTER 10

STEP 6

Select Improvement Ideas That Are Practical, Fast, and Cost Free

After steps 3, 4, and 5 have resulted in many dozens of suggestions for improving results, the next step is to categorize the ideas as: (1) practical, fast, and cost free, or (2) not. MVT experiments are done only with those ideas that meet all three criteria to ensure that we get easy, quick, and inexpensive results that provide immediate benefits in terms of business results.

Some people may be concerned that, by eliminating all ideas that are not practical, fast, and cost free, we are eliminating some ideas that could improve results. Although this may be true, our objective is to learn what improves results—safely, quickly, and inexpensively. Even after we narrow down the original list of suggestions, a long list of ideas to test will remain—usually about one-third of the original list. Ideas that are not judged to be practical, fast, and cost free may be shelved for review in later MVTs. They are not lost forever. However, consideration of any of these ideas should be done only as a last resort, after all the practical, fast, and cost-free ideas have been tested.

People have been tempted to use other means to narrow down the list of improvement suggestions and determine which ideas will be included in the MVT tests. For example, some people have wanted to vote on which ideas to include. Their rationale was that, by voting, we could include those ideas that we thought had the best chance of improving results. However, our empirical data, collected for over 20 years, show conclusively that although the local workforce, managers, executives, and technical experts can make great contributions by submitting ideas for improvement, they have poor ability to predict which ideas are going to be the most productive. QualPro consultants have often worked with clients to create contests in which the experts, managers, workforce members, and others are invited to rank the collected ideas in the order that they think the ideas will contribute, from the best to worst. When their votes are compared to the actual measurement of the impact of each idea through MVT testing, the results are surprising. There is no correlation between the ideas that everyone thought would work and the ones that actually did work.

By focusing MVT experiments only on those ideas that are practical, fast, and cost free, we are assured of identifying solutions that are easy, quick, and inexpensive to implement.

PRACTICAL

Practical means that we can actually experiment with an idea. It means that the change is physically possible without doing harm to the process, risking the safety of the workers, or risking the goodwill of the customers. For example, an idea for a chemical process might be to increase the temperature of the reaction from 170 degrees to 180 degrees. The local workforce and process engineer, who know the process best, are asked to make a judgment as to whether the change can be physically performed and whether it can be done safely. If the answer is yes (it can be physically performed safely), it is deemed practical. If it cannot be done physically and safely, it is not practical.

Practical also means that we are able to incorporate the idea into the process day in and day out. Sometimes an idea can be executed for a short time but cannot be sustained for the long haul. In that case, it is not practical.

In an MVT to improve response to a direct-mail package, an idea might be to change the wording in the letter. If the workforce that is responsible for designing the letter says that the rewording of the letter can be done, it is legal, and it is not expected to disappoint or anger customers, then the rewording is practical. Since the local workforce has the most knowledge about the process, its features, and how it works, the local workforce often decides whether or not a suggestion is practical. Keep in mind, however, that we are not asking the local workforce members if they think a suggestion will work. We are simply asking, "Can we actually experiment with this? Can we incorporate it into the process on a day-to-day basis? Is it safe?"

FAST

Fast means that, if we learn that a suggestion makes the results better, we can incorporate the idea into the process quickly. Quickly means a matter of days or weeks—certainly no longer than a month. Some ideas that have great potential but will take six months, a year, or two years to implement are left out of the experiment. Again, some will argue that good ideas may be left on the table, and they are right. However, the MVT process and its users can rarely wait six months, a year, or two years for improved results.

Fast also means that the factor can be tested during the time allowed for the experiment. Some may argue that if the MVT experiment is delayed only a few weeks or months, we can include this other factor that we really like. Since only 25 percent of factors will help, *no* factor should be viewed as a reason to delay experimentation.

COST FREE

If a proposed improvement is going to cost one dime more than the current cost of operating the process, it is not cost free. This means that any kind of a capital investment would not be considered cost free. It means that any idea that increases operating costs is not cost free. And if it is not cost free, it is not included in the MVT experiment. In essence, the MVT process is looking for huge payoffs for an investment of near zero. This is not to say that some ideas that cost money might not be helpful. But as long as we have "free" ideas, why spend money in an effort to improve results?

WHO IS INVOLVED IN CATEGORIZING IMPROVEMENT IDEAS?

Ideas should be separated into the two categories (Practical/Fast/Cost Free versus Not) by people who are familiar with the process to be improved. Typically, the practical criterion is assessed by the local workforce, the people who actually operate the process and work within it. The fast and cost-free criteria typically are determined by professional, technical, and management personnel, who may be more familiar with the timing of and cost of implementing an idea.

FACTOR LEVELS

As test factors (i.e., improvement ideas) are chosen through the categorization process, each factor's *levels* should also be determined. In an MVT experiment, factors typically have two levels: (1) status quo and (2) change. For example, a manufacturing MVT factor might be temperature, and its levels might be 150 degrees (status quo) and 175 degrees (change). In a sales experiment, a factor might be the time of week of a newspaper ad, and its levels might be Thursday (status quo) and Sunday (change).

The selection of the levels of each factor is very important. To maximize potential improvement, test levels should be made as bold as possible without experimenting recklessly or taking unnecessary chances.

While MVT experiments can include more than two levels (status quo versus change), we have found that testing more than two levels is not the most efficient approach. Since 75 percent of the test ideas are likely to hurt or make no difference, it is usually best to first determine if a test factor even makes a difference to the process, and then work on fine-tuning the level of the test factor if (and only if) it turns out to improve the process.

SUMMARY

For most people involved in an MVT project, the concept of using the practical, fast, and cost-free criteria to determine what ideas will be tested is foreign. Their instincts often are to use their knowledge and experience to narrow down the ideas. However, QualPro's data consistently show that using the practical, fast, and cost-free criteria is a far superior way to categorize and eliminate ideas and to determine the ideas to be tested. Ed Mueller, CEO of Williams-Sonoma, recently selected the 2005 Retailing Innovator of the year, who has more than a dozen years' experience using MVT, has said that "the concept of practical, fast, and cost free is the greatest genius in the entire MVT process."

Case Study: Step 6 (Continued from Chapter 9)

The list of more than a hundred potential improvement ideas needed to be narrowed to those that would be included in the MVT screening experiment. This narrowing of the list was achieved by categorizing the ideas into two groups:

1. Ideas that were Practical, Fast, *and* Cost Free.
2. Ideas that were not Practical, Fast, *and* Cost Free.

This categorization was performed by a group of people who, collectively, were knowledgeable of the entire retail process—merchandise selection/procurement, staffing models, training, advertising, pricing, signage, service policies, and so on. This group included the director of advertising services, a store manager, an assistant store manager, the director of merchandising, the manager of pricing, and the director of human resources.

The MVT consultant explained to the group that, to be included in the MVT screening experiment, an idea had to meet all three of the practical, fast, and cost-free criteria. If an idea failed to meet any one of the criteria, it was to be set aside.

Initially, the group felt that nearly every idea passed all three criteria. But as they considered the impacts across the business of going from a casual description of the idea to actually incorporating that idea into the process, many ideas were discarded.

Some members of the group were biased toward ideas that cost money. The feeling was widespread that only ideas that took substantial amounts of money and time could have substantial effects on sales and new customers. The MVT consultant gave examples from other MVT experiments to illustrate the fallacy of this thinking. The CEO happened to step into the meeting at an opportune time and was helpful in overcoming this tendency by sharing personal experiences of small but leveraged changes that had made a large business impact.

While there were 104 ideas prior to categorization, only 23 were found to be practical, fast, and cost free. The table on page 109 shows a portion of the group's categorization work.

As the group determined that an improvement idea initially passed the practical, fast, and cost-free filter, they then defined the levels that would be tested for that idea. Both the status quo level and the change level to be tested were defined and documented. The idea, with levels defined, was

Categorized Ideas

Brainstorming List	P	F	C
1 ~~Increase in-store special sales events.~~	✗	✓	✗
2 ~~Redesign stores according to adjacencies.~~	✓	✗	✗
3 ~~Highlight signage using lighting.~~	✓	✗	✗
4 ~~Use more newspaper (ROP) advertising.~~	✓	✓	✗
5 Conduct ongoing sales training in each weekly associate meeting.	✓	✓	✓
6 ~~Provide customer visit living room.~~	✗	✗	✗
7 ~~Bonus incentives for shoe department managers for sales.~~	✓	✓	✗
8 ~~Improve visual impact of displays using enhanced lighting.~~	✓	✗	✗
9 Award associates incentives by department rather than by individual.	✓	✓	✓
10 Call for help if more than one customer in queue.	✓	✓	✓
11 ~~Increase staffing in merchandise intensification areas.~~	✗	✗	✗
12 ~~Emphasize cosmetics staffing.~~	✓	✗	✗
13 ~~Have incentives (prize or dinner) for support associates.~~	✓	✓	✗
14 Play more upbeat background music.	✓	✓	✓
15 ~~Increase density of sales associates.~~	✓	✗	✗
16 Emphasize product "themes" in window signage rather than "items."	✓	✓	✓
17 ~~Increase number of managers on duty.~~	✓	✗	✗
18 Use more stylistic ROP advertising.	✓	✓	✓
19 Emphasize accessories in displays to increase cross selling.	✓	✓	✓
20 ~~Provide motivation training to all levels of staff.~~	✓	✗	✗
21 ~~Sponsor more community outreach programs.~~	✗	✗	✗
22 ~~Assist customers to other departments.~~	✗	✓	✓
23 ~~Increase communications to customer.~~	✗	✓	✗
24 ~~Expand store hours.~~	✓	✓	✗
25 ~~Relocate stores from declining areas to more upscale areas.~~	✗	✗	✗
26 Move directional signs into department locations, not central location.	✓	✓	✓
27 ~~Train associates to sell during catalog calls.~~	✗	✗	✓
28 ~~Increase level of support staff.~~	✗	✗	✗
29 Use broader play time for radio (not just drive time).	✓	✓	✓
30 ~~Intensify top selling merchandise, capitalizing on success for short term.~~	✓	✗	✗
31 ~~Use more television and radio advertising.~~	✓	✓	✗
32 ~~Implement better merchandise locator process across company.~~	✓	✗	✓
33 Use smaller sized ROP ads.	✓	✓	✓
34 ~~Institute new account rewards for associates.~~	✓	✓	✗
35 ~~Improve product placement and merchandising in shoe department.~~	✓	✗	✗
36 ~~Use billboards to advertise.~~	✓	✗	✗
37 Add runner from floor to assist in fitting rooms (during peak times).	✓	✓	✓
38 Consolidate pricing signage whenever possible.	✓	✓	✓
39 Require professional associate attire.	✓	✓	✓
40 Increase incentives for top 10% of managers (and lower for others).	✓	✓	
41 ~~Execute double/triple point loyalty~~			

MVT Test Factors and Their "Status Quo" and "Change" Levels

Factor Description	Status Quo "−"	Change "+"
A: Fitting room attendants	Current process	Add runner from floor during peak times
B: Dress code	Casual associate attire	Professional associate attire
C: Circular page count	2 page circulars	4 page circulars
D: Circular color style	Current	Bolder brighter colors
E: Circular paper stock	Current	Less expensive
F: Pricing signage	Current display signage	Consolidate signage
G: ROP message	Current	More stylistic
H: ROP size	Current	Smaller sized ads
I: Directional signage	Floor signage	Department signage
J: Store announce-ments	None	Use store announcements
K: Promotional location	Located with merchandise	Located near department entrance
L: Radio advertising	Target drive times	Broader play time
M: In-store product demos	Current	Daily demos in kitchenware
N: Checkout	Current	Call for help if more than one customer in queue
O: "Friendly" program	Current with no greeter	Emphasize customer service and assign greeter
P: Associate incentives	By individual	By department
Q: Cross selling emphasis	Current	Emphasize accessories in displays
R: Increased sales training	Current	On-going sales training in weekly associate meetings
S: Music	Soft music	More upbeat music
T: Management incen-tives	Standard reward	Increased weight for top 10%
U: Postcards versus telemarketing	Postcard messages to card holders	Automatic telephone messages to card holders
V: Associate schedul-ing	Current	Vary for peak traffic
W: Window signage	Emphasize individual items	Emphasize themes

then reexamined to make sure it was still practical, fast, and cost free. Sometimes, the group found that they had defined the levels in such a way that the idea did not meet one or more of the three criteria. The group would then work to redefine the levels so that they were practical, fast, and cost free; and, if that were not possible, the idea was discarded.

The final list of 23 test factors and levels created from the 104 ideas is shown in the table on page 110.

CHAPTER 11

STEP 7

*Design an MVT Screening
Experiment to Test Many
Ideas with Only a Few Tests*

The design of the MVT screening experiment is the most technically challenging step in the MVT process. Our experience indicates that a person needs to have strong quantitative ability, a strong background in statistics, and several years of experience in order to do a good job of designing an MVT screening experiment. QualPro consultants have designed complex experiments that tested more than 40 potential process changes involving 10,000 people in five states. We have designed experiments combining a supplier's process and a customer's process. Our experience training our own consultants and clients over the past 22 years tells us that most statisticians, even those who have PhD degrees, cannot do this type of design successfully unless they are trained extensively in the MVT methodology. Therefore, we strongly recommend that you not attempt to design an MVT screening experiment without the aid of an experienced MVT consultant.

DEFINING AN MVT TEST MATRIX

In MVT language, the potential process changes or improvement ideas that come out of Step 6 are "factors" to be tested. The material, subjects, organizational entity, or geographic entity that we experiment on for a given test is the *experimental unit*. The application of a pre-scribed combination of test factors to an experimental unit is called an MVT *recipe*.

THE PURPOSE OF THE SCREENING EXPERIMENT

The purpose of a screening experiment is to separate the potential process improvements (the factors) into those that help, those that hurt, and those that do not make any difference. Our objective always is to change the average of the key measure (for instance, raise the average sales level) or to reduce the variation in the key measure or both. For example, if we are trying to reduce defects, our objective is to lower the average. If we are trying to improve the performance of ball bearings, our objective may be to reduce the variation in diameter from bearing to bearing.

An MVT screening experiment requires that the number of potential improvements to be tested be at least one less than the number of recipes that will be tested. For example, we can test up to 31 improvement factors with only 32 recipes. Another way to say this is that a screening experiment with N experimental recipes will enable us to test up to N minus one ($N - 1$) potential changes to the process. The technique is analogous to surveying a small, carefully selected sample of likely voters in order to predict how millions will vote.

We will then be able to calculate the effects of each change in the process, independent of the effects of the other changes. We use a minus symbol (−) to designate the usual (status quo) level of a factor. We use a plus symbol (+) to designate the changed level that we are testing. In other words, a (+) means that an improvement factor has been "turned on" in a given experiment, while a (−) means that an improvement factor has been "turned off" in a given experiment.

EXAMPLES OF SCREENING EXPERIMENTS

Table 11.1 is an example of a simple screening experiment. We refer to the simple MVT screening design in Table 11.1 as a test matrix.

Table 11.1   Test Matrix for an Eight-Recipe MVT Screening Experiment

Test Recipes	Improvement Factors (Test Factors)						
	A	B	C	D	E	F	G
1	+	+	+	−	+	−	−
2	−	+	+	+	−	+	−
3	−	−	+	+	+	−	+
4	+	−	−	+	+	+	−
5	−	+	−	−	+	+	+
6	+	−	+	−	−	+	+
7	+	+	−	+	−	−	+
8	−	−	−	−	−	−	−

The pluses and minuses in any row, under the factors, define a test recipe. The capital letters (A, B, C, D, E, F, and G) represent different factors. For Recipe #1, Factor A is at the changed level. Factor B is at the changed level. Factor C is at the changed level. Factor D is at the status quo level. Factor E is at the changed level. Factor F is at the status quo level, and Factor G is at the status quo level. The other test recipes are defined in the same manner.

A defense contractor was having difficulty with the weld strength of a metal tab inside a missile housing. The function of the tab was to hold an assembly inside the missile housing in place and to stop it from rotating. In other words, the tab was an anti-rotation device. The weld strength of the tabs was so poor that the tabs kept falling off. The customer was ready to terminate the contract because the tabs fell off so often during assembly. The contractor blamed customer clumsiness and, of course, the customer disagreed. A team was formed to brainstorm factors that might improve the strength of the tab weld. Seven potential improvement factors were identified as practical, fast, and

Table 11.2   Test Factors for Improving Tab Weld Strength

Factor Description	Status Quo "−"	Change "+"
A: Tab material type	Recycle	Virgin
B: Electrode force	24 lbs	28 lbs
C: Energy	225 watt-sec	250 watt-sec
D: Size of electrode tip	$\frac{1}{8}$"	$\frac{1}{4}$"
E: Tab shape	Flat	Curved
F: Weld method	1-step	2 steps
G: Fixture	A	B

Table 11.3 Tab Weld Strength Test Matrix

Test Recipe	Material	Force (Pounds)	Energy	Tip (Inches)	Shape	Method	Fixture
1	Virgin	28	250	$\frac{1}{8}$	Curved	1-step	A
2	Recycle	28	250	$\frac{1}{4}$	Flat	2 steps	A
3	Recycle	24	250	$\frac{1}{4}$	Curved	1-step	B
4	Virgin	24	225	$\frac{1}{4}$	Curved	2 steps	A
5	Recycle	28	225	$\frac{1}{8}$	Curved	2 steps	B
6	Virgin	24	250	$\frac{1}{8}$	Flat	2 steps	B
7	Virgin	28	225	$\frac{1}{4}$	Flat	1-step	B
8	Recycle	24	225	$\frac{1}{8}$	Flat	1-step	A

cost free. The factors, along with their status quo (−) and changed (+) levels, are shown in Table 11.2.

An MVT test matrix was developed, defining the eight recipes in Table 11.3. Recipe #1 uses the virgin tab material, an electrode force of 28 pounds, an energy level of 250 watt-seconds, an electrode tip of ⅛-inch, the curved tab shape, the one-step weld method, and the fixture A.

This MVT screening design is about as simple as we have ever encountered in the real world. When you use MVT Steps 3, 4, 5, and 6 to produce test factors for an MVT screening experiment, you will usually end up with at least 20 factors to test. A typical list of factors, involving a sales rep example is shown in Table 11.4 on page 116. The screening design for that example, with 36 recipes that can test up to 35 factors, is shown in Table 11.5 on pages 118–119.

Typically, factors are tested in MVT screening experiments with two levels, the status quo and a change. Sometimes, it is desirable to test more than one change against the status quo. Although this creates complexities in MVT screening design and analysis, multiple changes can be tested if they are deemed important. However, in our experience, in almost all situations, testing a single change against the status quo is the most efficient path to success in a screening experiment.

CHOOSING THE EXPERIMENTAL UNIT

Choosing the experimental unit to be used in an MVT screening experiment is very important. As mentioned earlier, an experimental

Table 11.4 Test Factors to Improve Sales Rep Performance

Factor	Description	Status Quo "−"	Change "+"
A:	Provide reps better sales info	Same	New info
B:	Listing of special bundled promotions	No	Yes
C:	Free freight	Never	Selected
D:	Customer new product rewards	No	Yes
E:	Obtain input from reps on product promotion ideas	No	Yes
F:	$200 free samples of products	No	Yes
G:	Office hours	Standard	Extended
H:	Reverse directory for reps	No	Yes
I:	Notify reps if backorder	No	Yes
J:	Notify reps of product problems	No	Yes
K:	Personal visits to customers	Standard	More
L:	Mail material before visit	No	Yes
M:	Reps utilize (new) special discount prices	No	Yes
N:	Call ahead to confirm	No	Yes
O:	Company pays cost of equipment installs	No	Yes
P:	Free product with minimum purchase	No	Yes
Q:	Notify reps before phone-in orders are processed	No	Yes
R:	24-hour tech support	No	Yes
S:	Listing of commercial products sold by retailers and retailer address	No	Yes
T:	Follow-up visit	No	Yes
U:	Make top five product demos available to reps	No	Yes
V:	Small premium giveaway	No	Yes
W:	Listing of customers	Yearly	Monthly
X:	Follow-up/thank you letters	No	Yes
Y:	Inform customers of special financing	No	Yes
Z:	Daily sales plan approach	No	Yes
AA:	Applications glossary	No	Yes
BB:	Sales meetings Monday or Friday	No	Yes

unit is the material, subjects, organizational entity, or geographic entity that we experiment on with a test recipe. Following are several examples of experimental units:

- Material produced in a day's production.
- A group of four salespersons.
- A company's retail stores located in certain geographic area.

- A sales territory.
- A hospital.
- A manufactured roll of carpet.
- A shift's production of a chemical product.
- Material produced by a group of machines in a given time period.

An experimental unit should be something that is representative of the real world. We discourage the use of focus groups, laboratory scale models, pilot production plants, and the like. It is always possible to identify appropriate experimental units in the real world.

SELECTING EXPERIMENTAL UNITS

An extremely important component in the design of the MVT screening experiment is the random assignment of experimental units to MVT recipes. This is a three-step process:

1. The pool of experimental units must be determined.
2. The experimental units to be actually included in the test must be randomly selected from the pool.
3. Each experimental unit to be included must be randomly assigned to a test recipe.

We identify the pool of experimental units by analyzing the historical results for all potential experimental units and eliminating those that have exhibited unusual results and those that are expected to behave in an unusual manner during the time of the MVT experiment. For example, if a retailer has 800 stores and the key measure is sales, a statistical analysis is performed on historical sales, and any stores that are unusually good or bad are eliminated from the pool. Additionally, any stores that have renovations planned for the time of the experiment are eliminated from the pool. Similarly, if something like road construction is planned that will change customer access to a particular store, that store is eliminated from the pool.

Table 11.5   36-Recipe MVT Screening Test Matrix to Use with Table 11.4

Test Recipe	A	B	C	D	E	F	G	H	I	J	K	L	M	N	O	P	Q
1	−	+	−	+	+	+	−	−	−	+	+	+	+	+	−	+	+
2	−	−	+	−	+	+	+	−	−	−	+	+	+	+	+	−	+
3	+	−	−	+	−	+	+	+	−	−	−	+	+	+	+	+	−
4	−	+	−	−	+	−	+	+	+	−	−	−	+	+	+	+	+
5	−	−	+	−	−	+	−	+	+	+	−	−	−	+	+	+	+
6	+	−	−	+	−	−	+	−	+	+	+	−	−	−	+	+	+
7	+	+	−	−	+	−	−	+	−	+	+	+	−	−	−	+	+
8	−	+	+	−	−	+	−	−	+	−	+	+	+	−	−	−	+
9	+	−	+	+	−	−	+	−	−	+	−	+	+	+	−	−	−
10	−	+	−	+	+	−	−	+	−	−	+	−	+	+	+	−	−
11	+	−	+	−	+	+	−	−	+	−	−	+	−	+	+	+	−
12	−	+	−	+	−	+	+	−	−	+	−	−	+	−	+	+	+
13	−	−	+	−	+	−	+	+	−	−	+	−	−	+	−	+	+
14	−	−	−	+	−	+	−	+	+	−	−	+	−	−	+	−	+
15	−	−	−	−	+	−	+	−	+	+	−	−	+	−	−	+	−
16	+	−	−	−	−	+	−	+	−	+	+	−	−	+	−	−	+
17	−	+	−	−	−	−	+	−	+	−	+	+	−	−	+	−	−
18	−	−	+	−	−	−	−	+	−	+	−	+	+	−	−	+	−
19	+	−	−	+	−	−	−	−	+	−	+	−	+	+	−	−	+
20	+	+	−	−	+	−	−	−	−	+	−	+	−	+	+	−	−
21	+	+	+	−	−	+	−	−	−	−	+	−	+	−	+	+	−
22	−	+	+	+	−	−	+	−	−	−	−	+	−	+	−	+	+
23	+	−	+	+	+	−	−	+	−	−	−	−	+	−	+	−	+
24	+	+	−	+	+	+	−	−	+	−	−	−	−	+	−	+	−
25	+	+	+	−	+	+	+	−	−	+	−	−	−	−	+	−	+
26	+	+	+	+	−	+	+	+	−	−	+	−	−	−	−	+	−
27	+	+	+	+	+	−	+	+	+	−	−	+	−	−	−	−	+
28	−	+	+	+	+	+	−	+	+	+	−	−	+	−	−	−	−
29	−	−	+	+	+	+	+	−	+	+	+	−	−	+	−	−	−
30	−	−	−	+	+	+	+	+	−	+	+	+	−	−	+	−	−
31	+	−	−	−	+	+	+	+	+	−	+	+	+	−	−	+	−
32	+	+	−	−	−	+	+	+	+	+	−	+	+	+	−	−	+
33	+	+	+	−	−	−	+	+	+	+	+	−	+	+	+	−	−
34	−	+	+	+	−	−	−	+	+	+	+	+	−	+	+	+	−
35	+	−	+	+	+	−	−	−	+	+	+	+	+	−	+	+	+
36	−	−	−	−	−	−	−	−	−	−	−	−	−	−	−	−	−

R	S	T	U	V	W	X	Y	Z	AA	BB	CC	DD	EE	FF	GG	HH	II
+	−	−	+	−	−	−	−	+	−	+	−	+	+	−	−	+	−
+	+	−	−	+	−	−	−	−	+	−	+	−	+	+	−	−	+
+	+	+	−	−	+	−	−	−	−	+	−	+	−	+	+	−	−
−	+	+	+	−	−	+	−	−	−	−	+	−	+	−	+	+	−
+	−	+	+	+	−	−	+	−	−	−	−	+	−	+	−	+	+
+	+	−	+	+	+	−	−	+	−	−	−	−	+	−	+	−	+
+	+	+	−	+	+	+	−	−	+	−	−	−	−	+	−	+	−
+	+	+	+	−	+	+	+	−	−	+	−	−	−	−	+	−	+
+	+	+	+	+	−	+	+	+	−	−	+	−	−	−	−	+	−
−	+	+	+	+	+	−	+	+	+	−	−	+	−	−	−	−	+
−	−	+	+	+	+	+	−	+	+	+	−	−	+	−	−	−	−
−	−	−	+	+	+	+	+	−	+	+	+	−	−	+	−	−	−
+	−	−	−	+	+	+	+	+	−	+	+	+	−	−	−	+	−
+	+	−	−	−	+	+	+	+	+	−	+	+	+	−	−	+	−
+	+	+	−	−	−	+	+	+	+	+	−	+	+	+	−	−	+
−	+	+	+	−	−	−	+	+	+	+	+	−	+	+	+	−	−
+	−	+	+	+	−	−	−	+	+	+	+	+	−	+	+	+	−
−	+	−	+	+	+	−	−	−	+	+	+	+	+	−	+	+	+
−	−	+	−	+	+	+	−	−	−	+	+	+	+	+	−	+	+
+	−	−	+	−	+	+	+	−	−	−	+	+	+	+	+	−	+
−	+	−	−	+	−	+	+	+	−	−	−	+	+	+	+	+	−
−	−	+	−	−	+	−	+	+	+	−	−	−	+	+	+	+	+
+	−	−	+	−	−	+	−	+	+	+	−	−	−	+	+	+	+
+	+	−	−	+	−	−	+	−	+	+	+	−	−	−	+	+	+
−	+	+	−	−	+	−	−	+	−	+	+	+	−	−	−	+	+
+	−	+	+	−	−	+	−	−	+	−	+	+	+	−	−	−	+
−	+	−	+	+	−	−	+	−	−	+	−	+	+	+	−	−	−
+	−	+	−	+	+	−	−	+	−	−	+	−	+	+	+	−	−
−	+	−	+	−	+	+	−	−	+	−	−	+	−	+	+	+	−
−	+	−	+	−	+	+	−	−	+	−	−	+	−	+	−	+	+
−	−	+	−	+	−	+	+	−	−	+	−	−	+	−	+	−	+
−	−	−	+	−	+	−	+	+	−	−	+	−	−	+	−	+	+
+	−	−	−	−	+	−	+	−	+	+	−	−	+	−	−	+	−
−	+	−	−	−	−	+	−	+	−	+	+	−	−	+	−	−	+
−	−	+	−	−	−	−	+	−	+	−	+	+	−	−	+	−	−
−	−	−	−	−	−	−	−	−	−	−	−	−	−	−	−	−	−

Approximately 775 of the 800 stores typically would remain in the pool. The 32 stores to be included in the test would then be chosen randomly. Random selection can be accomplished by using a table of random numbers (each number representing a store), by using a computer program designed for that purpose, or simply by drawing numbers out of a container.

RANDOMLY ASSIGNING EXPERIMENTAL UNITS TO TEST RECIPES

The experimental units then need to be assigned to a test recipe. This too can be done very easily by simply drawing numbers out of a container. To do this, give a number (from 1 to 32) to each of the 32 recipes. Then assign a number (from 1 to 32) to each of the store locations. Put the numbers representing the store locations into a container, draw them out one at a time, and assign them to the 32 recipes in sequential order. Any shortcut or omission of these steps can result in a nonvalid experiment.

Sometimes, for reasons related to cost or timing, restricted randomization must be used rather than complete randomization. Restricted randomization should be avoided, if possible, but if the MVT screening experiment cannot be run unless we make concessions on randomization, we usually will make the concessions.

For example, in the store experiment described, a test factor may be the timing of television advertising. If two stores in the same city are randomly assigned to recipes that require different timing of TV advertising, a problem exists because the two stores would use the same television stations. In this case, one of the stores would have to be replaced by randomly selecting a store in a different city.

In manufacturing situations, a long, involved setup or cleanup process may be required between MVT recipes. In order to complete the experimentation in a reasonable time period, recipes may need to be completed in a particular order to minimize the setup or cleanup time. Even with restrictions on randomization, we have always been able to identify process changes that, when implemented, will improve results.

Table 11.6   Tab Weld Original and Reflected Design Matrix

Test Recipe	A	B	C	D	E	F	G
			Original				
1	+	+	+	−	+	−	−
2	−	+	+	+	−	+	−
3	−	−	+	+	+	−	+
4	+	−	−	+	+	+	−
5	−	+	−	−	+	+	+
6	+	−	+	−	−	+	+
7	+	+	−	+	−	−	+
8	−	−	−	−	−	−	−
			Reflected				
9	−	−	−	+	−	+	+
10	+	−	−	−	+	−	+
11	+	+	−	−	−	+	−
12	−	+	+	−	−	−	+
13	+	−	+	+	−	−	−
14	−	+	−	+	+	−	−
15	−	−	+	−	+	+	−
16	+	+	+	+	+	+	+

OTHER MVT DESIGN CONSIDERATIONS

Combining Original Screening Designs with Reflected Designs

If resources permit, we recommend combining an MVT *original* screening design with a *reflected* design. A reflected design is a design in which all the plus and minus signs in the original design are exchanged (all pluses are changed to minuses, and all minuses are changed to pluses). When we run the original design and the reflected design simultaneously and calculate the effects of the process changes over both designs, we get cleaner estimates of the effect of each test factor and the synergies among test factors. The original and reflected designs for the Tab Weld example are shown in Table 11.6.

Replicating Test Recipes with Different Experimental Units

There is also a need to replicate at least some of the test recipes in the MVT screening experiment. Replication means running a recipe more than once with different experimental units. Replication is needed to determine the inherent variation present during the experimentation. We can then calculate control limits to indicate whether the effect of each factor is significant. If replication is expensive or time consuming, we will do only partial replication. Sometimes we will not do any replication but will insert some dummy factors into the MVT screening experiment. A dummy factor is one for which no changes are made. The factor measures the impact of not doing anything differently. Dummy factor effects yield a measure of the data noise or variation present during the experimentation.

If the objective is to identify conditions that reduce variation in the key measure (as opposed to raising or lowering the average), it is essential that there be complete replication. This means that every test recipe is run with at least two different experimental units.

Determining the Size and Duration of the Experiments

We are always faced with the questions of what the MVT screening experiment duration should be and what the size of the MVT screening experiment should be. To answer these questions, we obtain estimates of the key-measure variation from the statistical process control charts of the historical data. We use these estimates of variation to determine what the duration of MVT experimentation should enable us to obtain a designated amount of improvement in the process. For example, if we would like to obtain an improvement of 1 percent in retail-store comp sales, we can use the historical comp sales variation to determine the needed size (number of stores) and duration (number of weeks) of MVT experimentation that will be necessary to detect a factor effect of 1 percent.

Playing the Game

Perhaps the most important phase of the design of an MVT screening experiment is what we call *Playing the Game*. This phase involves getting everyone together who has been involved in the categorization of factors and who is going to be involved in the MVT screening experiment, going through each recipe, and asking the question: "Can we run the conditions indicated by each pair of factors without any difficulty?" For example, in the experiment illustrated in Table 11.2, we would ask, "Can we run virgin material and high electrode force at the same time?" and "Can we run virgin material and 250 watt-sec. energy at the same time?" We continue this process until we have examined each factor-pair combination in the entire test matrix. We ask ourselves, "Can that be done?" and "Is there any problem in doing it?" Often, when we play the game, we determine that there are some factor combinations that we cannot test. Sometimes that necessitates the elimination of a factor. More often, it necessitates a change in a factor level.

SUMMARY

We have now taken the following actions:

- Defined the MVT test matrix.
- Chosen the experimental units.
- Randomly assigned the experimental units to test recipes.
- Determined the replication and reflection strategies.
- Set the size and duration.
- Played the game.

We are now ready to execute the MVT screening experiment.

Case Study: Step 7 (Continued from Chapter 10)

A total of 23 practical, fast, and cost-free test factors was defined in Step 6. Now the critical task of determining the design of the MVT screening experiment was undertaken by the MVT consultant.

His first activity was to determine the MVT matrix. Since 23 factors were to be tested, a matrix with as few as 24 recipes could be used. The MVT consultant did, in fact, create a 24-recipe MVT matrix that is shown in the table on page 124.

The MVT consultant considered reflecting the MVT matrix, which would have required 48 recipes. While this would have provided some additional useful information regarding synergies, the project leader was concerned with the organization's ability to execute 48 different recipes.

MVT Screening Matrix To Test 23 Factors Using 24 Recipes

Factors

Recipe		Store ID	A	B	C	D	E	F	G	H	I	J	K	L	M	N	O	P	Q	R	S	T	U	V	W
1	1681	1173	+	+	+	+	+	−	+	−	+	+	−	−	+	+	−	−	+	−	+	−	−	−	−
2	1416	0541	−	+	+	+	+	+	−	+	−	+	+	−	−	+	+	−	−	+	−	+	−	−	−
3	0636	0270	−	−	+	+	+	+	+	−	+	−	+	+	−	−	+	+	−	−	+	−	+	−	−
4	1791	0753	−	−	−	+	+	+	+	+	−	+	−	+	+	−	−	+	+	−	−	+	−	+	−
5	0544	0183	−	−	−	−	+	+	+	+	+	−	+	−	+	+	−	−	+	+	−	−	+	−	+
6	1449	0956	+	−	−	−	−	+	+	+	+	+	−	+	−	+	+	−	−	+	+	−	−	+	−
7	1687	1351	−	+	−	−	−	−	+	+	+	+	+	−	+	−	+	+	−	−	+	+	−	−	+
8	1571	0960	+	−	+	−	−	−	−	+	+	+	+	+	−	+	−	+	+	−	−	+	+	−	−
9	0485	1246	−	+	−	+	−	−	−	−	+	+	+	+	+	−	+	−	+	+	−	−	+	+	−
10	1488	0578	−	−	+	−	+	−	−	−	−	+	+	+	+	+	−	+	−	+	+	−	−	+	+
11	1328	0655	+	−	−	+	−	+	−	−	−	−	+	+	+	+	+	−	+	−	+	+	−	−	+
12	0606	1161	+	+	−	−	+	−	+	−	−	−	−	+	+	+	+	+	−	+	−	+	+	−	−
13	1932	1842	−	+	+	−	−	+	−	+	−	−	−	−	+	+	+	+	+	−	+	−	+	+	−
14	1226	0814	−	−	+	+	−	−	+	−	+	−	−	−	−	+	+	+	+	+	−	+	−	+	+
15	1613	1447	+	−	−	+	+	−	−	+	−	+	−	−	−	−	+	+	+	+	+	−	+	−	+
16	1933	1549	+	+	−	−	+	+	−	−	+	−	+	−	−	−	−	+	+	+	+	+	−	+	−
17	0235	1177	−	+	+	−	−	+	+	−	−	+	−	+	−	−	−	−	+	+	+	+	+	−	+
18	0699	1877	+	−	+	+	−	−	+	+	−	−	+	−	+	−	−	−	−	+	+	+	+	+	−
19	1737	1197	−	+	−	+	+	−	−	+	+	−	−	+	−	+	−	−	−	−	+	+	+	+	+
20	0318	0478	+	−	+	−	+	+	−	−	+	+	−	−	+	−	+	−	−	−	−	+	+	+	+
21	1415	0002	+	+	−	+	−	+	+	−	−	+	+	−	−	+	−	+	−	−	−	−	+	+	+
22	1853	1733	+	+	+	−	+	−	+	+	−	−	+	+	−	−	+	−	+	−	−	−	−	+	+
23	0361	1474	+	+	+	+	−	+	−	+	+	−	−	+	+	−	−	+	−	+	−	−	−	−	+
24	0279	0988	−	−	−	−	−	−	−	−	−	−	−	−	−	−	−	−	−	−	−	−	−	−	−

124

While the complexity of 48 recipes was not undertaken, the MVT consultant and project leader did agree to replicate the MVT. This meant that each recipe would be executed in two different stores, so 48 of the company's 1,000 stores would be included in the MVT screening experiment. Replicating the MVT increased its "statistical horsepower." But since only 24 unique recipes were necessary, the complexity of involving 48 stores was determined to be very reasonable.

Next, the MVT consultant determined what stores could be included in the MVT using statistical analysis of historical data. Seasonally corrected sales and profit data for each store were checked for stability and special causes. A few stores that had unusually high or low sales growth or profit levels were deleted from consideration as potential test stores. A few other stores recently showed very unusual trends up or down, and they were also removed from consideration. Store operations were asked to remove from consideration any stores that were known to have upcoming situations that might bias test results. They removed several stores that were undergoing renovation or changes in store management. This left a pool of 947 stores from which the stores to be included in the MVT screening experiment could be selected.

The specific stores to be included in the MVT screening experiment and the specific recipe to be executed for each store were then determined. The project leader decided to make this a public selection to eliminate the chance that anyone would think the test was rigged. First they made up 947 slips of paper, each with one store's identification number on it. They also prepared a flip chart with recipe numbers one through 24 listed and two blanks beside each recipe. During a meeting with headquarters employees, the CEO was asked to draw 48 stores from a basket containing all 947 stores. As each store was drawn, its number was placed beside the next recipe, until both slots beside each of the 24 recipes were filled. Since some of the test factors could only be executed on a market-wide basis (e.g., radio advertising), if a store was chosen from a market that was already represented, that selection was invalidated and another store was chosen.

The final MVT matrix and the two stores chosen to execute each recipe are shown in the table on page 124.

After the matrix and stores were identified, the critical "Playing the Game" exercise was completed. The recipe for each store was evaluated by the same group who categorized factors. They looked for any conflicts between factors or anything else that might prevent the successful execution of the recipe in that store. Often this exercise reveals problems that need to be resolved, but in this case, the design and store assignments were found to be usable without changes.

By analyzing the historical data for store sales and profits, the MVT consultant determined that if the recipes were implemented for six weeks, then the MVT screening experiment would be able to detect factor effects of approximately 1.7 percentage points worth of improvement in the key measure. In a typical scenario, only about 25 percent of the 23 factors would prove helpful (about six helpful factors). Six factors worth at least 1.7 percentage points each would total at least a 10 percent improvement in the key measure (sales). Since a 10 percent improvement in results would be viewed as a substantial turnaround in the company's performance, the MVT consultant and the project leader felt comfortable that the experiment had adequate power.

CHAPTER 12

STEP 8

Execute the MVT Screening
Experiment and Measure Test Results

The execution step of an MVT experiment is a really interesting time. You have 20 to 30 recipes in place, and the total results of each are beginning to surface. Data are accumulating. For the people who are involved in the recipes, excitement regarding findings is building. The key, at this time, is to take all that positive energy and channel it into a focus on perfect planning and execution of the MVT recipes.

WHAT TO EXPECT DURING AN MVT EXPERIMENT

Two things should be expected while an MVT experiment is being executed: improved results and problems.

Improved Results

Organizations using MVT for the first time often are fearful that their business results might suffer during an experiment. Fortunately, Qual-Pro has never been involved in an MVT experiment in which the overall results became worse. In fact, the opposite is almost always

Figure 12.1   Improvement in Direct Mail Response Rate
During MVT Experimentation

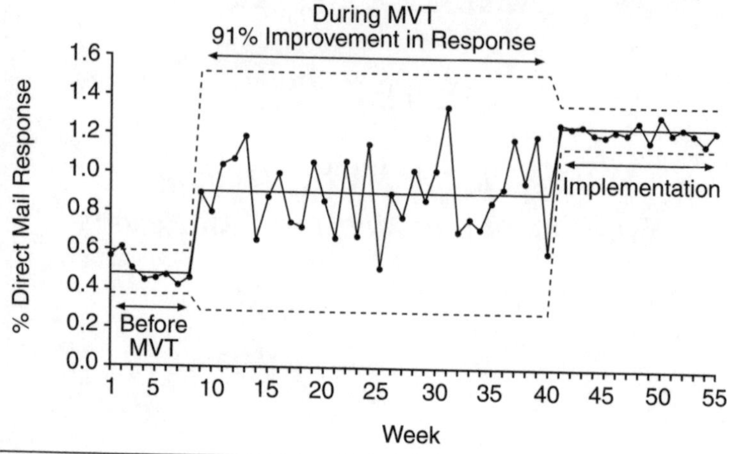

true. Results usually improve during the MVT experiment, and this is no accident. As previously indicated, almost as many test ideas hurt the key measure of performance as help it (22 percent hurt, and 25 percent help). However, the average impact of helpful factors tends to be larger than the impact of hurtful factors. This means that results during the experiment, on average, will be better than normal.

Another issue that contributes to improved results during MVT experiments is that, during an experiment, we are carefully controlling 20 to 30 aspects of the process (test ideas). This better–than–normal control of the process often leads to better execution and improved results. This does not interfere at all with MVT's ability to measure the impact of each of the test ideas, but it does provide a financial benefit that can be enjoyed.

Figures 12.1 and 12.2 use two charts to illustrate real business results achieved during MVT experiments. In both of these instances, the improvement experienced during the MVT experiment paid for all MVT-related costs, including consulting fees (many times over). In both cases, a positive return on investment (ROI) was established even before the MVT findings were known or implemented. Such improvement during the experiment is a common occurrence and, for many MVT users, an unexpected benefit.

Figure 12.2   Improvement in Metal Casting Yield
During MVT Experimentation

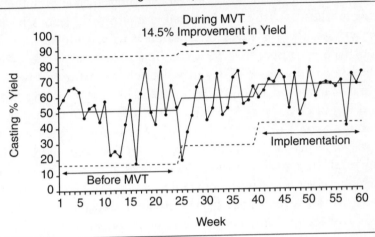

Problems

MVT experimentation is not without its challenges. Problems with the execution of recipes should be anticipated and addressed as they occur. There is no reason that an MVT user should be disappointed when problems develop. In fact, if no problems are identified, the monitoring system probably is inadequate. It would be very rare for the planning and preparations for an experiment to be so good that no problems occur during recipe execution.

Two types of execution problems are commonly seen: (1) lack of compliance (when factors or recipes are not executed as planned) and (2) situations in which it is not possible to execute a factor or combination of factors as those factors were defined.

Lack of Compliance.   This is very common, and it is very important that it be recognized quickly and dealt with effectively. By definition, MVT test ideas are different from the status quo way of operating, so it is no surprise that executing them correctly requires extra attention from management and employees.

There may be a poor ability to execute a test idea. Preparations may have been inadequate, training may not have been understood, materials may not have been made available, the labor schedule may not have been set up appropriately, and so on. However, remedying the problem is usually very straightforward (for example, supplementary training, arranging for the materials to be delivered, readjusting the labor schedule).

Sometimes, there is a lack of willingness to execute an idea. The persons who are responsible for executing a recipe may not "like" a factor that is being tested. They may not believe that it will work, or they may simply feel comfortable with the old way of doing things, even if it gives less desirable results. They may feel threatened by the potential outcome of the MVT process. For example, they may fear that any increases in productivity that would be achieved by MVT might result in a labor cutback. These issues also must be remedied quickly, but they often are more complicated to deal with. Actions to remedy such situations range from a simple re-explanation of the importance of recipe compliance to taking action to remove a person from involvement in the MVT experiment.

Compliance with test recipes does not happen automatically. It requires careful planning, communication, training, preparation, monitoring, and remedial action.

Situations in Which Factors Cannot Be Executed as Defined. In spite of people's best efforts at compliance, sometimes a factor or a combination of factors is impossible to execute as defined. When the test recipes begin to run, the process may not run properly, and it would be foolish to continue to execute the recipe. An example of this kind of problem is when a reaction temperature in a chemical process cannot be achieved without exceeding the reactor's safety guidelines for pressure. Because no attempt to raise the temperature had been made previously, this impossibility would not be discovered until the experiment begins. Or, in a marketing-related experiment, a factor might be to develop a short brochure that has only half the copy of the original brochures, but when the copy writers actually develop their copy, they discover that they cannot make the necessary sales points using the reduced number of words. One idea may interfere with another idea's execution in a way that could not be anticipated. For example, if one factor is increased TV advertising, and another idea is to purchase all advertising during network news, the two factors could be incompatible if there is not enough TV ad time available for purchase in those time slots. Or as another example, in a manufacturing experiment, one factor might be the use of a new machine tool; a second test factor might be higher RPMs using the tool; and those factors may work perfectly on an individual basis. However, the tool may break every time the high RPMs are used. In such a case, the recipes cannot be run with both ideas turned on.

If such a problem exists, action must be taken to allow the MVT recipes to be executed. Most often, the situation can be remedied by changing the definition of a factor while maintaining the spirit of the improvement idea. If the test factor is a 200-degree temperature instead of the normal 185 degrees, the temperature might be set at 195 degrees instead. If the factor is to decrease the copy in the direct mail piece by half, but a proper message cannot be constructed using so few words, perhaps reducing the copy by a third will still test the concept but allow a proper message to be constructed. If enough television time in network news cannot be purchased, perhaps the definition of the factor might be expanded to include cable news. If the new tool breaks every time the higher RPM is used, finding the highest RPM that will allow the tool to be used and changing the definition to test that RPM is the solution.

On a rare occasion, it may be necessary to remove a factor from an MVT test. The most common situation leading to factor removal is that someone dropped the ball in preparation of the test factor. If recovery would delay the entire experiment, the factor might be dropped, or another factor might be substituted. Usually, however, changing the factor definition will address a design flaw in a test idea.

IDENTIFYING PROBLEMS EARLY

It is very important to catch any compliance or design issues early. If recipes have been run, and a factor then needs to be changed or eliminated, testing of the recipes that contain the change will have to be repeated. This causes a loss of time, wasted effort, and frustration for those involved. Often, it is a good idea to run the most challenging recipes first, in order to identify any factors that cannot be executed. For example, if an experiment contains a recipe with all factors in the changed condition, it might be run first. If some factors just cannot be executed, the fact will be discovered quickly, and the need to repeat significant portions of the MVT will be avoided.

THE IMPORTANCE OF MVT EXECUTION

It is very important to execute each recipe as nearly perfectly as is possible. Poor recipe execution can result in a lack of findings or, even worse, in misleading findings. The data will always tell the truth, but if the recipe conditions that are tested are different from what was defined by the test idea, the wrong conclusions may be drawn.

The importance of recipe execution can be illustrated with a poker analogy. In poker, the best hand possible is a royal flush: that is, an ace, king, queen, jack, and 10, all of one suit. A royal flush is an incredibly powerful hand that also is extremely rare. The probability of achieving a royal flush in any given poker hand is infinitesimally small. An MVT experimental design is similar to a royal flush, in that a tiny fraction of the potential combinations represented by all the ideas is tested. If all combinations of 30 ideas were tested, over a billion recipes would be required. MVT experiments would use only 32 recipes to investigate 30 ideas. With the poker hand, if one card is exchanged—for example, if the jack of hearts is removed and replaced with the nine of clubs, the value of the hand does not drop slightly, it goes from being the most powerful hand in poker to being virtually worthless. Similarly, with an MVT experimental design, the poor execution of a single recipe or a small number of factors can dramatically reduce the value of the findings.

Steps in MVT Execution

Execution of an MVT experiment involves the following steps:

1. Develop an action plan.
2. Prepare factor materials and training.
3. Communicate the plans, roles, procedures, logistics, and importance.
4. Create and execute a monitoring process to measure recipe compliance.
5. Act to remedy any execution flaws.
6. Collect data.

Each of these steps requires adequate attention from management and employees.

Develop an Action Plan

The action plan to execute an MVT experiment is written documentation of who will do what and when. The "who" portion of the action plan is critical. Several roles must be filled. First, there must be an executive sponsor. The executive sponsor must communicate the importance of the project to those who will be executing the recipes. The sponsor also must ensure that resources are made available as required, and sometimes the sponsor may need to be involved in removing roadblocks that require executive involvement.

A project leader plays an especially critical role in the execution of an MVT. The project leader must communicate assignments, coordinate activities, ensure that the completion of tasks is monitored (for both timing and quality), and bring attention and action to bear when weaknesses are discovered. Usually, the best project leader is the line manager directly responsible for the day-to-day operation or process that is involved in the project. Sometimes, however, a key staff person or technical leader is chosen to fill this role.

Every test factor should be assigned a *factor owner*. This is a person who will be responsible for ensuring the proper planning, for development of materials for training in, and execution of a test idea. The factor owner should be the person responsible for the activity that is involved in the test idea on a day-to-day basis. This is not usually a special assignment for the person, but a change in the way that he or she does the job every day. Every factor must have a factor owner, but some factor owners may have more than one factor.

Another critical role is that of *data owner*. This is the person who will be responsible for ensuring that data are collected during the execution of the experiment. The data owner is responsible for making sure that data are gathered for every measure, that the measure has the proper timing per the correct operational definitions, and that the data are gathered in the defined format.

Another critical role in the action plan is that of the *MVT consultant*. Each MVT project should have the support and involvement of at least one person who has extensive MVT training and project experience. This person's role is to ensure that the MVT processes are followed properly; that practical, fast, and cost-free factors are developed; that appropriate MVT designs and recipes are created; that preparations and logistics do not inadvertently compromise the design; that data are collected properly and analyzed correctly; that proper conclusions are drawn from the MVT findings; and that implementation does result in the level of improvement indicated by MVT results. In short, the consultant is a steward of the process. It is not possible to develop the knowledge and skill to perform the MVT consulting function in a few months or by participating in a few weeks of training and completion of a single project. Extensive training and experience with many projects is necessary to develop this expertise.

With the exception of the MVT consultant, executing an MVT experiment should not require hiring people, removing existing personnel from their jobs, or outsourcing work. Persons already performing particular activities should do the MVT activities involving that work. They just do things differently during the MVT. If the need is felt to hire or reassign personnel, the categorization of test ideas as practical, fast, and cost free probably was not done properly.

The action plan is completed by the project leader, factor owners, and data owner by documenting the timing and resource involvement necessary to prepare, communicate, execute, and monitor each factor and each recipe.

Prepare Factor Materials and Training

Each factor owner reviews his or her factor's definition and determines what preparations are necessary to execute the test idea. Equipment may need to be relocated. There could be production schedules to work out or labor schedules to develop. There may be training to prepare. There could be materials to create or purchase and to distribute. There may be communications with vendors to execute. All the details required to execute each idea must be thought out and acted on. The project leader and MVT consultant are critical during this preparation phase because constant communication must occur with each factor owner to ensure that no factor is falling behind schedule and that the quality of preparations for each factor is adequate.

Communicate the Plans, Roles, Procedures, Logistics, and Importance

Recipes and the test ideas associated with them must be communicated to those who will execute them. They have to be told what test ideas their recipes will contain and exactly how each idea is to be executed. This usually is done by means of a meeting or conference call with the line managers or leaders responsible for executing one or more recipes. It is typically kicked off by the sponsor, who establishes the importance of the project and the critical need to properly execute the recipes. Instructions for the execution of each idea are then provided by the team leader, factor owner, and MVT consultant. The definition of each test idea, the plan, the materials, and the logistics associated with the plan should be documented in writing, and that written documentation should be distributed to those involved in executing a particular recipe. Confusion can be minimized by communicating only those factors that must be executed by a particular person in the recipe given to that person. A little more work is required to create documents that are specific to each recipe, but that effort will pay a good dividend in terms of minimizing confusion.

Each leader or manager who will be responsible for executing one or more recipes then works with his or her people, using the existing chain of command to put the recipe in place at the prescribed time and according to the defined procedures.

Create and Execute a Monitoring Process to Measure Recipe Compliance

Given the critical requirement to execute MVT recipes flawlessly, there must be a process to monitor recipe execution and identify shortcomings in recipe compliance. There are several ways to monitor recipes, including:

- *Check sheets:* For each recipe, a check sheet may be constructed on which the members of the local workforce indicate as they are doing their day to day work that the recipe conditions were in compliance. For example, if temperature is one factor, the temperature might be noted each hour. In a retail store experiment, if the use of a greeter is a factor, the greeter might initial a sheet at the greeter's location every 15 minutes to indicate his or her presence. A check sheet is a means of indicating continual compliance with a factor.

- *Self audits:* It often is useful to ask the manager who is responsible for a recipe to do his or her own audits and to indicate the proper execution of each factor on some routine basis (for example, daily or hourly).
- *Telephone audits:* In geographically dispersed MVT experiments, it often is useful for managers or staff members from headquarters to make routine telephone calls to the locations involved in implementing recipes and to ask questions to elicit indications of MVT recipe compliance.
- *Physical audits:* It is critical that compliance be checked by physically viewing recipes and assuring that each factor is in compliance. In geographically dispersed MVTs, doing so may necessitate spot checking or sampling of the recipes, as opposed to daily or hourly or even weekly audits. Physical audits, both announced and unannounced, are very important to the successful execution of an MVT experiment.
- *Data review:* As data are accumulated during the MVT, review of those data may reveal execution problems and/or influences by external events. The data should be reviewed as soon as it is available for each test recipe in order to search for anomalies that should be investigated.

Some combination of these activities should be used to monitor compliance for every factor within every recipe. The compliance results should be accumulated throughout the MVT so that a compliance percentage for each factor and for each recipe can be calculated. These data are used during the experiment to indicate the need for remedial actions. The data also have value during the analysis of the experiment later, in interpreting the findings.

Act to Remedy Any Execution Flaws

The monitoring process described should reveal most flaws in recipe execution. If incorrect recipe execution is uncovered, it is very important that remedial action be taken quickly and decisively. Again, recipe compliance should be put back on track as quickly as possible after an execution error is discovered. Every flaw should be documented and reported to the project leader. The MVT consultant then must decide whether data from the flawed recipe can be used. As indicated previously, it may be necessary to rerun an MVT recipe that experiences flawed execution.

Collect Data

The purpose of every MVT experiment is to maintain recipe conditions so that the important measures can be collected and analyzed. Care must be taken to ensure that data are being collected for the key measure and secondary measures. Assurance must be made that each is the correct measure; that it is collected per the operational definitions established in Step 2; and that the measures are for the correct time period, the correct location, and the correct products. In other words, all aspects of measurement must be executed very carefully to ensure that the MVT experiment has maximum value.

Usually, data can be collected daily or weekly during an MVT. Although daily and weekly (interim) data may not be adequate for analysis in order to draw reliable conclusions, they can be very useful anyway. Review of the data as they accumulate may provide insight into compliance issues. Analysis of the interim data also may have value in indicating measurement problems or compliance issues.

It is very important that the data be captured in the agreed-on format. Collecting data in an incorrect format can cause delays in analysis, create the need to reformat large volumes of data, and— even worse—introduce potential errors that could cause incorrect conclusions.

Although mentioned earlier, it is important to emphasize that there is value in performing analyses on interim data accumulated during the experiment. A word of caution, however: You must be very careful about communicating interim findings or results from analysis of interim data. The impact of a factor often may develop as the experiment goes on. Analyses that are performed part of the way through the experiment are useful, but the data are likely to change. Therefore, communication of interim results to MVT nonexperts may cause confusion and interfere later with the credibility of final conclusions. The results of interim analyses should not be communicated broadly within the organization.

MVT EXPERIMENTS ARE ROBUST!

This chapter emphasizes the critical importance of flawless recipe execution and the consequences of errors; however, it should be noted that MVT experiments are designed to absorb and accommodate a significant level of these types of problems.

Factors that involve human beings are almost never executed perfectly. In fact, less than perfect compliance is part of the experimental process. MVT findings will reflect results achieved by the "partial" compliance of these factors. This is a strength of the MVT process. Since perfect compliance on human factors will not be achieved in ultimate implementation, the MVT findings are very predictive of the real-world impact that will be seen.

Even in instances in which MVT experiments run into severe external problems, good results may be achieved. For example, MVT experimentation was run in a retail firm in which nine entire stores were destroyed by a hurricane during the experimentation! Yet, significant improvement was ultimately achieved.

The use of a well-qualified MVT consultant helps to ensure that every MVT is as durable as possible.

Case Study: Step 8 (Continued from Chapter 11)

With MVT recipes and store assignments in hand, the project leader and MVT consultant created their execution plan.

First, the test factors were divided up according to the department that was typically responsible for that activity. For example, Factor A (fitting room attendants) and Factor B (dress code) are store operations responsibilities. Factors C, D, and E (circular page count, color style, and paper stock) are responsibilities of marketing and advertising. With a list of factors in hand, the project leader and MVT consultant went to the head of each department and asked for the assignment of appropriate factor owners. These were usually persons who, on a day-to-day basis, control the area

Factor Owners for Each Test Factor

Factor	Department	Factor Owner
A: Fitting room attendants	Store Operations	Director of Store Operations
B: Dress code	Store Operations	Director of Store Operations
C: Circular page count	Marketing/Advertising	Creative Director
D: Circular color style	Marketing/Advertising	Creative Director
E: Circular paper stock	Marketing/Advertising	Advertising Manager
F: Pricing signage	Merchandising	Signage Manager
G: ROP message	Marketing/Advertising	Creative Director
H: ROP size	Marketing/Advertising	Creative Director
I: Directional signage	Merchandising	Signage Manager
J: Store announcements	Store Operations	Operations Project Manager
K: Promotional location	Store Operations	Operations Project Manager
L: Radio advertising	Marketing/Advertising	Advertising Manager
M: In-store product demo's	Store Operations	Operations Project Manager
N: Checkout	Store Operations	Director of Store Operations
O: "Friendly" program	Store Operations	Operations Project Manager
P: Associate incentives	Human Resources	Director of Compensation
Q: Cross-selling emphasis	Merchandising	Display Design Manager
R: Increased sales training	Human Resources	Training Director
S: Music	Store Operations	Operations Project Manager
T: Management incentives	Human Resources	Director of Compensation
U: Postcards versus telemarketing	Marketing/Advertising	Director of Marketing
V: Associate scheduling	Store Operations	Director of Store Operations
W: Window signage	Merchandising	Signage Manager

with which a factor is involved. The department head then communicated the assignment to the factor owner(s) and explained the importance of supporting the project. In just a couple of days, factor owners were identified for every factor. The department and factor owner for each test factor is shown in the previous table.

A brief meeting was held with the factor owners as a group. The agenda was to (1) explain the project objectives and timetable, (2) provide a brief overview of the MVT methodology, (3) explain the factor owner role, and (4) ask each factor owner to put together their individual action plan, with benchmarks, to prepare for the timely execution of their factor in appropriate stores per the MVT recipes.

Over the next few days, the project leader and MVT consultant reviewed the plans of each factor owner, ensuring that every plan fit the overall project schedule. They asked that each Friday the factor owners e-mail a copy of their plan with the completion status noted to the MVT consultant who would compile them and note any problems.

The factor owners then went to work on factor preparations, which mostly were just a part of their normal duties.

The MVT consultant worked with department heads to agree to a monitoring plan that would measure recipe compliance. The monitoring process had to be simple and was varied according to the nature of the factor. For example, circular color style, and page count could be monitored by reviewing the creative designs. Radio advertising was to be monitored by reviewing the media buy report received by the marketing department. In-store factors, such as fitting room attendants, dress code, and music, were to be monitored by a combination of self-reporting by each store manager and spot visits by operations management and/or the project leader or MVT consultant.

The status of preparations, both from a timing and quality standpoint, was continually updated until the MVT was officially launched. At that point, the monitoring system turned to a measurement of the actual conditions experienced by customers in each store.

On the first day of the MVT, a conference call was held with store managers who had self-audited their recipe compliance. Also attending were factor owners, the project leader, and the MVT consultant. They reviewed the audited status of each store and discussed any preparation problems that needed to be solved. Overall compliance was reported as 77 percent. One factor was not in place in any stores: Factor S, more upbeat music, was not being executed due to the fact that the music tapes had been created but had not been shipped to the stores as planned. The vendor was immediately contacted and they were mailed overnight. Several factors, including the fitting room attendant, checkout process, and promotional location were in place in some locations but were weak in others.

Several stores reported 100 percent compliance on day one. The MVT consultant told the group that, while 100 percent is certainly possible, it is highly unusual on the first day of an MVT and often can be a sign of a weak audit or misunderstanding of factor levels.

This conference call was then held weekly for the six weeks of the test and the self-audits were supplemented by store visits by non-store personnel on a spot check (sampling) basis. Compliance by store, by week, and by factor was closely observed, and problems were quickly addressed.

Early in the project, the CFO assigned a data owner. He selected an analyst who routinely collected data by querying her database using standard procedures. This person was charged with gathering and organizing the MVT data throughout the MVT screening experiment.

On a weekly basis, she pulled sales and margin performance for all MVT stores, for the week and on a cumulative basis since the beginning of the

MVT. She compiled the data into a simple table with store number down the left side of the page, one column of data for sales, and a second column for margin dollars. She provided this data to the MVT consultant, who closely reviewed the data each week looking for anomalies that might indicate a query problem to resolve, a recipe compliance problem to trouble shoot, or a special cause that needed to be investigated.

The MVT consultant reviewed the data with the project leader each week. Both were pleased to be able to report to the CEO that, beginning immediately upon the MVT launch, the comp sales and profit performance of the MVT stores were consistently better than the non-MVT stores by about 2.5 percentage points. The 48 MVT stores actually contributed several million dollars in improved performance to the company's coffers before the findings were even analyzed.

CHAPTER 13

STEP 9

*Analyze Screening Test Results to
Determine Which Ideas Help, Hurt, or
Have No Impact on Performance
(Prepare to Be Surprised)*

After executing the MVT screening experiment and gathering data for each recipe on the key measure(s), we analyze the data to determine the impact of each test factor.

EXAMINE THE MEASUREMENTS

The first thing we do when we begin getting the results from the MVT screening experiment is to carefully examine the data for each key measure to ensure that they represent what we think they do; that they came from the right recipe, the right time, and the right place; and that we truly have the right measure. In a recent situation in which we were concerned with paper sales, we had completed the MVT screening experiment and had data that we assumed represented paper sales. However, when we started to examine the data, we soon saw that something was wrong (or else the company was selling paper for unexpectedly high prices). We found that the client had inadvertently given us sales numbers representing furniture, not paper. We always need to examine the data carefully and make sure that it represents what we think it represents.

The other thing we must do is look at the data to make sure that all the values seem to be reasonable. If any of the values seem to be unreasonable—exceptionally low or high—they need to be investigated.

If the design is replicated (each recipe is executed two or more times), a range chart should be constructed using the ranges for each recipe. Any out-of-control points should then be thoroughly investigated to determine the presence of special causes. In the rare event that the special cause cannot be identified, or if the special cause was anything other than measurement error (that can be corrected), the recipe should be rerun.

It is best to review the data immediately, as soon as the measurements are available. This accomplishes two important things: (1) it allows us to quickly catch measurement errors, and (2) it helps us to identify flaws in the execution of recipes.

CALCULATE FACTOR EFFECTS

The next step is to calculate the effect of each test factor. For simplicity's sake, let us first look at the simple, eight-recipe example from Chapter 11. The weld-strength results of the recipes are indicated in Table 13.1.

The effect of factor A is simply the average of the responses at the plus level of factor A minus the average of the responses at the minus level of factor A. If we look at factor A for recipes 1, 4, 6, and 7, A is at the plus level. We calculate the average of these four responses. Next,

Table 13.1   MVT Screening Design—Tab Weld Responses and Effects

Test Recipe	A	B	C	D	E	F	G	y_1	y_2	$\bar{y}$
1	+	+	+	−	+	−	−	560	600	580
2	−	+	+	+	−	+	−	480	500	490
3	−	−	+	+	+	−	+	500	470	485
4	+	−	−	+	+	+	−	420	440	430
5	−	+	−	−	+	+	+	540	550	545
6	+	−	+	−	−	+	+	160	190	175
7	+	+	−	+	−	−	+	460	460	460
8	−	−	−	−	−	−	−	100	80	90
Effect	8.75	223.75	51.25	118.75	206.25	6.25	18.75			

Figure 13.1   Pareto Chart of Effects with Control Limit for Tab Weld MVT Screening Experiment

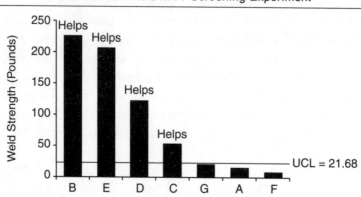

we calculate the average of the four responses for which A is at its minus level; that is for recipes 2, 3, 5, and 8. We then calculate the difference between the average response at the high level and the average response at the low level, and this result is the effect of factor A. The calculation is shown next:

$$\text{Effect of A} = \left(\frac{1645}{4}\right) - \left(\frac{1610}{4}\right) = 8.75$$

We can calculate the effects of the factors B, C, D, E, F, and G in the same manner. It is easy to see that, for a screening MVT, the calculation of effects is a very simple process. These effects can be shown graphically in a Pareto chart (Figure 13.1). Similar calculations for the sales rep example showed that 5 of the 28 factors were significant.

The procedure for calculating the effects of a reflected MVT screening design is the same.

If an MVT design is replicated, the average response is calculated for each test recipe, and that average for each recipe is used in the calculations of effects described here.

CALCULATE QUASI-INTERACTION EFFECTS

Not only can we calculate the effects of individual factors, we also can get worthwhile information about the interactions—or synergies—between pairs of factors. This simply means that the effect of one factor depends on the level (status quo or change) of another factor. In other words, factors work differently together than they do individually. For MVT screening experiments, we can get some idea of the large-magnitude synergies or interactions by calculating what we refer to as *quasi-interactions*.

The quasi-interaction between two factors, A and B, in a screening MVT is defined by:

$$\text{Quasi-Interaction AB} = \frac{1}{2}\left[\left(\begin{array}{c}\text{Effect of A at the}\\\text{high level of B}\end{array}\right) - \left(\begin{array}{c}\text{Effect of A at the}\\\text{low level of B}\end{array}\right)\right]$$

The quasi-interaction between factors B and E for the tab weld data shown in Table 13.1 is:

$$\text{Quasi-Interaction BE} = \frac{1}{2}\left[\left(\begin{array}{c}\text{Effect of B at the}\\\text{high level of E}\end{array}\right) - \left(\begin{array}{c}\text{Effect of B at the}\\\text{low level of E}\end{array}\right)\right]$$

This quasi-interaction between factors B (electrode force) and E (tab shape) can be displayed graphically, as is shown in Figure 13.2.

The BE quasi-interaction tells us that, if the 28-pound electrode force is used, the design of the tab weld is not important. The welds are sufficiently strong for both the curved tab and the flat tab, so that there is no danger of the tabs falling off. This synergy prevents the need for a time-consuming redrawing and retooling process.

The quasi-interaction effect for every pair of factors should be calculated to determine those quasi-interaction effects that may need to be considered for further investigation during the refining MVT experimentation.

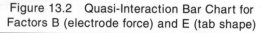

Figure 13.2   Quasi-Interaction Bar Chart for
Factors B (electrode force) and E (tab shape)

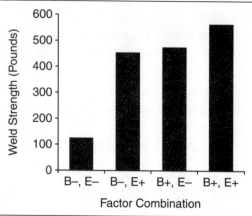

CALCULATE CONTROL LIMITS

After we have calculated the main factor effects and the quasi-interaction effects for each measure, we calculate the control limits for factor effects for each measure. The control limits are used to determine which of the factor effects and quasi-interaction effects are significant. We usually accept a 5 percent risk of being wrong, that is, of concluding that a factor helps or hurts when it really does not.

As is described in Step 7, there are several ways in which control limits can be calculated, but it is beyond the scope of this book to describe these. After the calculations are made, we can tell which factors help the key measure, which hurt, and which make no difference. The control limits can be shown on a Pareto chart to make it easy to see which ones are statistically significant. The Pareto chart with control limits for the tab weld example is shown in Figure 13.1.

CALCULATE EFFECTS ON VARIABILITY

As discussed in Step 7, in manufacturing, a major objective often is to reduce variation in addition to, or instead of, changing the key-measure average. If reducing variation is a major objective, it is stated in Step 1 when the project is launched. During the analyses of historical data in Steps 3 and 4, clues about impacts on variation are researched. During the brainstorming sessions in Step 5, ideas to reduce variation are surfaced. When the MVT screening experiment is designed in Step 7, the experiment is replicated (each recipe is executed with at least two experimental units).

To calculate the effect of each test factor on variation, we first obtain a range of the measurements for each test recipe. This is the numerical difference between the highest and lowest values for each recipe. The range for each test recipe is then used to calculate the effect of each factor on variation, using the same calculation as described earlier for calculating factor effects.

ANALYZING MORE COMPLEX DESIGNS

With more than 20 factors and multiple measures and with some of the factors at more than two levels, the analysis of an MVT screening experiment can become very complex. Most situations do not involve these complexities. QualPro has developed analysis software to handle these situations and teaches advanced seminars to deal with these concepts.

Case Study: Step 9 (Continued from Chapter 12)

When he received the sixth week's sales and profit data for each MVT store, the MVT consultant examined the data. Since he had been reviewing the data every week, his search for anomalies by an assessment of the data was completed in only a couple of hours. He discovered a store with zero sales for the week. A few minutes of investigation determined that the store had changed store numbers for administrative reasons and queries now had to reference the new number. This was quickly resolved and the data were corrected.

He then used standard MVT procedures to calculate the effect of each test factor on comp sales and comp profits. The MVT matrix and the comp sales data for each of the two stores in each recipe is shown in the table on page 148.

He then used standard MVT calculations, including the average of the two stores for each recipe, to determine the individual effects of each test factor on comp sales and comp profits. He also calculated the control limit for the experiment using the ranges (the difference between the two stores) for each recipe. A Pareto chart showing the magnitude and direction of each

MVT Screening Matrix and Comp Sales Data for Each Recipe

	Factors																										
Recipe	A	B	C	D	E	F	G	H	I	J	K	L	M	N	O	P	Q	R	S	T	U	V	W	Store 1	Store 2	Average	Range
1	+	+	+	+	+	+	+	+	+	+	+	−	+	+	−	−	+	−	+	−	−	−	−	1.03	1.15	1.090	0.12
2	−	+	+	+	+	+	+	+	+	+	−	+	+	+	−	−	+	+	−	+	−	−	−	1.27	1.19	1.230	0.08
3	−	−	+	+	+	+	+	−	+	−	+	+	−	+	+	−	−	+	+	+	+	−	−	1.18	1.10	1.140	0.08
4	−	−	−	+	+	+	+	+	+	+	+	+	+	−	+	+	+	+	−	−	+	−	+	1.12	1.08	1.100	0.04
5	−	−	−	−	+	+	+	+	−	−	−	+	+	−	−	+	+	+	−	+	+	+	+	1.06	1.14	1.100	0.08
6	+	−	−	−	−	−	+	+	+	+	+	−	+	+	−	−	−	+	+	−	−	+	−	1.18	1.11	1.145	0.07
7	−	+	−	−	−	−	+	+	+	+	+	+	+	+	+	+	−	−	+	+	−	+	+	1.15	1.20	1.175	0.05
8	+	−	+	−	−	−	+	+	+	+	+	+	+	+	+	+	+	+	+	+	+	−	+	1.00	1.08	1.040	0.08
9	−	+	−	+	−	−	−	−	+	+	+	+	+	+	+	+	+	+	+	−	+	+	−	1.13	1.17	1.150	0.04
10	−	−	+	−	+	+	−	−	+	+	+	+	+	+	+	+	+	+	+	+	−	+	+	1.09	1.11	1.100	0.02
11	+	−	−	+	−	+	−	−	−	−	+	+	+	+	+	+	+	+	+	+	+	−	+	1.20	1.23	1.215	0.03
12	+	+	−	−	+	−	+	−	−	−	−	−	+	+	+	+	−	+	+	+	+	+	−	1.10	1.09	1.095	0.01
13	−	−	+	+	−	+	−	+	+	−	−	−	−	−	+	+	+	+	+	+	+	+	−	1.04	1.20	1.120	0.16
14	−	+	−	+	+	−	+	−	+	+	−	−	−	−	−	+	+	+	+	−	−	+	+	1.27	1.15	1.210	0.12
15	+	+	+	−	−	+	+	−	−	+	+	−	−	−	−	−	+	+	−	+	+	+	+	1.01	1.05	1.030	0.04
16	+	+	+	+	+	−	−	+	−	−	+	+	−	−	−	−	+	+	+	−	+	+	+	1.23	1.24	1.235	0.01
17	−	−	+	+	+	+	−	−	+	−	−	+	+	−	−	−	−	+	+	+	+	+	−	1.08	1.13	1.105	0.05
18	+	+	+	−	−	+	+	+	−	+	−	−	+	+	−	−	−	+	+	+	+	+	+	1.20	1.28	1.240	0.08
19	−	+	−	+	+	+	−	−	+	−	+	+	+	−	+	−	−	−	+	+	+	+	+	1.12	1.13	1.125	0.01
20	+	+	+	+	−	−	+	+	−	+	+	+	+	+	−	+	−	−	−	−	+	+	+	1.15	1.28	1.215	0.13
21	+	+	+	+	+	+	−	−	+	−	−	+	+	+	+	−	−	−	−	−	+	+	+	1.20	1.21	1.205	0.01
22	+	+	+	+	+	+	+	+	−	+	+	−	+	+	+	+	+	−	−	−	−	−	+	1.11	1.34	1.225	0.23
23	+	−	+	+	+	+	+	+	+	+	−	−	−	−	−	−	−	−	−	−	−	−	−	1.07	1.05	1.060	0.02
24	−	−	−	−	−	−	−	−	−	−	−	−	−	−	−	−	−	−	−	−	−	−	−	1.08	1.12	1.100	0.04

Factor Effects from Retail MVT Screening Experiment

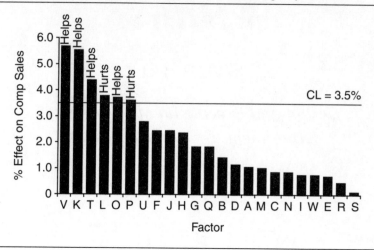

effect on comp sales as compared to the control limit is shown in the figure above.

Finally, he calculated quasi-interactions. One large quasi-interaction was identified that involved factor A (fitting room attendants) and factor V (associate scheduling). This quasi-interaction is shown in the figure below.

Because the MVT screening experiment was fully replicated, the MVT consultant could have calculated the effect of each factor on variation between stores. Since reducing store-to-store variation was not an objective of the project, this analysis was not performed.

Quasi-Interaction from Retail MVT Screening Experiment

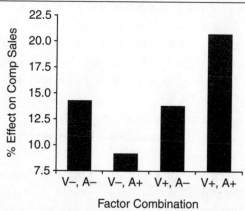

CHAPTER 14

STEP 10

Design and Execute an MVT Refining Experiment to Optimize Results

There are several purposes of an MVT refining experiment. In the earlier MVT *screening* experiment, we identify some process changes that improve results. However, we are not certain that those things that we think will help will do so. There is at least one chance in 20 that a factor change that appears to help will not do so, because control limits typically are set at a 95 percent confidence level. Also, the quasi-interaction effects (even those that appear to be large in the MVT screening experiment) need to be further investigated. So one major purpose of a *refining* experiment is to increase our confidence in the findings. We will be at least 20 times more confident if a process change exceeds the control limit in a refining experiment as well as in a screening experiment. The chance that a process change tests as significantly improving results in both screening and refining MVTs, but is not actually helpful, is extremely low—$\frac{1}{20} \times \frac{1}{20}$ or $\frac{1}{400}$. If a factor appears to be significantly helpful in both the screening and refining experiments, we feel comfortable that we will be able to take that improvement to the bank.

Another major purpose of a refining experiment is to identify conditions even closer to the optimum. In 22 years of experience, we have found that approximately 70 percent of the improvement is revealed in the initial screening experiment, and another 30 percent of the possible improvement is revealed in the refining experiment.

A third purpose of the refining experiment is that we can determine useful synergies between factors. In screening experiments, we can only estimate quasi-interactions that we know are mixed up with other factor effects; in refining, we can estimate interaction effects with more confidence.

FULL-FACTORIAL EXPERIMENTS AND FRACTIONAL-FACTORIAL EXPERIMENTS

MVT refining experimentation usually involves testing all possible combinations of five or fewer factors that were revealed to improve results in the MVT screening experimentation. Such a test of all combinations is called a *full-factorial experiment*. In cases in which we run a very large MVT screening experiment with 30 to 40 factors, the refining experiment may be a fraction of a full-factorial MVT experiment, with 10 or fewer factors. A fractional-factorial experiment allows us to estimate individual factor effects and some, but not all, interaction effects.

REFINING EXPERIMENTS VERSUS DESIGN OF EXPERIMENTS

Refining experiments in the MVT process are the same as the classical design of experiments (DOE) that have been used sparingly in industries, especially in manufacturing, over the past few decades. The key difference is that the MVT refining experiments always test the correct improvement factors. The screening MVT analysis separates the factors that help results from those that hurt or do not make any difference. The only factors that we include in the refining experiments are those that are helpful. Classical DOE has not generated great enthusiasm in industry, because it starts with factors that prove to be not helpful 75 percent of the time. Most DOE experiments in industry over the past 40 years have tested two to five improvement factors, and most of these experiments have revealed one or two things that help. This approach is not nearly as successful as the MVT process, which commonly tests 20, 30, or more factors.

REVIEW THE RESULTS OF MVT SCREENING EXPERIMENTS AND DETERMINE APPROPRIATE ACTIONS

After an MVT screening experiment, the effects of each factor on the performance of the process are calculated and reviewed. Three options are possible for each factor, based on the results of the screening experiment:

1. The factor may be included in the MVT refining experiment if it improved performance.
2. The factor may be implemented immediately if it improved performance in a reflected experiment.
3. The factor is left in the status quo condition if it did not improve performance.

After the screening experiment, we choose factors to test in the refining experiment if they meet the following criteria:

- The factors significantly improved performance. This means that the factor effects were greater, in the helpful direction, than the control limit.
- The factors did not improve performance in the screening experiment but can reduce costs without hurting performance.
- The factors were involved in quasi-interactions in which either (1) the quasi-interaction effect was larger than every one of the individual factor effects or (2) the quasi-interaction effect was larger than two times the screening MVT control limit.

In rare instances, in small MVT screening experiments, such as the tab weld example, most of the factors may test as helpful. Some factor effects are likely to be much larger than others. In these instances, only a few of the factor effects may be large enough to solve the problem, so only a few of the factors would be included in refining experiments.

If the MVT screening experiment was reflected, and if the factor effect was greater than the control limit, the factor may be implemented immediately. In situations in which the screening design was not reflected, we never recommend implementing the factor unless the factor also shows up as significant and helpful in the refining experiment.

If a factor showed no potential to improve results, it should not be changed from its current level unless it offers an opportunity to reduce costs.

Typically, the appropriate action to be taken for each factor is determined by the project leader and MVT consultant and is recommended to the executive sponsor for review and approval.

DESIGN THE REFINING MVT

The procedure used for designing the refining MVT is very similar to the procedure used for designing the screening MVT.

Define the Factor Levels

We first define the factor levels, using the improvement factors that the executive sponsor has agreed to include. These factor levels are almost always the same as those used in the screening experiments.

Choose the Proper Test Matrix

We next choose the proper test matrix. The test matrix for the two factors B and E (electrode force and tab design) and the resulting refining-test matrix for the tab weld example are shown in Table 14.1. The refining test matrix for the five factors that proved effective in the sales rep example in Chapter 11 are shown in Table 14.2.

Table 14.1   Tab Weld MVT
Refining Test Matrix

Test Recipe	B	E
1	−	−
2	+	−
3	−	+
4	+	+

Table 14.2   Sales Rep MVT Refining Test Matrix

Test Recipe	L	N	T	V	Y
1	−	−	−	−	−
2	+	−	−	−	−
3	−	+	−	−	−
4	+	+	−	−	−
5	−	−	+	−	−
6	+	−	+	−	−
7	−	+	+	−	−
8	+	+	+	−	−
9	−	−	−	+	−
10	+	−	−	+	−
11	−	+	−	+	−
12	+	+	−	+	−
13	−	−	+	+	−
14	+	−	+	+	−
15	−	+	+	+	−
16	+	+	+	+	−
17	−	−	−	−	+
18	+	−	−	−	+
19	−	+	−	−	+
20	+	+	−	−	+
21	−	−	+	−	+
22	+	−	+	−	+
23	−	+	+	−	+
24	+	+	+	−	+
25	−	−	−	+	+
26	+	−	−	+	+
27	−	+	−	+	+
28	+	+	−	+	+
29	−	−	+	+	+
30	+	−	+	+	+
31	−	+	+	+	+
32	+	+	+	+	+

Randomly Assign Experimental Units to the Recipes

After the proper refining test matrix has been chosen, the next step is to randomly assign experimental units to the recipes. Just as with the design of the screening experiment, we want to randomly select experimental units from all those possible and randomly assign the experimental units to the recipes.

As with the screening MVT, sometimes we also will have to be concerned about restricting randomization, and we will have to decide whether to do partial replication of the experiment, complete replication, or no replication. The answer will be determined by the constraints on time and money. Next, we have to determine the MVT duration or size. Finally, we have to *play the game,* going through each recipe and asking everybody concerned, "Do these two-factor combinations present a problem?" We must do that for all pairs of factors in each recipe.

Execute the MVT Refining Experiment

Execution of the MVT refining experiment is identical to that of the screening experiment, except that it is easier. There are fewer factors, and the logistics and factor preparation have been done previously. Therefore, the work is not as involved.

As with the MVT screening experiment, compliance must be closely monitored. Measurements should be evaluated as soon as they are available. Test recipes that are not properly executed (i.e., there was poor compliance) must be redone.

Case Study: Step 10 (Continued from Chapter 13)

After calculating the individual and quasi-interaction effects on performance of the improvement factors tested in the MVT screening experiment, the MVT consultant met with the project leader and reviewed the findings.

Six of the 23 factors had significant individual effects on sales as indicated in the figure on page 149. Four factors were helpful—factor V (peak hour associate scheduling), factor K (promotional location near department entrance), factor T (management incentives weighting adjustment), and factor O ("friendly" program with greeter).

Additionally, two factors tested in the screening MVT experiment were shown to actually hurt performance—factor L (radio advertising timing) and factor P (associate incentives based on department results).

The large quasi-interaction involved factor V (peak hour associate scheduling) and factor A (adding fitting room attendants during peak times). This quasi-interaction shows that scheduling additional associates had virtually no impact on sales unless they are used as fitting room attendants. Conversely, adding fitting room attendants actually hurt sales if additional associates were not scheduled.

Findings for comp profits paralleled the comp sales findings almost exactly and are not presented here.

MVT Refining Experiment Matrix for Retail Project

Recipe	Store ID		Promotional Location K	"Friendly" Program O	Management Incentives T	Associate Scheduling V	Fitting Room Attendants A
1	0338	1048	−	−	−	−	−
2	0828	0966	+	−	−	−	−
3	1193	0357	−	+	−	−	−
4	0740	0170	+	+	−	−	−
5	0522	0842	−	−	+	−	−
6	0543	0557	+	−	+	−	−
7	0709	0504	−	+	+	−	−
8	0599	1439	+	+	+	−	−
9	1788	1544	−	−	−	+	−
10	1966	1092	+	−	−	+	−
11	0341	0754	−	+	−	+	−
12	1347	0808	+	+	−	+	−
13	0101	1277	−	−	+	+	−
14	1195	1007	+	−	+	+	−
15	0723	1263	−	+	+	+	−
16	1731	1360	+	+	+	+	−
17	0116	0702	−	−	−	−	+
18	1283	1313	+	−	−	−	+
19	0794	0722	−	+	−	−	+
20	1703	0623	+	+	−	−	+
21	0027	0704	−	−	+	−	+
22	1714	1085	+	−	+	−	+
23	1550	0329	−	+	+	−	+
24	1002	0481	+	+	+	−	+
25	0322	0813	−	−	−	+	+
26	0459	0000	+	−	−	+	+
27	0325	0967	−	+	−	+	+
28	0095	0627	+	+	−	+	+
29	0819	1329	−	−	+	+	+
30	1977	0094	+	−	+	+	+
31	1820	1574	−	+	+	+	+
32	0023	1942	+	+	+	+	+

    The project leader and MVT consultant then called a meeting to review the findings with factor owners and department heads. They went through the effects of each factor one-by-one along with the quasi-interaction. The same questions were asked for each result. Does this make sense? Can we rationalize this result? Is there any reason why we should question its accuracy?

    This exercise was very important to build buy-in. If someone challenged a finding, it was resolved. And there were a few challenges. For several of the factors, execution was questioned. Compliance data were reviewed, building comfort on that issue. Someone questioned whether the location of promotions near department entrances could actually make such a big impact on store-level sales. The head of operations quickly spoke up and said that she had personally seen this factor in several stores, and the new location seemed to always draw a crowd of shoppers. After two hours of intense discussion, the group was satisfied that the screening MVT findings were very credible.

One simple question was then asked for each factor. Should this factor be carried into the MVT refining experiment?

They also decided to refine the four helpful factors (factors V, K, T, and O) as well as factor A, which was involved in the large quasi-interaction.

They agreed that execution of the MVT refining experiment could begin within two weeks. Since only five factors would need to be executed, and all the procedures for these factors were already available, the refining MVT was not expected to be a big execution challenge. The MVT consultant pulled out the basket of store numbers from which he had selected stores for each screening recipe and the group randomly selected 64 stores to be included in the MVT refining experiment.

After the meeting, the MVT consultant prepared recipes for a five-factor MVT refining experiment. The experiment included 32 recipes that tested every combination of the five factors. Each recipe was executed in two stores. This powerful MVT design would leave no ambiguity regarding the effects of each factor, by itself and in combination with other factors. The matrix for the MVT refining experiment is shown on page 156.

The next day, the entire plan was presented to the CEO and executive management team. They endorsed the refining plan and expressed their excitement regarding the potential benefits of the findings, given that there were four statistically significant factors plus a significant quasi-interaction with potential impacts on comp sales and profits exceeding 3.5 percent for each factor.

Execution of the six-week MVT refining experiment and the collection of data went very smoothly using the exact same process as used with screening. This included a kick-off phone call with the stores involved, distribution of recipes and review of factor procedures with store managers, self-audits; weekly phone calls, "sampling" visits by managers, factor owners, and the MVT consultant, and weekly review of data to look for problems.

CHAPTER 15

STEP 11

Analyze the Results and Decide
Which Ideas Will Make the Biggest
Impact on Your Business

As with the MVT screening experiment, as the MVT refining experiment progresses, we need to examine the data to confirm they represent what we think they do. Did they come from the right recipe, at the right time, and the right place? Do we have the right measures in the correct units? We need to examine the range chart for all test recipes that were included in the refining experiment. If the range between replicated runs or any test recipe is outside the upper control limit, we need to thoroughly investigate the cause of this condition.

A range chart for the sales rep refining experiment is shown in Figure 15.1. The chart shows two out-of-control points. Point number 14 was caused by the fact that one of the sales reps in that recipe was sick three weeks of the four-week experiment. This caused his sales to suffer greatly, as compared to other sales reps in that recipe. Point number 22 was caused when one of the sales reps in that recipe had exceptionally high sales versus others in the recipe. Investigation revealed that he had talked to sales reps participating in other recipes, and he had actually executed almost all of the helpful test factors. These special causes made it appropriate to leave results for those two sales

Figure 15.1   Range Chart for the Sales Rep MVT Refining Experiment

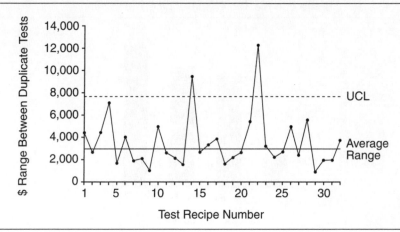

reps out of the analysis. The average for the remaining sales reps in each of these recipes was used for the MVT analysis.

CALCULATE THE EFFECTS

We next calculate the effect of each test factor for each measure. Usually, the test factors each have two levels: a status quo level (what we have been doing) and a change level (what we think will yield better results). When there are two levels, the calculation of factor effects, is the same as for the MVT screening experiment. The effect of changing levels of factor A is simply the average of the responses at the plus level of factor A minus the average of the responses at the minus level of factor A. It is the same for the other factors. The refining experiment for the tab weld example verified the conclusions of the screening experiment. For the sales rep example, four of the five factors that helped in the screening MVT also helped in the refining MVT.

Most of the time, all the factors in MVT screening experiments have just two levels each. However, in refining experiments, there often are some factors at more than two levels. For example, in the tab weld example, we might have chosen a refining experiment with electrode force at four levels: 28 pounds, 30 pounds, 32 pounds, and 34 pounds. When factors have more than two levels, it is not as easy to

Figure 15.2   Interaction Bar Chart for Factors
B and E in the Tab Weld Refining Experiment

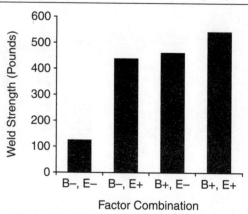

determine the conditions that test significantly better than the other conditions. For such cases, we have developed MVT-analysis software that performs the complex calculations required.

The following step is to calculate the effect of each two–factor and higher-order interaction for each measure. Unlike the analysis of the MVT screening experiment, in the analysis of the MVT refining experiment, we are able to calculate real interaction effects. The interaction effects are calculated in the same manner as the quasi-interaction effects. How these are calculated is described in Chapter 13. The interaction between factors A and B is defined as one-half the difference between the effect of A at the high level of B and the effect of A at the low level of B. The interaction between factors B and E in the Tab Weld experiment is shown in Figure 15.2. It is virtually identical to the quasi-interaction seen in the screening experiment.

For the Sales Rep refining MVT the single largest effect was a two-factor interaction effect. This interaction combined with four helpful factors increased sales by an astonishing 48 percent.

The interactions between factors A, B, and C are defined as one-half the difference between the interaction effect of A and B at the high level of factor C, and the interaction effect of A and B at the low level of factor C. A typical interaction between three factors (A, B, and C) is shown in Figure 15.3.

Figure 15.3   Typical Interaction Bar Chart for Factors A, B, and C

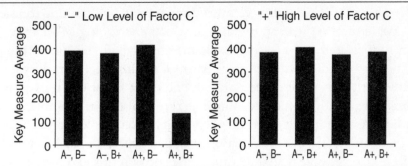

SUMMARIZE THE FINDINGS FOR MANAGEMENT REVIEW

The next step is to summarize the findings for all key measures in a simple format that can be reviewed by managers. A Pareto chart of the improvement factor effects in descending order of magnitude, with the control limit shown, is an effective way to communicate the results. Using statistical process control (SPC) charts that show key-measure performance results prior to the MVT, during the MVT screening experiment, and during the MVT refining experiment also is an effective way to help managers understand the overall results, which are usually very impressive. If there are multiple key measures, the Pareto chart and the SPC chart need to be redrawn for each key measure.

After this, we calculate the effects on consistency. As in the analysis of an MVT screening test, if we can identify a changed level of a factor that yields significantly less variation than we experienced with the original process, that usually is a very valuable finding.

COMPARING REFINING RESULTS WITH SCREENING RESULTS

On rare occasions, we will observe a significant factor effect in the screening MVT, but the same factor will not test as significant in the refining MVT. When this happens, we must examine the results closely. In some instances, when the factor effect in the refining test results is almost significant, we may want to implement it anyway. If we have adhered to the practical, fast, and cost-free criteria, the chances are that we will have everything to gain and nothing to lose.

We have never seen an instance in which a screening MVT experiment indicated that a factor was significantly helpful but the refining experiment indicated that it was harmful to the process in question. Ninety-three percent of the time, we find that a factor that tests as significantly helpful in the screening experiment also tests as significantly helpful in the refining experiment. Seventy-seven percent of the time, a quasi-interaction effect that is greater than any individual factor effect and/or greater than two times the control limits also tests as significant in the refining experiment.

CREATING THE PREDICTIVE EQUATION

Once the results of the MVT refining experiment are assessed, they can be consolidated into a predictive equation. This allows us to predict key measure improvement results based on the factors that will be implemented. The predictive equation, for a key measure that we are attempting to maximize (e.g., sales) is constructed by taking the overall MVT refining experiment average and adding half of the absolute value of each significant factor effect and interaction effect. For a key measure that we are attempting to minimize, we subtract half of the absolute value of each significant factor effect and interaction effect. This equation can be used to calculate the predicted value when implementing all helpful factors. To do a what-if analysis, where not all helpful factors will be implemented, an MVT consultant can use a similar equation to calculate the expected results.

IF NO FACTOR HELPS

Many people ask what happens if we perform a screening MVT experiment and do not find any significantly helpful factors. The only way there can be failure to identify anything that helps is if: (1) no one in the entire organization has a good idea about what might improve the process; (2) too few factors are tested; or (3) the experiment is run for too little time. These things will never happen if you have an MVT consultant guiding the improvement effort. The only times that we have seen such occurrences is when companies have attempted to design their own experiments using unqualified personnel.

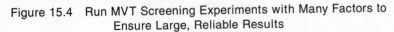

Figure 15.4   Run MVT Screening Experiments with Many Factors to Ensure Large, Reliable Results

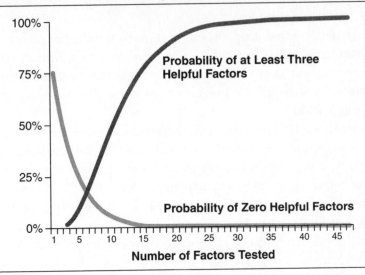

The probability of finding no helpful ways to improve a business process when testing a varying number of factors is shown in Figure 15.4. As can be seen, there is virtually no chance of finding no helpful factors if we test as many as 15 factors. If we test as many as 20 factors, there is almost a 100 percent chance that we will find at least three helpful factors that improve the process.

REVIEW THE RESULTS WITH MANAGEMENT

The purpose of MVT is to help managers make informed decisions on how to improve performance, based on the results of the MVT experiments. We show the company's managers the improvement factor effects from the screening and refining experiments. We show them the control charts from before the MVT, during the screening MVT, and during the refining MVT. We show them how much their process will improve, on average, depending on which combination of tested factors they implement. We review the effect of each improvement factor and help the managers, process experts, process owners, and decision makers to buy in to and make sense of the results. After we review the effect of each factor on the key measure(s) of performance, and we review the effect of each significant inter-action, we help management decide what to do, and which process changes to implement.

We make sure that proper thought is given to whether or not each improvement factor should be implemented. On a rare occasion, a factor that was deemed practical, fast, and cost free prior to the experiments will fail to meet one of these criteria during the experimentation.

Sometimes it is not necessary to implement all of the helpful factors. In some situations, one factor, or a small subset of the significant help-ful factors, can completely solve the problem. In the tab weld exam-ple, the managers quickly saw that implementation of the 28-pound electrode force and either of the tab weld designs (Figure 15.2) would produce welds so strong that they could not be removed with a ham-mer and screwdriver. Since the curved tab weld design would require more effort, and the impacts of the other factors were small, only the increased electrode force was implemented.

Some decisions require trade-offs. Sometimes, for example, we will find that one set of conditions will yield the highest sales but that an-other set of conditions will yield the highest profit margins. In the manufacturing industry, we often find that the best factor conditions for one product characteristic is not the best set of conditions for an-other product characteristic. In such situations, we encourage the managers to think carefully, make decisions about necessary trade-offs, and aim for the best overall conditions for the company. Although they make trade-off decisions every day, managers are relieved to be able to make them based on empirical evidence, not on hunches, com-pany politics, or best guesses.

Case Study: Step 11 (Continued from Chapter 14)

The sixth week of the MVT refining experiment was completed, and the MVT consultant received comp sales and comp profits data for each of the 64 stores in the retail MVT.

Before analyzing the MVT results, he first reviewed the data for that week, just as he had done for the previous five weeks. He visually reviewed the data looking for obviously unusual values, and then created a range chart that compared the ranges (the difference between the comp sales/profits of the two stores in each recipe). Review of these charts for the sixth week, and for the cumulative data containing all six weeks, showed no evidence of data anomalies or execution errors that would skew MVT findings.

The MVT consultant then calculated the effect of each test factor on both comp sales and comp profits. He very carefully double- and triple-checked the accuracy of his data entry to ensure that he did not enter an incorrect value; he got a coworker to help him make sure that he had not entered a data value into the wrong recipe; and he went back after making the calculations once and redid them all so that he had an independent calculation of each effect to compare to his first calculation.

With the stakes for the project being as high as they were, he knew that this was a situation where the adage "measure twice before you cut once" was very applicable. And it was good that he did! Because when he did the independent calculation, he discovered that he had exchanged entries for two of the recipes. Because of his careful checking, he discovered the error and corrected it before anyone had even seen it. He benefited from a Qual-Pro cliché—"When it comes to data integrity and calculations, paranoia is always warranted."

Because the MVT refining experiment was a full factorial design (it included every combination of the five test factors), no separate calculation of interactions was necessary. The refining MVT analysis precisely calculated the effect of each test factor individually; it calculated the impact of every pair of factors; it also calculated the impact of all combinations of three factors, four factors, and five factors. He constructed the Pareto chart on page 166 that shows all these effects, as compared to the control limit.

The MVT consultant was extremely pleased with the agreement between the MVT screening experiment effects and the effects calculated for the refining MVT. All four factors helpful in the screening MVT were also significantly helpful in the refining experiment. Additionally, the quasi-interaction between associate staffing and use of fitting room attendants was confirmed.

Just as in the MVT screening experiment, profit effects closely mirrored factor effects on sales.

From the results of the MVT refining experiment, the MVT consultant was able to construct a predictive equation that would forecast the collective impact of the five test factors on sales and profit. The equation and calculation of the potential impact of the five factors are shown on page 166.

The project leader and the MVT consultant then presented the findings to the CEO and executive management team. The findings were quickly accepted. Management was extremely excited by the potential of a 10 percent

Pareto Chart Showing the MVT Refining Experiment Factor Effects

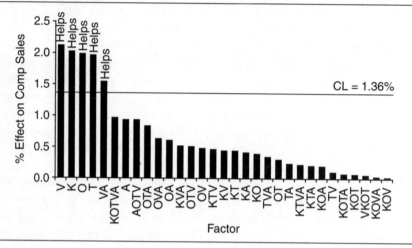

comp sales impact. The MVT consultant was quick to remind the group that the improvement could be realized only by thorough implementation of the five helpful factors identified by the MVT process.

Every member of the executive team recognized the enormous effect that this level of improvement could have on the stock price. As each of them mentally calculated the impact of the improved profits on the value of their own stock options, they promised full implementation support.

Predictive Equation Used to Perform Retail What-If Analysis

Overall MVT average for comp sales +	5.17%
($\frac{1}{2}$ effect of promotion location) +	1.01%
($\frac{1}{2}$ effect of friendly program) +	1.00%
($\frac{1}{2}$ effect of management incentives) +	0.99%
($\frac{1}{2}$ effect of associate scheduling) +	1.06%
($\frac{1}{2}$ effect of interaction for associate scheduling and fitting room attendant)	0.78%
= Predicted comp sales	10.01%

CHAPTER 16

STEP 12

*Carefully Implement the Most
Powerful Ideas, Calculate the
Bottom-Line Impact, and Take the
Money to the Bank!*

The first 11 steps of the MVT process will have surfaced numerous improvement ideas, tested them, and determined exactly what combination of improvement ideas will create the business results that best meets the company's objectives. However, successful MVT experiments and useful findings do not contribute to an improved financial picture unless the findings are implemented. An MVT project is deemed successful when its findings are implemented and there is a positive effect on the company's financial picture.

Unfortunately, there have been occasional examples of great MVT findings that were never put into practice. The reasons for this are varied: there was no solid agreement among the members of the management team as to exactly what was going to be implemented; there was insufficient planning and monitoring; no one had true accountability for implementation; the ball was dropped; or no one followed up to determine whether effective implementation actually had occurred. There even have been a few examples of sabotage, when a particular employee group favored a different set of actions or their goals were not aligned with the corporate goals and they actively worked toward preventing implementation of the MVT findings.

Regardless of the obstacles, it is clear that implementation, the last step of the MVT process, is absolutely necessary before the company can enjoy the benefits of MVT. The steps used in implementing findings from MVT experiments are virtually identical to those used in the process of executing MVT experiments. The difference is that, in an MVT experiment, there are many recipes, each with different conditions to be executed. During implementation, there is only one recipe, with only one set of conditions to be executed. The recipe represents the best conditions to achieve the company's objectives.

To recap, the steps are as follows:

1. Develop an action plan.
2. Prepare factor materials and training.
3. Communicate the plans, roles, procedures, logistics, and importance.
4. Measure and report recipe compliance.
5. Act to remedy any execution flaws.

DEVELOP AN ACTION PLAN

In Step 11, decisions were made as to what factors were to be implemented. In Step 12, plans must be laid out in detail as to who will do what, and when, to put the optimum conditions in place in the organization. An aggressive plan has great value in the implementation of MVT findings. In many business situations, every day that implementation is delayed represents large sums of money that are lost.

Roles and Responsibilities

The same roles that were important during the MVT experimentation are equally important during final implementation.

An executive sponsor continues to be critical to communicate the importance of implementing the MVT findings. This is even more important now, because the financial stakes are known very precisely. The executive sponsor needs to continue to ensure that resources are shifted as needed and to remove roadblocks that require executive involvement.

There continues to be a need for a project leader. Usually, the project leader for the MVT will continue to lead the effort during implementation. The project leader will communicate assignments, coordinate activities, monitor completion of tasks (for both timing and quality), and bring attention and action to bear when weaknesses are discovered.

Each factor to be implemented needs a factor owner. Because there is a much smaller number of factors at this stage, there may be only a handful of factor owners. These often are the same persons who were factor owners during the MVT experimentation.

It is critical that every factor be implemented just as it was tested. "Improving" a test factor can have a catastrophic impact on results. (Remember, 22 percent of improvement ideas actually hurt the desired result.) Never, never change a successful test idea; any "improvement" at this stage is just as likely to hurt the result as to help. Any new ideas should be saved for the next round of MVT experimentation.

A data owner also continues to be necessary, because key-measure data and secondary-measure data will be captured and reported on an ongoing basis. These data will verify that the improvements are happening as projected and serve as the reconnaissance system to ensure that MVT gains are maintained over the long term.

The MVT consultant's role in implementation is to ensure that the practical, fast, and cost-free factors that helped during MVT experimentation are those that are actually implemented; that preparations and logistics do not inadvertently compromise the original factor definitions; that improvement data from the final implementation are collected properly and analyzed correctly; and that the level of improvement forecast by MVT results is achieved. The MVT consultant also helps to troubleshoot any shortcomings in improvement as compared to the MVT forecast.

The implementation action plan is completed by the project leader, factor owners, and data owners, who document the timing and resources necessary to prepare, communicate, execute, and monitor each factor's implementation.

PREPARE FACTOR MATERIALS AND TRAINING

Just as in the execution of MVT recipes, during implementation, equipment may need to be relocated; production schedules need to be worked out; labor schedules need to be developed; training needs to be prepared and delivered; and materials need to be purchased, created, and distributed. These preparations should be relatively easy to do, as they have been done twice previously, during the screening and then the refining MVT experiments. Now, however, the preparations may be performed on a larger scale around the organization, and care must be taken to ensure that the materials, training, and so on for each factor are exactly the same as the preparations for the factor during the successful MVT experiments.

COMMUNICATE THE PLANS, ROLES, PROCEDURES, LOGISTICS, AND IMPORTANCE

As before, the definition of and the plan, materials, and logistics for each factor to be implemented must be communicated to those involved in implementing it. The sponsor must communicate the importance of proper execution. The sponsor is supported by the team leader, factor owners, MVT consultant, data owners, and/or line managers, who provide implementation instructions to all appropriate persons in the organization. Each manager who will implement MVT factors works with his or her employees to put each factor in place, using the existing chain of command along with the logistics and materials that have been prepared for the implementation.

MEASURE AND REPORT RECIPE COMPLIANCE

Flawless execution is just as important during implementation as it was in testing MVT recipes. During implementation, however, every percentage point of noncompliance may directly cost the company thousands or even millions of dollars. Therefore, it is vitally important to create and execute an effective monitoring process to measure factor execution and to identify shortcomings in compliance. The implementation and monitoring of compliance must be driven by line management; these functions rarely are successful if delegated to a non-line staff group.

The monitoring process must measure compliance on every factor within each organizational entity. Compliance should be monitored on an ongoing basis, and compliance percentages should be entered into a statistical process control (SPC) chart, for each factor for each organizational entity, and watched closely. The monitoring system may be very similar to that used during MVT experimentation. It may involve check sheets, self-audits, telephone audits, announced and unannounced physical audits, and review of the data.

ACT TO REMEDY ANY EXECUTION FLAWS

Any flaws in factor execution should be documented and acted on immediately. Action should be taken quickly and decisively. You can afford to put a lot of effort into actions to remedy flaws in execution. It pays big dividends.

HOW GOOD IS GOOD ENOUGH?

The target for factor compliance is 100 percent. Every incident of noncompliance takes money out of the company's bank account. Strive for perfection!

There should be an SPC chart to report measurements of compliance percentage for each factor being implemented. SPC charts are very useful in ensuring that day-to-day attention is focused on monitoring results. An SPC chart also should be maintained for the key measure that represents the original project objective. This is the ultimate measure of success. Have business results improved? Only if this chart moves in a favorable direction can the project be viewed as a success. This chart should be maintained forever. It is an executive reconnaissance system that will alert management if additional attention to the project or process is necessary.

WHAT IF WE DO NOT GET THE RESULTS WE EXPECT?

If the results achieved are below the expectations that were indicated by the MVT, lack of compliance in implementing the factors is almost always the cause. By carefully reviewing the data regarding business results and compliance, the MVT consultant usually can determine where line management should focus its investigation efforts and remedial actions.

One of our retail clients put an implementation plan into place. The CEO was interviewed on CNBC and indicated that the company was taking several actions to improve results. A month went by. Two months went by. The expected sales and profits did not occur. Qual-Pro then audited 26 of the stores and found that none of the actions were actually being performed in any of stores. The lesson to be learned here is that one can never assume that, just because a memo comes from headquarters, people will do what they are told to do. You have to have an implementation plan and you must monitor implementation and quickly address shortcomings to ensure compliance.

We had another, more comical instance, involving a group of direct salespeople. After completing the MVT process, an implementation meeting was held with all the direct sales representatives from a five-state area. The findings of the MVT process were presented, and hard copies of implementation instructions were handed to each salesperson. A question-and-answer session lasted an hour and a half. Finally, the sales managers were convinced that every salesperson knew what he or she needed to do. Then the meeting adjourned. On the way out of the meeting room, almost one-third of the salespeople dropped their implementation instructions into the trash container. During the next two months, the company achieved two-thirds of the improvement that the MVT process forecast. SPC charts for individual salespeople revealed that one-third of them experienced no significant increase in sales. These salespeople were talked to individually (the rumor was that they were threatened with termination). Within another two months, they too experienced the dramatic improvement in sales.

WANT EVEN BETTER RESULTS?

Your organization may want to achieve even better results than those indicated by your screening and refining MVT findings. For example, when screening and refining MVT experiments were completed in the carbon-foam example described in Chapter 1, the proportion of defective product still remained at 15 percent. This was dramatic

Figure 16.1   Results of MVT Process including Multiple Refining
Experiments for the Carbon-Foam Example

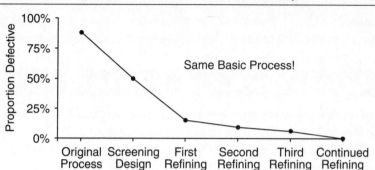

improvement from the original 85 percent defective product, but there remained plenty of room for additional improvement. And there was no reason to believe that the factor levels indicated by the refining experiment were at their optimums. For example, a mixing time of 30 seconds was found to be better than 60 seconds, but there was no reason to believe that 30 seconds was the optimum time. The same was true for several other factors including blade position and turntable speed. In situations like this, additional refining experimentation that focuses on fine-tuning earlier findings can be very fruitful. Several additional refining experiments were run to nail down the optimum settings for these factors. The end result was five years of production without a single defective casting. The improvement with each successive round of MVT experimentation is shown in Figure 16.1.

If additional refining still does not appear to offer enough improvement, then go back to Step 3 and implement the MVT process again from there. Generate and assess more test ideas. Run more MVT experiments. Identify more improvement actions. Implement more helpful actions. In this way, you can drive your business performance even higher.

If you think that all of the possible improvement already has been accomplished, the good news is that you are probably wrong! Time and time again, our experience shows that additional improvement is almost always possible. Driven by the feeling of success and by knowledge of the process, your organization is likely to surface more ideas for the second and third rounds of MVT than it did for the first one. The ideas probably will become increasingly aggressive and more creative. Additional MVT experiments often achieve larger results and gain momentum, making even larger gains than those of the first round.

Case Study: Step 12 (Continued from Chapter 15)

After gaining executive team agreement to implement five actions, the project leader and MVT consultant launched the implementation process.

They immediately called a meeting of the factor owners of the five factors and the department heads involved. The CEO kicked off the meeting by congratulating the group on an excellent MVT project. He then went on to explain that, if the company did not implement the five factors in an effective and sustained manner, all their hard work could be wasted. He promised full support of the executive team and challenged them to have every factor implemented in all stores within one month. He reminded them that the factors all had been categorized as practical, fast, and cost free. He said that he was confident they could achieve this goal since they had executed the factors during MVT screening and refining experiments already.

The implementation process was virtually identical to that used to execute the MVT experiments. In this case, however, there was only one recipe—the one that contained the five implementation factors.

After the charter of the group was established, each factor owner quickly created an action plan for the factor(s) for which he or she would be responsible. Each plan was reviewed with the project leader and the MVT consultant, and then execution of the plans was immediately initiated.

Every one of the factors was implemented, according to the factor owners, prior to the CEO's one-month goal.

They also developed a long-term compliance monitoring plan for each implementation factor. For example, "promotion location at department entrances" was permanently written into the merchandising standards, operations audit documentation was changed to include this standard, and control charts were established by district and for the company overall to track the portion of the audited stores each month who were in compliance. Similar monitoring and control processes were put in place for each factor, and the CEO insisted that presentation of these SPC charts become a part of his monthly operations review.

When all factor owners declared "implementation complete," comp sales results had indeed improved, but only to a little less than half of the level

Improved Comp Sales Using the MVT Process

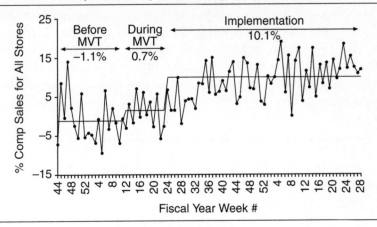

predicted by the MVT. Remembering the advice of the MVT consultant, who had explained to the executive group that shortfalls in results versus MVT predictions were usually caused by lack of factor compliance, the CEO took decisive action. He first reviewed the recent compliance monitoring results and saw that, while there was evidence that the factors were being put in place, the rate of compliance was only 53 percent. He then placed an unprecedented conference call to all store managers and district managers and explained in very straightforward language that these five actions were not optional. Not only were they critical to the company's success, but they would help the store managers meet their individual sales/profit goals. He required every store manager to verify by e-mail to the CEO's assistant that the actions were in place in their store. The e-mail was due in seven days.

This resulted in action; compliance data improved very quickly, and comp sales improved at the same time. While comp sales results varied on a week-to-week basis, they continued to average about a 10 percent gain throughout the year (see the chart above).

These improved comp sales increased revenue by more than $20 million per month, or about $250 million per year. After two quarters of substantially improved sales, the stock market believed that the improvement was sustainable, and the stock price doubled over the next quarter. This created a dramatic win-win-win with (1) shareholder stock values growing by over 100 percent, (2) the management team's stock options becoming extremely valuable, and (3) the employee profit-sharing retirement plan benefiting greatly.

Later that year, the CEO reminded his executive team that, by definition, the actions that improved comp sales in one year could not contribute to the next year's success. This was because the actions were already built into the year-over-year comparison. Given their dramatic MVT success that year, the executive team quickly concluded that they needed to initiate an ongoing program of MVT experimentation so that new, effective improvement actions were continually being fed into their system. . . . But that is another story.

CHAPTER 17

WHAT IT ALL ADDS UP TO

Putting the Twelve Steps of the MVT
Process in Perspective

In this chapter, we discuss what to expect when you use the MVT process: what to expect in the way of improvement and what to expect in the way of required work. We also identify the minimum requirements for getting breakthrough results with the MVT process.

EXPECTED IMPROVEMENT FROM THE MVT PROCESS

The dedicated application of the MVT process yields quantum leaps in improvement, the likes of which no one in the company would ever have thought possible. In QualPro seminars, we often use graphics to communicate the typical payoffs from using the MVT Process. Although Figure 17.1 may seem a bit extreme, it reflects what we have observed within companies in the United States. Figure 17.1 compares improvements obtained with the MVT process versus those obtained with other improvement approaches.

This figure shows a high mountain. The other popular improvement approaches are struggling through the trees at the bottom of the mountain, never even getting started up the path to the top. The MVT process attains the peak of the mountain. The screening MVT

Figure 17.1   MVT Gets Us to the Top of the Mountain

gets us about 70 percent of the way up the mountain, and the refining MVT gets us to the top.

As we have pointed out previously, the MVT process includes elements of many of these other approaches.

Again, although this illustration may seem far-fetched, it illustrates exactly what we have observed in 22 years of using the MVT process. When MVT-proven factors are implemented, a company usually gets better results than have been seen in the history of the process that is being improved.

Figures 17.2 and 17.3 show typical examples of real-life results.

The sales results shown in Figure 17.2 are results (1) pre-MVT, (2) during the screening MVT, (3) during the refining MVT, and (4) during implementation. During the screening MVT, we usually see results that, on average, are a small bit better than what has been observed previously in the process. During the refining MVT, we usually see results that are considerably better than those that have been seen in the recent past. During implementation of the results

Figure 17.2   Business-to-Business Sales
Tripled Using the MVT Process

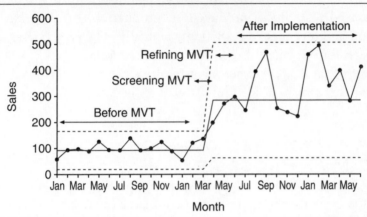

from the refining experiment, we see improvements that are dramatically better than those achieved prior to the MVT experimentation.

Figure 17.3 illustrates a manufacturing situation and shows the improvement in NOx emissions. Prior to the MVT process, emissions were at a high level, 4,500 ppm. During the screening MVT, the emissions improved a small amount. During the refining MVT,

Figure 17.3   Environmental Emissions Reduced from
4,500 ppm to 140 ppm Using the MVT Process

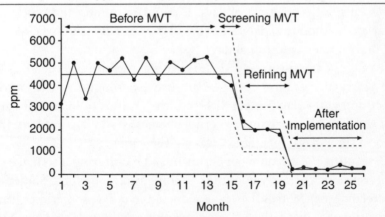

the emissions improved considerably. After implementation, the emissions were reduced dramatically to 140 ppm. Additionally, the company saved $80,000 in product loss, production was increased 17 percent, and revenues rose $850,000 annually. The project was win-win-win for the state, the company, and the workers.

Most of the 13,000 experiments that we have been involved with in the past 22 years yielded results such as these.

WORK REQUIRED DURING THE MVT PROCESS

The 12 steps of the MVT process may appear to represent a lot of work, and the first time they are used in an organization, they could seem like a lot of work. However, nobody we have ever worked with has hired any extra people to perform the MVT experimentation or to implement the results. The even better news is that it gets easier with practice.

In many instances, the creation of the environment involves just having someone sufficiently high in the management hierarchy say, "We are going to do this." Identification of the key measure is not difficult because it usually is obvious. Developing a capable and controlled measurement system requires a little checking and some work, but it usually does not take long if the company has the right help.

Using SPC charts to identify instances of uncontrolled variation and the underlying special causes, obtained from the historical measurements, takes a couple of days. Using data mining and other multivariate methods to analyze historical data usually takes an expert no more than a few additional days.

Doing the brainstorming and identifying the proposed changes that are practical, fast, and cost free are usually fun and can be accomplished in a few days, in parallel with the analysis of historical data.

Designing the screening experiment takes an MVT consultant from two to three days, including "playing the game."

Executing the screening experiment and monitoring it to make sure that it is done correctly does require some time and work. Sometimes a screening experiment can be conducted in a day; sometimes it may take a month. Nevertheless, monitoring to make sure that the MVT is done correctly and seeing the actual change in the levels usually is exciting, and is later seen as fun, for the people involved. An MVT consultant usually can analyze the results of the MVT screening experiment in one day.

Designing the refining experiment and getting the appropriate management personnel on board usually can be achieved in one or two days. The execution of the refining experiment is always much easier than the execution of the MVT screening experiment. In most instances, the results observed in the refining experiment are much better than any that have been obtained in the past, so seeing them is an exciting, upbeat experience for all concerned.

By the time the MVT refining experiment has been completed, all involved usually are eagerly awaiting the analysis so that they can implement the best conditions. Fortunately, the MVT consultant can often do the analysis of the refining experiment results within a day. The overall results are reported to the managers as soon as they can be assembled, and discussions held on what will be implemented are then conducted.

Implementation is always an exciting time. Implementation of the helpful factors is not very painful, as they are all practical, fast, and cost free. Financial results immediately begin to improve, and everybody involved feels as if they are members of a winning team. The overall feeling is that of having accomplished something significant, something outstanding. This is why MVT is used time and again within the same companies.

MINIMUM REQUIREMENTS FOR GETTING BREAKTHROUGH RESULTS WITH THE MVT PROCESS

The first 12 chapters of Part II describe how to use the MVT process to get dramatic improvements every time. Some of the 12 steps do not have to be performed in some situations. For example, a company may have no historical data to analyze. In some cases, we have achieved such dramatic improvements during the screening experiments that the clients did not want to wait before implementing the best conditions observed in the screening experiments; consequently, we never performed the MVT refining experiments. However, the minimum requirements for getting good results from the MVT process are as follows:

- Someone at a sufficiently high level in the organization has to communicate to the organization's members that it is going to do the MVT project.
- Results must be measurable.
- Everyone who could have any worthwhile suggestions participates in the brainstorming and the categorizing processes.
- An MVT consultant designs and analyzes the MVT experiments.
- MVT screening and refining experiments are properly executed.
- Findings are implemented completely and quickly.

SUMMARY

What this all adds up to is that proper, dedicated application of the MVT process will yield staggering improvements. The work involved in going through the 12 steps is not as difficult as it may first appear. The typical result of using the MVT process is a little bit of improvement during the screening experiment, considerable improvement during the refining experiment, and dramatic improvement when the results are implemented. Finally, in certain circumstances, some steps of the MVT process can be omitted, and dramatic improvements still can be obtained.

PART III

BREAKTHROUGH MVT SUCCESSES IN THE REAL WORLD

CHAPTER 18

HOW LOWE'S REDUCED ADVERTISING EXPENSES BY $50 MILLION WHILE INCREASING SALES*

Lowe's, the home improvement retailer based in Mooresville, North Carolina, was doing well in the 1990s, before it discovered MVT. By any measure, it was a force in retailing, with 470 stores—almost all of them over 100,000 square feet; $12 billion dollars in annual sales (with a double-digit growth rate for several years); 65,000 employees who were highly motivated both to serve the customer well and to improve the buyer's experience in the future; and a ranking as the number-two home improvement and building materials retailer in the world. For five years, Lowe's had been averaging an annual growth of 22 percent and earnings of about 30 percent. The market had been mostly respectful of the company's performance, and the stock price reflected this. Lowe's had been named one of the best 100 companies in the United States to work for by *Fortune* magazine. Despite the constant challenges of a highly competitive industry, the future seemed bright.

Bob Tillman, Lowe's chairman of the board and CEO, had done an excellent job of creating the environment for improvement. He

---

* All the information in Part III examples was either publicly presented at a QualPro MVT Symposium and/or printed in a third-party publication such as *Forbes*, the *Wall Street Journal*, *BusinessWeek*, etc.

motivated everyone to be continually thinking: "What can we do to improve our business performance? What can we do to better satisfy customers?" So Dale Pond, Lowe's executive vice president of marketing, was looking for ways to improve the business when he went to a QualPro MVT Symposium and heard a story about one company's MVT experience that hit very close to home. He decided to give MVT a try. The following year, Dale presented the results of two MVT projects at Lowe's to the 1998 QualPro MVT Symposium. Dale Pond explained, "We didn't come to QualPro with a problem. We came to QualPro with, really, a desire to be better. That is somewhat inherent in our culture. We're never satisfied. Bob Tillman makes it a point to never, ever, on Monday morning, say— 'Boy what a great sales week. It's always, what could we have done different and to have been better.' "

The company's culture supported continuous improvement in the stores and throughout the organization. Anything that seemed to be improvable was fair game for change. But it was thought that functions such as marketing and advertising could not be measured objectively, so performance in these areas was assessed more subjectively: for example, what did the managers think about the advertising? Like other retailers and businesses that depend on advertising, Lowe's relied on consumer research to determine the effectiveness of an ad campaign. However, retail marketing professionals will tell you that you can't pinpoint how much of a store's performance is related to its advertising. Despite significant investment in measuring top-of-mind awareness, image and attribute scores, and the attitudes of customers and employees, and in attempting to correlate this information with sales performance, Lowe's could not, in Dale's words, "make indisputable, irrefutable connections between our advertising and our investment."

Dale knew that there were good reasons to try to make those connections. Lowe's primarily attracts customers through television and radio commercials and through printed advertisements: newspaper ads, Sunday newspaper inserts (weekly flyers), and mailbox circulars. The company produces 25 preprints each year and distributes 30 to 40 million copies of each. In 1996/1997, the preprint was 72 pages. Large retailers like Lowe's spend between 2 percent and 5 percent of sales dollars on advertising and promotion. With $12 billion in annual sales, advertising and promotion adds up to a major investment.

Dale wasn't satisfied to hear that "you can't measure" ad performance precisely and wanted a reliable method for measuring the impact of advertising on sales. He had done the math on the preprints and knew that because of the huge volume, even small improvements that saved money would be significant. He found his answer in MVT when he came to our MVT Symposium and heard how MVT was used to redesign the cover of the *National Enquirer.*

You might not think that Lowe's and the *National Enquirer* have much in common, but they both rely on flashy covers for their printed material to entice consumers to pick them up. *National Enquirer* covers are designed to attract readers in the grocery line, while Lowe's tries to get consumers to pull Lowe's "preprint" circular from their mailboxes or the Sunday paper. Consumer research had demonstrated consistently that, the more the cover entices the reader, the more of the preprint each reads, and, if the preprint appeals to the reader, the more likely it will influence the reader to visit the store and buy. What the research had not been able to tell was how to make the cover more effective at hooking the consumer at first glance.

The *National Enquirer* used MVT to test dozens of cover design ideas and achieved a dramatic impact. Inspired when he heard about this, Dale was convinced that the MVT methodology could help him at Lowe's. He asked QualPro's Art Hammer to perform an assessment of Lowe's marketing and advertising functions. As a result of the assessment, Lowe's decided to undertake two initial projects: the first involving the cover design and its effectiveness, and the second to determine the most effective media mix (the allocation of television spending versus radio versus print ads) to increase sales and fully exploit the $100 million annual media buy. It was believed that these projects would have immediate and obvious returns and would contribute to the development of the 1999 marketing and advertising plans—the latter becoming the time-line driver of the MVT project. The project had high visibility and complete senior management commitment to go with the aggressive schedule. It involved an expert team of Lowe's personnel and a focused, experienced project manager to go with the SWAT Team from QualPro. The SWAT Team approach was the only way to get a project of this complexity completed in a few months.

To get the projects off the ground, Dale and QualPro worked together to define the key measure: sales at each store—pure, raw, simple sales. Dale explained, "That's one that everyone in the company could relate to. That's what we use every Monday morning, when we go before the executive management committee and we talk through where we are and what we are doing."

Dale Pond described the formal launch of the project, "In order to get buy-in and support, we held a kick-off meeting. We invited everyone and anyone who could be directly, or indirectly, affected by the project, now or even in the future. At the meeting, I set the stage regarding the importance of the project, from a strategic point of view. What will it mean to us as we move forward as a company over the next few years ahead."

The QualPro MVT consultants then began a review of past sales data and current sales-department functions. The consultants constructed control charts of the historical data and used multiple linear regression and various multivariate methods to analyze for possible cause and effect relationships, including possible synergies. Several test factors were identified.

Meanwhile, Lowe's held brainstorming sessions that would involve everyone who came near the processes and wanted to participate. The success of an MVT project almost always can be traced to the participation and involvement of many people in the organization—people whose experience and knowledge ensure a deep well of ideas about what might make something work better.

The brainstorming sessions involved people from marketing, advertising, merchandising, store operations, logistics, and other areas and accomplished two primary goals: (1) getting buy-in and some ownership of the outcome from all the people involved, and (2) developing a list of ideas that might be helpful and could be tested in an MVT experiment. MVT brainstorming rules were applied; no idea could be rejected because it was unusual or hadn't been done before. But the ideas did have to be practical, fast, and cost free.

The brainstorming activity produced astounding results, verifying the outstanding job that Mr. Tillman and the Lowe's management team had done in creating the environment for improvement. More than 2,000 potential process changes were identified.

The MVT process requires experimenters to cut the idea list by applying the practical, fast, and cost-free criteria. Qualifying ideas have to be easy to test and implement, using existing people and facilities and processes. They also must be fast, able to be implemented as soon as whatever materials or instructions the experiment requires can be prepared. Many ideas are deemed not practical or not fast, even though they may have tremendous potential and perhaps should be considered for another project. The ideas that are left must be cost free; they cannot cost more than what we are currently paying to do something else. It was the no-cost aspect of the cover project that interested Dale Pond. He knew that if some of the ideas worked on the cover, implementation of them would cost nothing and generate new, better sales. Little did he know that the MVT project would also uncover ways to save major dollars in production expense.

Dale stated that the MVT consultants from QualPro held their feet to the fire during the categorization process: "We could not throw out any idea just because it didn't fit conventional wisdom. As bizarre as an idea might be, as out-of-the-box as it might be, if it was cost-efficient, practical, and feasible, then it was still considered. . . . Ideas could only be rejected if they couldn't be done within the time line, if they were too expensive to implement on a continuing basis, or if we simply were incapable of getting them done."

Twenty-nine design or process ideas made the cut. Testing all possible combinations of these factors would require examining more than 536 million potential combinations. The mathematics in the screening MVT, designed by the MVT consultants from QualPro, provided most of the knowledge of the effects of each of the factors—with just 36 versions of the cover. Some of the factors seemed almost too simple. For example: Should the cover be in color, or would black and white be just as effective? Do consumers react differently to the number of items on the cover? (No one in merchandising wanted to see fewer items on the cover, as they were convinced that front-page exposure would move more of the featured products.) What kind of products should be on the cover? Do cartoon characters make a difference, versus pictures of real people? Does it matter whether Lowe's sends out a preprint on Wednesday or Saturday? Because MVT science could construct the correct combinations of the 29 factors to measure the effects in only 36 versions of the cover, these questions could all be answered. (Other testing and improvement methods fall far short of the capability to test this level of complexity.) The test covers stretched everyone's creativity both in design and in managing the external production and distribution of the preprints.

The current cover already had "patch areas"—areas that vary for seasonal products—and was subject to geographical pricing variations based on related costs. The challenges were great for the external production partners: the ad agency, the prepress company, and the printers. Testing 36 different covers in different markets with local pricing with different product patches with multiple vendors was not easy to pull off, but the Lowe's project participants made it happen.

The paring of the list of ideas for the media-mix project resulted in 16 factors to be tested, including how much radio time should be purchased and what time of day it should run, whether newspaper run-of-press (ROP) advertising should be in color or black and white, and how much television coverage was enough and whether it should be purchased at all.

Using sales data collected from each of the markets executing an MVT recipe, the analysis of the experiment made it clear which changes improved sales results and which changes hurt results. It confirmed that most of the factors made no difference, which created the opportunity to stop doing things that didn't help sales and reallocate the resources to things that did. By identifying practices that hurt sales results, it made it possible to avoid or eliminate them, creating huge cost savings.

WHAT LOWE'S LEARNED FROM THE MVT PROJECTS

Lowe's performed MVT refining experimentation that further clarified which ideas made an impact on sales. Dale Pond explained, "What we found were some surprises. There were a number of things that we knew would be winners. They either made no difference or may have even hurt. In fact, one of my colleagues summed it up nicely when he said that the results we're seeing sure slaughtered some sacred cows."

Surprisingly, one finding of the MVT experiments was that three or four product items on the circular's cover worked far better than seven or eight. Using pictures of real people instead of cartoon characters made them seem more informed and authoritative to the customers, who preferred that confidence-inspiring trait over humor. (Early on, the proponents of the cartoon characters thought that the MVT tests should be used to determine if the characters should be rounder, if they should be male or female, what they should wear, and so on, but they never questioned whether the characters should be eliminated.)

A key discovery that ultimately saved both prep time and printing costs was that more product pages in the circular did not sell additional products. Cutting the size of the circular from 72 pages to no more than 48 pages saved millions of dollars annually in printing and postage expenses and did not hurt sales.

The results of the MVT projects led to dramatic changes. In the next year, Lowe's saved millions of dollars in advertising and marketing expenses, and improvements in sales directly related to the MVT-acquired knowledge added millions in new revenue. As Dale said at the 1998 QualPro Symposium, "This is powerful stuff."

> Our front cover project clearly indicated savings [on advertising spending] in the tens of millions of dollars when we take into account what we've learned from the "doesn't matter" column [i.e., advertising costs proven by MVT to have no business impact]. We believe that we can capture additional sales in the tens of millions as well, which means that there's savings and incremental sales, and that's significant leverage. So this is really good stuff. And our media mix project also showed some great promise. Currently, with only the preliminary results, we're confident that the revisions that we're making to the media mix next year will increase our advertising effectiveness significantly and lower our advertising cost. And that again is more leverage. We think we can lower our costs by a number in the tens of millions of dollars. All totaled it's very possible that we can increase sales and reduce our advertising expense by nearly $50 million next year and reapply those resources in other more productive areas.

Dale also pointed to unexpected insights that real data can produce. Instead of sales projects based on theoretical models and sales history, Lowe's learned that, with real data, it could manipulate sales patterns and improve revenue by taking advantage of its new understanding of how its advertising actually worked. It could measure performance and relate it directly to sales—another goal of the MVT process.

Dale cited several other lessons:

- *You can unleash creativity.* When asked how the creative types reacted to the MVT Process, Dale said, "Slowly initially. I think they were threatened, and thought if we got too scientific in our approach or too narrowly focused in our approach, that it would inhibit their creativity. But as it turns out, the brainstorming sessions really overcame all that. Frankly, I think most of our creative group, both internally and externally, felt that it was probably one of the more stimulating, exciting exercises that we have been through in years. It really took all the shackles, all the conventional wisdom, out of the picture and allowed people to put crazy ideas up there and then actually test some of those crazy ideas. In many ways, the creativity, I think, exploded—became greater in scope."
- *Don't wait.* Lowe's was convinced that an MVT project could produce results but, in the absence of a particular problem to solve, there was no urgency to start the project, so it waited a while, letting other things take precedence. After the project, Dale concluded that waiting to implement MVT cost the company sales and hurt performance. "Don't wait! I think the right time is immediately. That is the lesson we learned. I said earlier, and I will say it again, that once you get into it, you will be sorry that you did delay. . . . You are losing sales. You are losing valuable resources. And you are probably continuing to do things that actually hurt your company."
- *Plan for the unexpected.* Lowe's did plan for the unexpected and still managed to be surprised a few times. A hurricane, an unplanned inventory closeout, and a calendar variation—Labor Day was a week later than usual in 1998—all made the project more challenging. Dale said, "Up front, good planning, geographically dispersed test stores, and the structure of the tests themselves protected the integrity of our results."
- *Emphasize communication and involvement.* Coordinating any project of this magnitude and complexity requires frequent and effective communication of goals, techniques, and requirements. In the case of Lowe's projects, and all MVT experiments, people

become involved and take interest in and ownership of the efforts and results because they participate in the process.

- *Some ideas help, some hurt, and most don't matter.* It was never difficult to get people to accept the idea that approximately one-fourth of the suggested ideas would help to improve performance, one-fourth of the ideas would actually hurt results, and about half of the ideas (or current practices) would make no real difference in results. The problem was that each person had a different opinion about which ideas belonged in which category. Real data from the MVT experiment ended the speculation. In some cases, people didn't know why one idea worked better than another or were surprised that something they took for granted to be important didn't help at all, but which ideas worked was no longer a subjective opinion. Lowe's knew (with a certainty no one had believed possible) exactly what did work with their customers and produced improved sales.

Lowe's learned that the MVT techniques used so effectively on the cover design and media-mix projects could be applied to almost anything and enable significant process and performance improvements.

CHAPTER 19

How DuPont Achieved $26 Million in Increased Production with No Capital Investment

DuPont makes many different materials that consumers call "plastics" but which are actually far more specialized and differentiated than that term implies. One particular line of products is called engineering polymers; these are used primarily to replace metal in applications in which rigidity, stress tolerance, and weight reduction are key goals.

In the mid-1950s, DuPont developed a material that was a tough and heat-resistant metal substitute—an inflexible polymer synthesized from formaldehyde. DuPont patented it as Delrin® and, in 1960, completed construction of a production plant at Parkersburg, West Virginia. Parkersburg, a traditional town of 33,000, is a base of operations for many members of the Fortune 500, and the local workforce is made up of well-educated, highly motivated, productive, and loyal employees.

The plant was designed for an annual production capacity of 20 million pounds of Delrin; and by the time it began manufacturing, DuPont's investment had reached $50 million. The investment was a good one, and today, Delrin is a mainstay of DuPont's engineering polymers line and is widely acclaimed as a lightweight but durable, low-wear, low-friction plastic for use in electronic office equipment; advanced conveyor technology; and automotive applications, such as window glides, gas caps, dashboard parts, and many heat-resistant parts under the hoods of cars. It is found in the buckles on backpacks, hiking boots, ski bindings, and other sports products. It comes in several grades, with specific qualities that optimize its use for specific needs. It is also a complex and potentially dangerous product to make.

A Problem in the Delrin Production Process

A polymer is a large molecule made from the combination of many similar (or identical) smaller molecules called monomers in a process called polymerization. A useful analogy is to think of a single link in a chain as a monomer and the chain itself as the resulting polymer. To produce Delrin, formaldehyde gas (the monomer) is pumped through a series of pipes into the polymerizer and, when all goes well, a controlled reaction starts that "chains" the monomer molecules to form the polymer.

The problem at DuPont was that, over a very short production time (often a few days), the buildup of particulates in the pipelines caused the polymer to begin forming within the pipes that fed the gas to the polymerizer, and the company was forced to take the machine offline to clean the pipes. The problem was labeled monomer head adhesions (MHA) because the monomer (formaldehyde gas) began seeding and chaining prematurely on the polymerizer head assembly. Once formed, the clogs were sticky and difficult to remove. Of the three Delrin polymerizers at the plant, at any given time, two ended up operating 24 hours per day, seven days a week, and one was offline for maintenance or cleaning. With the resulting loss of production, minimizing the time for the cleaning process was critical. The downtime was costing DuPont an estimated $8 million annually. The operators called the cleaning process "The Beast," and taming the beast was a high priority.

For more than two years, a great deal of effort was expended on the problem. According to Darren Bro, process improvement leader,

DuPont had spent $1 million on having four teams conduct 22 different plant tests, based on the traditional, one-factor-at-a-time experimental method. The tests were designed and conducted by experts in the process who provided instruction to the operators but rarely sought the operators' input on the problem. The tests were not successful, and the problem was considered, at least informally, to be unsolvable. In 1995, the technical experts recommended a capital investment of $1.5 million in the hope of solving the problem, but there was no guarantee.

A DIFFERENT APPROACH: THE MVT PROCESS

DuPont eventually could not make enough Delrin. The demand was so strong that the company had sold product it had not yet made and might not be able to make. Fortunately, DuPont had used MVT at several locations on other projects that had tremendous success, generating more than $100 million in cost savings and new or enhanced revenue. Project manager Randal King and Delrin superintendent Ron Lee were anxious to find a solution and enthusiastic about the opportunity to try MVT. Ron moved quickly to form the project team and create an environment in which improvement was inevitable.

The cross-functional team included participants from each area involved in the process: materials, methods, machines, measurements, and people. This M&Ms team was composed of engineers, operators, supervisors, and mechanics. There was particular benefit in recruiting engineers who were new to the Delrin process, as they came to the project without biases or preconceived notions or the experience of previous failures. The process also required the engineers to listen to the operators, and that helped to engender a spirit of cooperation and involvement for everyone. Within the first three weeks of the project, participants completed a basic process improvement seminar and an MVT seminar, taught by QualPro.

Alan Newberry was an operator assigned to the team. As the MVT consultants from QualPro explained the MVT Process in the initial meeting, the team was told to expect surprises from the testing, and Alan thought to himself, "There are going to be surprises for somebody all right." Alan felt sorry for the consultant assigned to the project, as he was sure that the optimism of the moment would fade, as it had in previous one-factor-at-a-time tests run by DuPont.

The team's first goal was to establish common operational definitions, so its members could communicate effectively about the process, and to define the key measures that would form the target objectives for the experiments. This part of the process took some time. There were many points of view and extensive discussion; the conclusion was that "run life"—the amount of time that a polymerizer could operate continuously between cleanings—was the key measure that had to be extended. In the sold-out market that existed then, every pound of good Delrin that DuPont could make was needed to meet the backlogged demand, and increasing run life would provide needed production hours to generate more product.

The team members knew when to get ready for a polymerizer cleaning. When the pipes began to clog, the pressure would drop in the pipes leading to the polymerizer head, and the vacuum would increase relative to the inlet pressure, which was easy to measure. Experience had taught the operators that when the differential between the inlet pressure and the vacuum reached three psi, they were operating on borrowed time. So the goal of the MVT project was to increase the amount of time the polymerizer could operate before the vacuum reading reached three psi.

The next steps for the team members were to assess their measurement systems and to determine if the process was stable as it operated then. Alan found another benefit here to the MVT process. The team accepted the principle that decisions would be made based on data, not on opinions or conjectures. Management was more than willing to hold the team to this standard. In fact, when the team asked for money for a new measurement system based on a perceived, but unproven, belief that one was necessary, management turned them down, because they did not have data to support their request. Instead, management provided existing electrical and instrumentation resources to help analyze the current system and discovered that it was far more reliable than had been thought. But was the system stable? Alan and the other operators didn't think so. Sometimes run life was 20 hours; other times, it was a hundred hours.

Operators and mechanics were genuinely afraid of the process, for two reasons. First, it was dangerous. With the formaldehyde, solvents, and various alcohols involved, a mistake could cause an explosion. Loss of life and property were ongoing threats. Second, with 350 adjustable valves in the polymerizer, no one wanted to touch the system when it was working for fear that they might inadvertently shut it down. As for stability, Alan put it this way: "I would hate to drive a car that would go 10 miles today and a hundred miles tomorrow."

The QualPro consultants began an in-depth analysis of more than two years' worth of historical data to see what patterns of stability were hidden under the surface of everyday experience. However, much to their surprise, there were no instances of uncontrolled variation. The longest run life achieved was 122 hours, and the shortest was only 32 hours. An average of 72 hours of run life was calculated, but the problem remained of predicting the run life. The operators never knew if the next run life cycle was going to be average, long, or short. It came as a surprise to the team that, despite the highly variable performance, statistically, the process was stable. Also, the use of multiple regression indicated no test factors to be included in the MVT screening experiment.

Brainstorming Yields 300 Ideas

Step 5 in the MVT process consists of brainstorming ideas that might improve the process. For the brainstorming sessions, the project team sat with various groups, from operators to technical experts, and collected over 300 valid ideas that might reduce monomer head adhesions. As in all MVT projects, the ideas were subjected to the practical, fast, and cost-free criteria review. This cut the list to 23 testable ideas, and the team's excitement grew.

Eric Brown, the team leader, took the plan to management, who pushed back. A 23-variable, 24-run experiment would take four months to complete. Management wanted a quick, big hit that would get senior management's attention for this first (for this plant) MVT project. Because a 12-run experiment would meet the time requirements, the question was how to cut the list of 23 ideas down to 11. In a stroke of brilliance that would ensure their attentive cooperation during the test, Eric went to the operators who had participated in the brainstorming sessions and presented them with the 23-idea list. He asked for each operator's input, and from the results, he identified 11 items to test. The brilliant part of Eric's action was that it increased the involvement of the operators who would have to run the tests. Making the process adjustments required to fulfill the various recipe conditions is challenging, and, in previous tests, the engineers often had blamed the operators for running tests incorrectly, thereby invalidating the results. Through their involvement in generating the ideas to test, Eric had helped the operators to take extra pride in their efforts, which ensured that the changes that had to be made from one test to the next were done correctly.

As the process involved hazardous materials, the team paid special attention to the tests and the combinations of factors that each contained. The team wanted to make sure that nothing in the recipes would jeopardize continued production or result in an environmental or safety issue for the employees of the plant. Then, with test factors set and test recipes provided by the MVT consultant from QualPro, the project team set up staffing to support the around-the-clock tests and began the two-month experiment.

Of the 11 test factors, three had significant impact: polymer temperature, start-up procedure, and PC mix flow; the other factors had no appreciable effect on run life, although almost everyone thought that some of the factors surely would. Eric was ecstatic. QualPro had promised him that, if he performed a 12-run test, he was sure to get one big hitter. After testing, the team changed seven factors—the three that had significant impact and four where the changed level was easier for the operators to perform. A few months into the effort, the team had reduced the occurrence of monomer head adhesions to a point that the monthly losses disappeared. The run life was extended from an average of 72 hours to an average of 139 hours, almost double the starting point and well above the 120-hour goal the team had set.

The changes produced a 15-percent increase in the amount of Delrin produced, which generated an additional $18 million annually in new revenue. The MVT process had increased run life, reduced downtime, generated more time for cleaning and maintenance of the off-line polymerizer, and eliminated the $8 million annual loss that the polymer buildup caused. With the additional revenue generated by this new level of production, the annual (and recurring) benefit of this project to DuPont was $26 million—without any capital investment.

Another benefit was an improvement in operator performance: by reducing the number of time-consuming and complicated turnarounds of the polymerizers by about 13 per month, the M&M team eliminated a major burden. Each turnaround required adjusting about 350 valves; if you multiply that by the 13 turnarounds eliminated, that is a significant reduction in the chance for an operator to make an error. The MVT process led to fewer mistakes and less opportunity for a catastrophe to occur.

A final benefit was the overall attitude in the plant. The polymerizer problem had been the major bottleneck on which attention was focused. After their successful resolution of that problem, the team members and others at the plant were anxious to move on to the next bottleneck, and to try their new MVT skills there.

CHAPTER 20

A SMALL COMPANY IMPLEMENTS MVT IN ITS SELLING PROCESS

It was through a love of Georgia Tech football that I met Jeb Bell, the president of Equipment Controls Company (ECCO). As Jeb explained at a QualPro Leadership Symposium, "It was during the course of half-times and pregames that Chuck and I would discuss what we do and become familiar with each other's businesses." Jeb understood that QualPro's mission was to help solve problems with processes such as manufacturing. After listening to Jeb discuss his company's problems in early September 1998, I asked him about its sales and margin. Larry Brown, ECCO's sales director, and Jeb had just been discussing problems in the margin area. I said, "We can fix that; come to the QualPro Leadership Symposium in Atlanta next month and see."

MVT WORKS JUST AS WELL FOR SMALLER COMPANIES

Jeb and Larry came to the symposium, and as Jeb later related, "We walk into a meeting and you've got Lowe's Home Improvement, you've got DuPont, you've got every major public company in the world, and us. And we're sitting there thinking, 'Maybe this isn't the right thing for us.' But we listened to the various presentations and started saying, 'Yeah, this is applicable. We can do this; we can do that.' And so we said, 'Okay, let's get them in.' " Jeb Bell became convinced that the power of MVT isn't just for billion-dollar corporations; it works just as well for smaller companies. In his case, it resulted in improved performance that enabled ECCO's expansion from its existing southeast market into the western states and Mexican markets.

ECCO'S EXPERIENCE

At the time, as the primary distributor of measurement and control products to natural gas utilities in the Southeast, ECCO was a third-generation, family-owned business that had been in operation for more than 30 years. With only 13 employees, ECCO had annual sales in the neighborhood of $5.5 million. As Jeb said at the next QualPro Leadership Symposium, when he presented its success story, ECCO excelled in virtually any business-performance measure you could name: sales per employee, accounts-receivable collection rates, inventory turnover, and so forth—everything except gross margin and, thus, profit. As he put it:

> This was a real concern to us, considering that we were spending a ton of money operating every year and not getting the rewards that we felt were justifiable for what we were doing. We were always this company with a lot of potential. Our fiscal year starts in October, so when we went to the first QualPro seminar, this time in September last year, we said, "This year is going to be the year of reality. We're going to reach our potential or be well on the way to reaching our potential, because we're really tired of saying, 'Gee, we've got a lot of potential.'"

"WE'RE GOING TO REACH OUR POTENTIAL"

When it comes to Step 1 and creating the environment, you can't get more creative than ECCO did. Its MVT project kicked off at 6:30 in the morning, with everyone in the company attending—as Jeb put it, "From myself to the person answering the phone; the warehouse, everyone. Because, quite honestly, if we were getting the margins we needed based on the decisions made basically by me, we wouldn't have needed QualPro or that meeting!" From day one, everyone at ECCO knew the importance that was placed on the MVT project (and the hope that the company's owners were placing on its success). Jeb announced, "They're going to tell us one of two things: that we all should be working at McDonald's or that we're going to reach our potential."

Based on our review of ECCO's performance data, Steps 2 through 4 indicated that margin would be the key measure for the MVT experiment, as the company's managers were primarily interested in improving profit as a basis for future expansion. Interviews with those reps who had achieved higher sales were important in identifying some ideas for testing. Correlating successful territories with sales approaches led to other ideas, but the bulk of factors that were tested came from Step 5, brainstorming, which began at the 6:30 A.M. meeting. The goal of the brainstorming was to develop as many ideas as possible for driving up the gross margin percentage. During the meeting, 65 to 70 ideas were generated by the 13 employees.

SELECTION AND TESTING OF THE FACTORS

During the categorization of the ideas to select those that were practical, fast, and cost free, several of the ideas that were obvious (called "gimmes") were selected to be implemented without being tested. Two of these were: (1) implementing an accurate order-entry method to better tie "outside" sales to "inside" sales and (2) covering UPS-red (expediting) fees for last-minute shipments. Both ideas had direct impact on the bottom line and could be used to help raise the gross margin percentage. In the end, after all the raw ideas were categorized, 14 factors were selected for testing (Table 20.1).

To test these factors in Step 8, QualPro opted to use a 20-run test, but because of ECCO's small size, it was necessary to be creative in setting up the experimental test units. Because there were only five outside salespeople and there would be 20 different recipes (combinations of factors) to test, each sales representative would need to be in four recipes. To accomplish this, each sales territory was divided into

Table 20.1   ECCO's Screening MVT Improvement Factors

Factor Description	Status Quo "−"	Change "+"
A: Mailing program	No line sheet	Line sheet mailed
B: Contact customers who didn't buy recently	N/A	See inactive customer list
C: Customer survey	N/A	Survey mailed
D: Monthly sales specials	None	Mailed to customers
E: Sales call follow up, increased customer service	Nonspecific	Call office and gain agreement to follow up
F: Product demonstration	Business as usual	Plan specific event
G: Quote follow up	Business as usual	Phone follow up
H: Consolidate products (high $ focus)	Business as usual	High margin item list
I: Weekly schedules, enhanced controls	Business as usual	Itinerary 7 days in advance
J: "Lower" discounts	Business as usual	Some customers have adjusted discount levels
K: Market breakthroughs	No specific plan	Identify targets in territory and plan sales call
L: Giveaways	None	Calendar/other giveaway
M: Call ahead every time	Business as usual	Call for appointment
N: Simple, improved order-entry form	Business as usual	Use new form

four areas, according to past sales and zip code. Anyone who dealt with customers during the time of the experiment would identify the territory and then apply the correct mix of factors while dealing with a customer. This required some additional attention to compliance with the correct recipe. The approach that ECCO selected, with QualPro's assistance, was a simple monitoring sheet that identified the customers contacted by the representatives and identified the recipe used with each customer. This reinforced the use of the correct level (±) for each of the factors.

Step 8, the screening MVT, ran for 45 days. Six factors were found to be successful: A: Mailing Program; D: Monthly Sales Specials; F: Product Demonstration; L: Giveaways; M: Call Ahead Every Time; and N: Simple, Improved Order-Entry Form. Two of these, A and F, also significantly improved sales, and none of the factors hurt sales. Three factors were found to hurt the margin; these were C: Customer Survey, H: Consolidate Products, and J: "Lower" Discounts. Two of them, C and J, also hurt sales. In analyzing the results, it was found that

ECCO was deficient in the execution of two of the "hurtful" factors, C and H, during the MVT experiment, which could explain their adverse impact.

THE NAYSAYER STEPS IN

As is often the case in Step 9, naysayers stepped forward to question the conclusions. At ECCO, the chief argument centered on the fact that the sales representative who normally had the best results seemed to have the best recipes during the test. This raised the question of whether the factors were driving the results or the sales representatives were.

THE FINDINGS ARE CONFIRMED

Steps 10 and 11 would resolve this question, and a refining MVT experiment was designed to confirm the screening results and to convince any doubters. The refining MVT tested four factors: D: Monthly Sales Specials (which was combined with A: the Mailing Program), F: Product Demonstration, M: Call Ahead Every Time, and N: Simple, Improved Order-Entry Form. Factor L: Giveaways was not tested in the refining MVT because the screening results confirmed that the factor was not hurtful, which was what the company wanted to show (this factor was about the only marketing that ECCO performed, and the company wanted to use the giveaways to keep its name in front of its customers by means of calendars and hats). In addition, for the refining MVT, only four states were used in defining the experimental units, because other concerns that could skew results precluded using Alabama during the refining-test time period. The results of the refining MVT confirmed the findings from the screening MVT.

After implementation, ECCO found that its margin was running about 8 percent above what it was prior to the MVT project and that, although not an objective, sales had improved by 5 percent. Additionally, other feedback from the testing indicated that other benefits were possible. The analysis pointed out that one salesman had a sales cycle that was 15 to 25 days slower than that of everyone else. The company worked with that individual, and, within a month, he was selling products in the same time frame that the other sales reps did. Interestingly, the naysayer salesperson made a large sale between the screening and refining experiments that proved, according to him, that his success was independent of QualPro's work. After reviewing with him the actions taken to secure the new customer, Jeb pointed out that the salesman had actually used several of the winning factors during the sales process, which, if anything, further validated the test results.

In concluding his remarks at the QualPro Leadership Symposium, Jeb reflected on the past year, starting with his attendance at the previous symposium, when his initial reaction was, "Why am I here?" which gradually turned into the realization "This can work for us!" He never expected to return just a year later to publicly describe the success that his small company had achieved: improved profits and sales, growth, and expansion into new markets.

CHAPTER 21

HOW SBC-AMERITECH CUT ITS INSTALLATION AND REPAIR BACKLOG IN HALF AND ELIMINATED A PUBLIC RELATIONS NIGHTMARE

SBC Chairman of the Board and CEO Edward Whitacre Jr. inherited a mess! SBC acquired Ameritech in late 1999, and it quickly became obvious that Ameritech had deep-seated operational problems. Telephone repairs were running at exceptionally high levels, and Ameritech was struggling mightily to keep up. Installation of new service was being delayed by these large service backlogs, with some customers waiting weeks for new telephone service to be installed.

After assessing the situation, Whitacre took decisive action. He moved his most experienced executive, Ed Mueller, from a position as CEO of SBC international operations to take over Ameritech operations as CEO. Mueller had previously been extremely effective as CEO of Southwestern Bell Telephone and CEO of Pacific Bell. Whitacre also moved Dennis Harris, SBC's most experienced network services executive, into the role of president of network services at Ameritech. In a recent QualPro Symposium, Harris said that Whitacre gave himself and Mueller a set of simple instructions, "Fix it!" Whitacre had just done a very effective job of creating the environment.

Before looking at the actions that SBC-Ameritech took to achieve this fast fix and the critical roll played by MVT in that success, it is necessary to know what led to such a dire situation. The Communications Workers of America union warned Ohio regulators in late 1995 that a pattern of understaffing had already put Ameritech, a corporation covering five Great Lakes states, on a dangerous road. The union documented thousands of problems with Ameritech's equipment that indicated infrastructure deterioration. It estimated that it would take 10 years in Dayton, Ohio, alone to rehabilitate plant facilities.

Reports filed with the Federal Communications Commission indicated that the average waiting time for phone-service repairs by Indiana residential customers grew from 14.4 hours in 1994 to 32.6 hours in 1997 and remained above 27 hours for the rest of the decade. This increase was consistent across the entire Ameritech region, including Illinois, Indiana, Wisconsin, Ohio, and Michigan.

Problems continued after SBC Communications, Inc., acquired Ameritech in late 1999. An unusually wet spring led to a rash of service failures, and some neighborhoods went weeks without repairs as tens of thousands of customers sat helplessly waiting for service. Understaffed offices were overwhelmed, and customers typically were left on hold for an hour or more and were often cut off after that. Technicians found cracked and rotted cables that had failed underground and in terminal boxes. Installations for new service were backed up for weeks. The company also lost a sizeable percentage of its technician workforce because of unexpected retirements, which increased from 1 percent per year in the mid-1990s to 10 percent per year in 1999. When Mueller and Harris took over, more than 220,000 Ameritech customers were waiting for installation or were without satisfactory service. Ameritech undertook a six-month initiative to improve installation and repair times, which included bringing in 4,000 new technicians, and a planned $2.8 billion investment in the physical plant for the next year, as well as enhanced training and deployment of equipment to increase employee productivity.

By the middle of 2001, after a sizeable investment (as well as tens of millions of dollars paid in fines—settlements in Ohio and Wisconsin alone that year were $10 and $11 million, respectively), the backload of work (called "load" or "inventory") was reduced from

220,000 to 85,000 customers, and the service crisis was averted. Nevertheless, Mueller and Harris felt that better performance than this was needed to preclude future crises. They set a goal of cutting the 85,000 customer backload in half, even though most managers in the company thought that a 70,000 load was the lowest that could theoretically be achieved.

Conventional wisdom among Ameritech managers was that, even if the load were reduced to 70,000, doing so would raise other issues, such as excessive overtime rates and problematic scheduling of technicians. So Ameritech found that it had a cultural and psychological barrier to overcome, in addition to the technical issues. Any changes had to be implemented through thousands of managers over hundreds of thousands of square miles of territory. There were 30,700 network people working for Ameritech in five states at the time that Harris set out to get service problems under control.

EMPIRICAL TESTING IS THE ANSWER

He knew that to succeed in permanently reducing the load farther, he would need a foolproof method that would convince his team and overcome preconceived notions. While at Southwestern Bell, Harris had the opportunity to see MVT improve business processes, including the turnaround of performance at SBC's DSL business unit. He believed empirically testing many possible improvements was the answer. Harris had no problem convincing Mueller that MVT was the right solution. Mueller had worked with QualPro to use MVT dozens of times during his own tenures at Southwestern Bell and Pacific Bell.

Both Mueller and Harris wanted to break the backload cycle and drive the inventory much lower to enable Ameritech to be more flexible and responsive to its customers. The president of Consumer Services recognized that she was involved in this effort, because the issues touched her operations as well. She committed her resources to the effort, and Network Services and Consumer Services (the two largest organizations in Ameritech) formed a joint partnership to reduce the 85,000 backed-up orders even farther by using the MVT process. With the blessing of Whitacre, the environment had been created for implementing real process improvement.

Table 21.1   Three Load Reduction MVTs

Indirect MVT	Direct MVT	Implementation MVT
Standardization	Load management	Effective implementation
Enhancement of existing field force procedures		Sustained effort

Functional areas involved: Business offices, central offices, customer service bureaus, central operation groups, installation and repair technicians, infrastructure maintenance organization, and construction and engineering.

The approach taken was a SWAT-like, three-pronged approach that included three separate MVTs, all part of the load-reduction initiative. The approach is shown in Table 21.1.

The first prong was the indirect MVT; it attacked issues of standardization and existing procedures used by the workforce that could indirectly reduce load volumes. The second prong was the direct MVT; it focused on what could directly reduce the load volumes or the inventory. The third prong of Ameritech's approach was the implementation MVT; it was designed to identify what steps would best ensure effective implementation and sustain any improvement gained.

The load (backlog) and the percent of the load that required dispatches were the two key measures that were adopted for the MVT testing.

Prior to launching brainstorming for improvement ideas, historical-data analysis was performed using control charts and multiple regression analysis. Several possible test factors were surfaced for each of the direct and indirect MVT experiments.

The Indirect MVT

The objective of the indirect MVT was to indirectly reduce the load through standardization and enhancement of existing field force procedures. It was conducted across functional areas in parts of all five Ameritech states. The indirect MVT effort is overviewed in Table 21.2.

To determine factors to test in the MVT, Ameritech completed 33 separate brainstorming sessions across the five-state region in each of the functional areas and generated 1,100 ideas. Many people from each of the functional areas, including local technicians, customer-service

Table 21.2   Overview of Indirect MVT Effort

Indirect MVT

Objective: To indirectly reduce the load through standardization and enhancement of existing field force's procedures.

Indirect MVT process:
- Completed 33 brainstorming sessions
- Generated over 1,100 ideas
- Determined that 25 of the ideas were practical, fast, and cost free
- Placed those 25 ideas into the screening experiment

Key measures: Installation and Repair Inventory, Percent Dispatched

---

representatives, engineers, and top and middle managers, helped to generate the ideas. The challenge was to reduce the 1,100 ideas to a manageable number of practical, fast, and cost-free (testable) factors. In the end, Ameritech chose 25 ideas as test factors for the indirect MVT, with each functional area having test factors applicable to its business area. Table 21.3 shows the test factors for the indirect MVT experiment.

There were only two key measures for the indirect MVT: (1) the load or inventory (how much work to do each morning) and (2) the percent of that inventory that required a dispatch. The goal for the inventory was to achieve a level of 40,000, with 6,000 to 7,000 daily dispatches for trouble and 30,000 to 35,000 additional service orders. "Percent dispatch" means how many truck rolls are needed (the proportion of the time a truck is sent out to complete the job). Not every service order or trouble case results in physically dispatching a technician to the field. The goal for the second key measure was to reduce the percentage of trouble cases that ended up requiring physical visits to customers' premises. With 10,000 technicians available to be dispatched every day, there is an optimum load necessary to keep them productive. The key is to find the optimum mix of number of employees and service intervals while still allowing for special cases, such as weather and economic aberrations that affect telecommunications.

Because of the complexities of intermingling so many different functional areas into a single experiment, special attention was taken in assigning the different MVT recipes and maintaining the balance

Table 21.3   Test Factors for Indirect MVT Experiment

Factor Description	Status Quo "–"	Change "+"
Business office job aid	Status quo	Designated service reps use business office job aid
Swing team job aid	Status quo	Business office swing team uses swing team job aid
Weekend frame wiring	Status quo	Central office techs complete frame wiring on Friday
Dialtone verification	Status quo	Central office techs complete dialtone verification by 8:00 A.M.
Heat coil testing	Status quo	Central office techs verify dialtone through heat coil
N/T/C job aid	Status quo	Customer service bureau reps use N/T/C job aid
NA re-dispatch job aid	Status quo	Customer service bureau reps use NA re-dispatch job aid
MDU repair job aid	Status quo	Customer service bureau reps use MDU job aid
CBC job aid	Status quo	Customer service bureau reps use CBC job aid
Feature trouble job aid	Status quo	Customer service bureau reps use feature trouble job aid
MR job aid	Status quo	Customer service bureau reps use MR job aid
Repair dispatch	Status quo	Central operations groups controllers do NOT dispatch repair techs before access window
Tech job assignments	Status quo	Central operations groups controllers assign business orders after 9:00 A.M.
Installer notification	Status quo	Central operations groups controllers notify techs of order changes
Pre-call checklist	Status quo	Central operations groups controllers use pre-call checklist
PDF status	Status quo	Central operations groups controllers do NOT change PDF to PDO
Skill match	Status quo	Central operations groups managers match tech qualifications to work assignments
Weekend service orders	Status quo	Central operations groups managers notify CO manager of weekend requirements
Close DSOs	Status quo	Installation and repair cable techs close DSOs with field assistance
Future trouble repair	Status quo	Installation and repair techs repair observed potential future problems requiring more than one hour
Tech check list	Status quo	Installation and repair techs use technicians' daily activity check list
Installation job aid	Status quo	Installation techs use installation job aid
Jack stress tests	Status quo	Installation techs test all jack locations during installation
Troubleshooting job aid	Status quo	Repair techs use troubleshooting job aid
Repair repeats job aid	Status quo	Repair techs use repair repeats job aid

necessary to test multiple factors. For the indirect MVT, a 32-run reflected design was used, resulting in 64 different recipes or combinations of test factors. Following QualPro's guidance, Ameritech opted to use the central offices as the experimental unit for the test.

After completing the screening MVT, Ameritech found five helpful factors that it carried forward into a refining MVT. These were actions that helped to standardize fieldwork or interactions with customers, which will be explained shortly.

All five factors proved to be effective during the refining experiment, which was completed in early October. Ameritech ended up with:

- *A business office job aid:* Business office customer service representatives used this to help ensure that they clarified exactly what the customers' requests were, in order to preclude unnecessary dispatches.
- *A multidwelling unit (mdu) repair job aid:* This was used by Customer Service Bureau customer representatives to differentiate between single-unit and multiunit locations. Single-unit locations have accessible locations outside the home or business where the phone line enters the structure. This location is always accessible to a repair technician. Multiunit customers could include either apartment buildings or large businesses. Many times, the lines entering a multiunit structure are located at a central point that is not accessible to a technician unless prior arrangements are made with the building manager. If the right questions were not asked and arrangements made, unnecessary dispatches could result because the equipment in multiunit locations might not be available to a technician.
- *A repair dispatch:* This was used by Central Office Group controllers who dispatched repair technicians so that they did not dispatch them before or after the customer-access time window.
- *An installer notification:* This was used by Central Office Group controllers to notify technicians of order changes before the technicians were dispatched.
- *An installation job aid:* This was used by installation technicians (generally the least experienced of all technicians) to focus

Table 21.4   Overview of Direct MVT Effort

Direct MVT

Objective: To reduce the load through direct management of the inventory

Direct MVT process:
- Completed supplemental brainstorming sessions, primarily in Ohio
- Determined that five of the ideas were practical, fast, and cost free
- Placed these five ideas into the screening experiment

Key measures: Percent Change in Inventory

---

them on some critical issues associated with their jobs and to preclude sending help to many locations. Essentially, this was a
checklist of suggestions for troubleshooting installation problems
to help them exhaust possibilities prior to calling in a repair technician to assist.

With these identified, Ameritech-wide implementation was
planned for immediate execution. The five factors that were confirmed in the refining experiments reduced both the installation and
repair loads by 15 to 20 percent and reduced dispatches for both installation and repair.

The Direct MVT

At the same time that the indirect MVT was being performed,
Ameritech executed another MVT, the direct MVT. The objective
was to reduce the load through direct management of the inventory.
Historically, Ameritech had dealt with inventory by attempting to reduce what was coming into the inventory rather than by dealing with
what was already on hand. This direct MVT looked for factors that
would focus on the inventory itself and drive it down. The direct
MVT is depicted in Table 21.4.

In Ameritech, there are many "separate and distinct" geographic
areas or "clock" areas that control installation and repair dispatches.
Each of these areas is managed by a district manager, who works independently in terms of setting intervals (response times) relative to
managing the load. The direct MVT was run in Ohio, where there
were eight of these areas, but the company again generated ideas from

Table 21.5   Test Factors for the Direct MVT Screening Experiment

Factor Description	Status Quo "–"	Change "+"
Reset installation intervals	Status quo	3 days retail, 2 days wholesale
Set Monday target at 1.5 cases of trouble per repair tech and 4 orders per installation tech	Status quo	Work weekend as required to meet Monday target
Go to 1-day interval for affecting service	Status quo	Use the same target for affecting target as out of service
Assign all I&M personnel to I&R on Mondays	Status quo	Routine assignment of I&M to be worked right into the force
Assign I&M and C&E personnel into I&R based on pre-set inventory targets	Status quo	Set targets based on specific inventory levels and say assign 33%, 66%, and 100% of the I&R and C&E force into I&R

across Ameritech and came up with the five practical, fast, and cost-free factors shown in Table 21.5 for the test.

The key measure for the direct MVT was the percent change in inventory. Rather than focus on how to change the incoming volumes, as was done in the indirect MVT, this test looked at improving productivity while controlling the inventory.

After completing the screening MVT, Ameritech carried two helpful factors forward into a refining MVT. These were resetting the installation intervals and going to a one-day interval for service, the first and third factors in Table 21.5. The direct MVT reduced the load directly by reducing the service and repair intervals, essentially changing the allowed time for dealing with new service orders or repair orders. The experiment resulted in reducing the install load by 12 percent to 15 percent and the repair load by 20 percent to 30 percent. Combined, this resulted in a 15 percent to 17 percent reduction of the total load. Taken together, the indirect and direct MVTs indicated that, after implementation, inventory would drop by 40 percent.

The Implementation MVT

Satisfied that MVT was working, Ameritech moved on to its implementation MVT. The objective was to determine, not only for the

Table 21.6   Overview of Implementation MVT Effort

Implementation MVT

Objective: To implement factors identified from the direct and indirect MVT in such a way that the factors are effective and sustained.

Implementation MVT process:
- Completed supplemental brainstorming sessions
- Selected seven of the ideas that were practical, fast, and cost free

Key measures: Percent Compliance with Implemented Factor

---

earlier completed MVTs, but also for any initiatives that might be implemented in the future, how to make sure that changes implemented (in this case, the winning factors identified from the direct and indirect MVTs) were effective and sustained. Basically, this MVT focused on identifying actions to ensure compliance when MVT findings are implemented. In Table 21.6, the implementation MVT effort is overviewed.

Additional brainstorming generated many ideas to be tested, seven of which were included in the implementation MVT. The test factors are shown in Table 21.7.

The key measure was percentage of compliance. Compliance meant successfully executing the factors that were implemented and sustaining them.

Ameritech found that there were significant factors that were clearly efficient and effective in implementing and sustaining the improvement gained in the earlier MVTs. These significant factors were used to implement direct and indirect MVT factors, but also will be used on an ongoing basis to implement other initiatives. Training activities, management involvement, two-way feedback, and employee involvement were the winning factors for the implementation MVT.

Figure 21.1 on page 219 reflects the dramatic improvement experienced after Ameritech implemented the effective factors found by the direct and indirect MVTs.

Overall, Ameritech reduced the total load from the 85,000 level "that couldn't be broken through" to below the 40,000 level. The graph was presented at the 2002 QualPro Leadership Symposium by Dennis Harris, a keynote speaker. The cost for Ameritech of this

Table 21.7   Test Factors for the Implementation MVT

Factor Description	Status Quo "–"	Change "+"
Accountability	Status quo	(A) On the date that applicable factors are implemented, communicate to your employees their content.
		(B) Approximately one week following the implementation date, distribute a copy of the Self-Test (covering the content of each factor) to each of your employees during a meeting or at some other convenient time and ask them to take the test and check their answers before the end of that day. (You *may* follow up to see if your employees have followed your instructions, but these tests are *not* to be collected or evaluated by management.)
Training management	Status quo	(A) Create and maintain a training log that includes the distribution of materials, attendance at training sessions, and coaching sessions on the "Helpful Factors."
		(B) Provide makeup session for any of your employees who miss the initial training to ensure that they all receive the materials and training.
Training activities	Status quo	(A) When training your employees on the applicable factors they are expected to implement, incorporate any identified special training devices into your training sessions.
		(B) Use the special promotional activities identified by management to kick off the implementation of the applicable factors.
Project information	Status quo	(A) On the date that the applicable factors are implemented, verbally communicate to your employees the provided background and potential impact of the factor.
		(B) After describing the content, distribute to them a written copy of the information.
Management	Status quo	Each week during the test, spend a total of involvement 20 to 30 minutes engaged in one-on-one discussions or small group meetings with your reps to inquire regarding their understanding and use of the "MDU job aid" and to offer your assistance in carrying it out.
Two-way feedback	Status quo	(A) Each week during the test, at regularly scheduled or specially called meetings, ask your employees for feedback regarding how the implementation of the applicable factors is going.

(continued)

Table 21.7 *(Continued)*

Factor Description	Status Quo "–"	Change "+"
		(B) At these same meetings, communicate information regarding the status and/or progress of the implementation effort.
		(C) Inform your area manager of what you learn from these discussions.
Employee involvement	Status quo	(A) Before implementation, appoint one or more of your experienced employees to serve on a local peer group.
		(B) Provide your local peer group with detailed information regarding the applicable factors and the name and phone number of points of contact for assistance.
		(C) Encourage other employees to approach members of the local peer group if they have questions, concerns, or problems associated with implementing the factors.
		(D) Communicate regularly with the peer group to ensure that there are no conflicts between what you and the peer group are telling employees about the applicable factors.

intervention was less than any one of the many fines that were levied by regulators during the period of out-of-control service performance. The gain was savings in the neighborhood of $30 million per year and satisfied customers, which (important during this time of increased competition) translates into more retained customers. As Vic Grabill, general manager of the Ohio I&R and project manager for the MVTs, noted:

> I measure the effectiveness of anything that I do in my business based on my perception of two primary bodies, customers and employees. Our customers have clearly told us by the interviews that we have done, the feedback we have solicited, that they are thrilled with reducing intervals and reducing volumes. Our ability to service them in a more timely manner is key.
>
> The second measuring stick that I like to use is what do our employees, our team members, have to say about it. At all ranks of the organization, people understand now that there is great value to reducing inventories and reducing intervals. And, as a result of that,

Figure 21.1   Impact of MVT Process on Ameritech Load

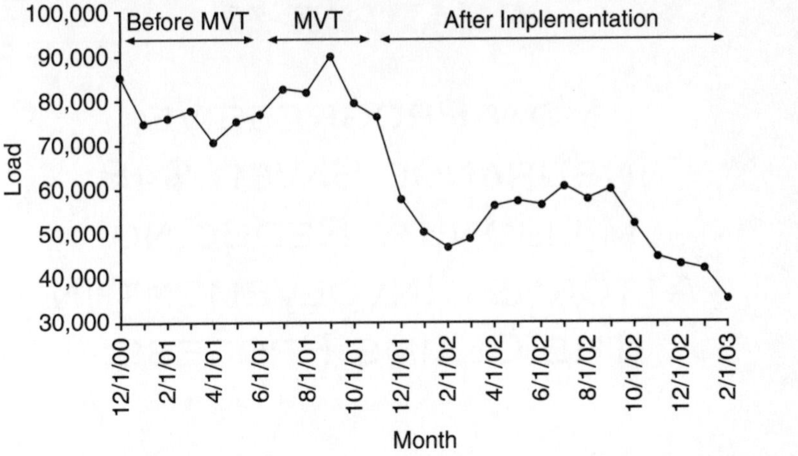

as we effectively manage the load, it allows them to probably more effectively do their jobs, whether they're technicians in the field, whether they're a maintenance administrator taking a trouble report, or whether they're an officer in the corporation trying to effectively manage the organization from a physical response. And one of the key initiatives associated with that improvement certainly were the efforts of QualPro and the MVT process. So we appreciate our partnership with them.

CHAPTER 22

HOW PROGRESSIVE INSURANCE SAVED $48 MILLION BY REDUCING ATTORNEY INVOLVEMENT IN THE CLAIMS PROCESS

The 1990s were important and exciting years for Progressive Insurance. With an annual growth rate of 15 to 20 percent during that time, Progressive grew from a relatively small company to a $3.5 billion company by the end of 1997. That was when Tim Madden, Claims Process Controller, described Progressive's attorney representation project at a QualPro MVT Symposium.

Progressive was a Fortune 500 company, the sixth-largest private-passenger automobile insurer and the largest independent-agency insurer in the United States, with more than 5,000 employees, 300 locations, and more than 30,000 independent agents. Active in 48 states and Washington, DC, with more than 60 years of experience, Progressive consistently received superior ratings from A. M. Best and had earned an industry-wide reputation for innovative business practices. Progressive introduced the first immediate response vehicles and became the first publicly held company to report results monthly. It established the first auto insurance web site (www.progressive.com), was the first to sell insurance online, and introduced the first toll-free 24/7 comparison rating service.

CREATING THE ENVIRONMENT AT PROGRESSIVE INSURANCE

Progressive's success was built, to a great extent, by clearly and aggressively targeting the market for nonstandard and high-risk auto insurance. In that area, it had become the number two company in the United States. With such a large share of the high-risk market, the only way to grow the business was to broaden the company's target audience by going after the standard auto insurance market. To achieve this goal, while maintaining and enhancing its competitive position, Progressive was looking for ways to drive down its costs and improve its revenues. So it was no surprise when Progressive turned to MVT to optimize its business processes—especially considering Progressive's history as a data-driven company that respected sound research and was eager to apply what it learned to all aspects of its operations.

Following an initial contact in the early 1990s, Progressive and QualPro teamed up on several MVT process efforts. They effected a wide range of internal and external processes, resulting in millions of dollars of cost savings and increased sales, which helped establish a positive environment and a workforce motivated to embrace the MVT process. Using the MVT process, Progressive was able to identify the most effective method for motivating independent agents to sell Progressive products, the optimal media-buying strategy for its national advertising campaign, and the most effective strategies for reducing insurance fraud. It was able to stimulate faster claim filing by customers, improve the performance of customer service reps in the company's call center, and increase customer retention by identifying and acting on those things that most affected customer satisfaction and loyalty.

Although all results were unique to Progressive, the designs for the MVT experiments might be considered typical, in that most of the targeted processes—sales, marketing, customer service, and customer loyalty—would be recognized by any organization with a product or service to sell.

In 1996, however, Progressive embarked on a project that, while targeting a problem that is probably unique to the insurance world, illustrates the versatility of MVT and the extent to which it can be adapted to just about any type of business process.

IMPROVING THE CLAIMS PROCESS

In his presentation at the MVT Symposium, Madden explained that, "Progressive's objective is to reduce the human trauma and economic costs of automobile accidents. It is absolutely what we are about. That's a phrase that comes from our Chairman, Peter Lewis. It is what he talks about. It is what you read in our annual report year after year of what we do. And when we have claims adjusters in the room, that's what we talk to them about, and tell them that's their job."

The customer's experience filing claims plays a big role in reaching this goal. For most customers, once a policy has been purchased, there is little or no interaction with the insurance company until a claim is filed. So Progressive works hard on its claims process.

The strategy is to provide an immediate response to all claims, operate efficiently, achieve accurate settlements, and delight customers. By reducing the cycle time, the company increases its capacity. By controlling payouts and other costs, it remains competitive.

According to Madden, Progressive's previous efforts created a narrow and clear focus on speed of response. Immediate response, Madden says, is "giving the customer whatever we can do at that point and time to help them out of this terrible situation they are in. Our benchmark for that, our key number that drives our whole company, is how fast we can get out and see your car." The target was set at nine hours, which would be the fastest in the industry—an objective the company was achieving about 50 percent of the time.

The faster the start, the quicker the claim is settled, and that improves customer satisfaction. In recent years, Progressive had been able to cut the total claim time for third-party injury from 90 days to 43 days and the claim time for damage to the customer's car from 18 days to 9 days. During that time, the automobile insurance industry's costs increased by 50 percent, but Progressive's cost increased only 20 percent, and its cost as a percentage of premiums dropped from 14 percent to 10 percent.

Both speed and costs were gradually coming down until around 1994, when both began creeping up again. This increase was, in part, a result of the company's writing more standard insurance policies in big cities, in which attorney involvement was more frequent.

COSTS OF ATTORNEY INVOLVEMENT

When attorneys become involved in insurance claims, speed goes down and costs go up. It takes longer to settle the claim, and the insurance company has to pay more. The immediate-response effort by Progressive had reduced the attorney representation rate from around 40 percent to 36 percent, but, as it began to creep up again, there were growing concerns that the ultimate effect could be devastating.

In 1994, the average payout was $1,808 when there was no attorney involved: $891 to the injured party for pain and suffering and $917 for other expenses (doctors, towing, rental cars, and so on). When a claimant retained an attorney, Progressive immediately incurred about $1,600 in legal expenses to pay its own lawyers to handle the case. In addition, medical costs generally increased by 200 to 300 percent, because attorneys usually requested that their clients consult chiropractors or physicians.

One might argue that Progressive did not have the claimant's best interests at heart in its desire to reduce attorney involvement, but the truth is that the claimant generally did not benefit from hiring an attorney. In fact, even though the amount paid by Progressive for an injury went up, the actual amount received by the claimant, was around $107 less. The additional money, of course, went to the attorney. In addition, the payment to the injured person often was delayed by six months to over a year because of the additional time it took to settle a claim when an attorney was involved—even when there was no litigation. As a result, the claimant, on average, had to wait six months longer to receive $107 less.

With these issues in mind, Progressive decided to work with MVT to develop and implement a targeted process improvement effort, with the goal of minimizing the factors that led to attorney representation in claims.

THE MVT PROCESS

The Key Measure

The key measure was very simple. It was the percentage of claimants who hired an attorney within 60 days of the date of loss. It had been running 36 percent, and every 1 percent cost Progressive $6,000,000. The measurement system was evaluated and found to be adequate.

Identifying Test Factors

Progressive recognized that accident victims generally do not retain attorneys just because they like attorneys. By identifying specific actions it could take to minimize attorney involvement in the claims process, the company estimated a financial benefit of $6 million for every percentage point the representation rate could be reduced. So its task was to identify the reasons that people retained attorneys in the first place.

It began by conducting a survey of Progressive employees who had considerable knowledge of the claims process. It also contacted people who had retained attorneys to close their claims with Progressive and asked them (1) what had motivated them to do so and (2) what might have prevented them from doing so.

The company also talked with the defense attorneys that worked for it and with plaintiff attorneys who were asked, very specifically, "Why do people come to you when they're involved in a bodily injury claim?" In addition to all this, the company commissioned an independent survey of 1,200 people in Texas, New York, Florida, and Ohio to identify the conditions under which they would consider retaining an attorney.

This research led to the conclusion that the factors contributing to the retention of an attorney were the seriousness of the injury, the need for protection, and the actual processing of the claim. A long list of suggestions regarding what could be done to resolve these issues was assembled. The historical data was analyzed using SPC charts and multiple linear regression to hunt for additional ideas for driving down the rate of attorney use. To its credit, Progressive didn't blindly implement the feedback and ideas it got from customers, attorneys, and historical data. It wanted to test the real-world results of these ideas, instead of acting on opinions.

Armed with insights into the reasons for hiring an attorney, a large group of Progressive employees from throughout the company participated in a three-day, on-site training program conducted by

QualPro consultants. During these sessions, the participants brainstormed ways in which the potential reasons for retaining attorneys could be "neutralized."

The potential changes from the historical data analysis and brainstorming produced 59 ideas. Excluding ideas that were not "practical, fast, or cost free" reduced the number to 19. "Playing the Game" brought the final total to 13.

The MVT Experiments

The 13 suggestions were incorporated into a 16-run MVT screening design that was conducted in 16 different branch offices for a total of six months.

The branch locations were selected to match claimant demographics as much as possible, but the recipes were randomly assigned to the branches. Everyone involved in the test was informed of its nature and purpose. This communication was vital to the success of the project because of the special challenge created by conducting an experiment in such diverse locations. It is much easier when all the employees who are expected to carry out a given recipe are located within the same location.

Four factors helped, one factor hurt, and eight made no difference. The four helpful factors were then included in a subsequent refining MVT experiment.

Results of MVT Analyses

What proved to be the most helpful idea was to simply pay for the disputed property damage. When people are involved in an accident that is serious enough that they are injured, their vehicle usually is pretty badly damaged. Disputes over how much to pay to replace a vehicle often arise when the vehicle is relatively new and the owner has financed the entire amount. Suppose John Doe puts $100 down on a $37,000 new car and finances the rest. On the way home from the dealership, his new car is totaled in an accident that is not his fault. He is hurt, and the other driver's insurance company offers its sympathy and then offers to John the blue-book value for his car, which, for a "used" vehicle, is $28,000. You can imagine how well that will satisfy John. If the insurance company is not willing to replace his new car, how do you think he will feel about its handling his bodily injury claim? His response is likely to be, "I'm calling a lawyer!"

This improvement idea—being more willing to pay for or replace vehicles rather than offering strictly book value—was difficult for Madden to even agree to when it was first proposed in the MVT process. "One of the things I was trained in from day one," says Madden, "was that you don't overpay anything." He especially believed that you don't overpay the PD (property damage) to control the BI (bodily injury). So the factor challenged conventional wisdom in the insurance industry. However, the districts in which this factor was tested showed a drop of five percentage points in the attorney representation rate, which more than made up for the additional payouts involved.

The second most helpful factor was using an open-ended release form (where legally permissible). Instead of settling a claim by offering a "take-it-or-leave-it" sort of option, agents in the districts in which this factor was tested would say, for example, "We're going to pay you $X for your bodily injury claim. We know that it may turn out later that there may be a more serious injury that hasn't been detected yet. This is not final. You can come back to us, and we'll renegotiate this if you are diagnosed with further injury." This idea resulted in a drop of two percentage points in the attorney representation rate.

The third most helpful effect was achieved by increasing the number of in-person initial contacts with a claimant. Although a face-to-face meeting was Progressive's "standard operating procedure," it was being carried out only a fraction of the time. The extra effort to make in-person contacts resulted in a further reduction of the attorney representation rate.

The fourth helpful factor, increasing the range and discretion allowed agents in settling bodily injury claims, further reduced the rate.

One idea that Progressive believed would be helpful actually hurt. Progressive claimants were given a brochure designed to reduce the likelihood that someone would retain an attorney, and a Progressive rep explained it. It had the opposite effect. The claims brochure was a well-reasoned and professionally illustrated and printed document that listed the pros and cons of retaining an attorney to settle a bodily injury claim. Although it acknowledged that there were times when an attorney would be necessary and/or helpful, it did an excellent job of demonstrating why retaining an attorney, in most circumstances, is not in the customer's best interest. It came as a big surprise to most of those involved in the project that the districts in which this brochure was distributed had significantly higher attorney retention rates than those districts in which the brochure was not distributed. Madden said that not only did use of the brochure actually drive up attorney representation by two percentage points, he was paying $150,000 in printing costs to achieve this hurtful effect!

In spite of the high hopes that many Progressive personnel held out for the other eight factors, they had no effect at all on the attorney retention rate.

Taking into account the five significant factors—four helpful and one hurtful—MVT results predicted that the attorney representation rate would drop from 36 percent to 26 percent.

Implementation

To translate the results of the MVT into effective action, the first step was to meet with the highest levels of management to communicate the results and develop a plan for further refinement and implementation. It was agreed that two of the four helpful factors (in-person contacts and open-ended releases) would be implemented immediately and the other two (paying for disputed property damage and increasing the discretion allowed agents when dealing with bodily injury claims) would be put into a second refining experiment for further testing.

To effectively implement the first two factors, Progressive developed a videotape, to help sell the plan to managers and agents. In addition, these new best practices were the basis for an ongoing consultative process to ensure that everyone understood the purpose for the changes and the anticipated results. The requirement for 100-percent in-person contacts was theoretically already in effect, but was not actually happening, so a plan was implemented to make this MVT-proven success factor a reality, and Progressive succeed in doubling its rate of in-person contacts. The open-end releases were easily implemented. By mid–1997, with both factors firmly in place, the at-torney representation rate dropped by four percentage points, and there was a potential for even more improvement by getting even more in-person contacts.

The two remaining factors (paying for disputed property damage and increasing the discretion allowed agents when dealing with bod-ily injury claims) were the most promising and also the most contro-versial. A refining MVT confirmed the beneficial effects of these ideas and they were then implemented.

Madden concluded, "If you look at it six months into implementa-tion, we had a cumulative total of four percentage points of improve-ment from the first two factors and four more from the second two factors. That's eight points. If you go back to our original math, you see that for each point of reduced attorney representation . . . we proj-ect a savings of $6 million. This is a huge, huge return."

PART IV

USING MVT
TO SPREAD
BREAKTHROUGH
RESULTS
THROUGHOUT
YOUR COMPANY

CHAPTER 23

THE KEYS TO SUCCESSFUL ORGANIZATION-WIDE IMPROVEMENT

Many organizational-improvement approaches teach employees a number of statistical, logical, or motivational techniques but do not provide a truly effective way to improve a process quickly and reliably. The preceding chapters in this book tell how and why the use of MVT is more effective in improving processes than any other performance-improvement approach. In Parts I, II, and III, the focus was on improving a single process. This focus is very important, because there can be no realistic hope of improving results reliably and dramatically on a broad basis if you cannot first improve results on a narrow basis.

Part IV focuses on using MVT to improve processes company-wide or organization-wide. Such an effort can help an organization in amazing ways, both financially and culturally. Organizations (such as SBC, Lowe's, and DuPont) that have applied the MVT process broadly across their companies have fared extremely well and increased their competitive abilities.

After top executives learn about MVT and gain an appreciation for its power, the next question is invariably, "How do I roll this out to my entire organization?" Fortunately, QualPro has over two decades of experience in helping companies implement hundreds of rollout efforts. We have performed formal surveys to determine the elements that are common to the most successful ones. We have even performed MVT experiments of our own to learn the key actions that drive roll-out success.

Our experience and investigations have allowed us to develop an understanding of the things that are necessary in using MVT to quickly and reliably improve a company's competitive position and financial performance, with a side benefit of improving its culture. Following are the keys to success that we have identified for an organization-wide rollout of the MVT process.

KEY ASPECTS OF AN ORGANIZATION-WIDE ROLLOUT OF MVT

1. *It is critical to achieve early success.* No matter how many examples are provided that illustrate MVT successes in similar companies, even in the same industry, people do not really believe in the effectiveness of MVT until they see "knock-your-socks-off" MVT successes in their own organization.

2. *Early MVT projects should focus on the right objectives.* When choosing early MVT projects, focus on objectives that are (1) significant (can make significant financial contributions to the organization), (2) relatable (are recognized by most people in the organization as being important), and (3) doable (can be done for no cost in a reasonably short time frame).

3. *The right people must be selected to lead MVT projects.* It is important that the selection of people to participate in MVT projects sends the right message. Those selected should be people who are viewed as top performers and effective leaders. Staff personnel who "have the time" or "don't have something important to do" are never the right people to serve as MVT project leaders or key participants.

4. *Expert MVT consultants must guide initial MVT projects.* Initial projects must have the guidance of MVT consultants who have years of MVT experience. Attempting to get by with the support of newly trained novices or persons whose expertise or experience is in other process-improvement ap-

proaches is likely to lead to a painful experience that does not achieve breakthrough results.

5. *Initial success stories should be documented.* The initial successes will serve as the proof of the MVT concept for your organization. They should be documented carefully so that the details can be transmitted to others. These stories will be the first of many legends that will make up the MVT folklore that will help to transform the process improvement culture of the organization.

6. *Line managers must accept responsibility for achieving breakthrough results.* Line managers must drive the improvement efforts, and everyone in the organization should know that continuous improvement is a critical role of line management. If it is delegated to a staff group, such as a quality- or process-improvement department, the effort will not succeed in the long term. The support of such a group may be useful in executing MVT projects, but that support should never replace the leadership and participation of the line management.

7. *The local workforce must take responsibility for executing the process.* The MVT process is a management tool. It enables the organization's management to define processes that have the capability to deliver breakthrough results. It is critical, however, that those who work within those processes (the local workforce) execute the processes as they have been defined. The local workforce must not alter procedures, times, or measurements that have been defined using the MVT process. Also, whenever outside influences (special causes) change process results, the local workforce must be observant and help to identify the cause(s) of the changed results.

8. *Senior managers must gain some knowledge of the MVT process.* In order to provide effective leadership of the MVT process, top managers must gain some knowledge of the process. This requires some training, but not a lot. As the MVT process is introduced to the organization, the top managers must learn enough about it to demonstrate to the organization that they are knowledgeable enough to recognize and reward proper use of this powerful tool.

9. *Senior management must insist on the use of the 12-step MVT process.* The message sent from top management, throughout the organization, must be that MVT is not optional. The message must be: "This is the way in which we are going to make breakthrough improvements in our results. Everyone is expected to participate appropriately. Our organization will focus on the MVT approach, not on other options." Letting people choose not to participate in the MVT process or use their own favorite improvement approaches at this point will result in negative to disastrous outcomes.

10. *Senior management should adopt a new paradigm: Expect dramatic improvement.* The MVT process is not designed to achieve small, slow, or incremental progress. Managers should expect dramatic breakthroughs. They should be dissatisfied with progress that is not fast or large. The payoff will be remarkable if an organization applies the MVT technology to all its key processes.

11. *Senior management should communicate a "proof-of-the-need" message.* To generate enthusiasm for the broad use of the MVT process, it is useful for top managers to develop and communicate a message that proves that the organization needs to achieve breakthrough improvements. This message should clearly demonstrate to all employees that the success and, ultimately, the health of the organization relies on successfully improving its productivity, costs, market share, profitability, and competitive position, and that the MVT process can deliver such improvements.

12. *Senior management should communicate a breakthrough results plan.* Top managers should develop and communicate a breakthrough results plan. This plan should include: (1) numerical objectives for improvements in financial and operations results, (2) a prioritized schedule for the involvement in the MVT process of the various operating units, (3) the reward and recognition system that will support execution of the plan, and (4) an outline of key infrastructure components (success measures, project selection, and monitoring system). The plan should be simple and concise, comprised of no more than four

pages. It should identify who is going to do what to make the
MVT rollout happen.

13. *The breakthrough results plan should be aggressive and call
    for rapid, significant MVT projects in every segment of the
    organization.* Top management needs to resist the temptation
    to allow some segments of the organization to defer launching
    their MVT efforts. Many division or department heads will
    have reasons or excuses for not starting immediately. Some will
    say that they want to implement MVT learnings from other
    segments of the organization. However, MVT findings should
    never be taken from one part of an organization and applied to
    another that was not a part of the MVT experimentation. To
    get organization-wide performance breakthroughs, MVT
    projects should be performed in parallel in every segment.

14. *The environment does not have to be perfect.* Some approaches
    have been built on the philosophy that, before dramatic im-
    provement can occur, the organization's environment or cul-
    ture must be optimized. The fact is that the environment or
    culture will improve as a result of breakthrough process im-
    provement, not the reverse. It is foolish to wait for the envi-
    ronment to be improved before launching MVT projects.

15. *Measures of success should be defined that link every level of
    the organization.* Every segment of the organization should
    develop success measures that are linked to the business indi-
    cators for the overall organization. Key measures should be de-
    veloped for every management level. All of these measures
    should be linked so that the success of each employee is tied to
    the objectives and strategic direction of the organization.

16. *A process should be put into place to identify and prioritize
    opportunities for improvement.* In order to maximize the ben-
    efits that the MVT process brings to the organization, a pro-
    cess must be developed to select the most potentially significant
    MVT projects. Evaluating the current status and potential for
    improvement of key measures can help in identifying poten-
    tial projects. These can then be prioritized, based on short-
    and long-term benefits. Top management input to and review
    of project selection is absolutely critical.

17. *A process must exist or be developed to capture the customers' wants and needs.* No organization succeeds over the long term unless it satisfies its customers or clients. Some MVT projects are directly focused on improving customer satisfaction. In order to improve its ability to satisfy its customers, an organization must learn what they want and what they need. Clues can be gained though customer surveys. Evaluation of sales data may provide indications of customers' wants and needs. Direct customer involvement in the brainstorming phase of the MVT project may be useful. The ultimate answers, however, are gained by customers voting with their sales dollars.

18. *The system for rewards, recognition, and promotions should reinforce the use of MVT to achieve breakthrough results.* Employees should be motivated by means of the organization's rewards, recognition, and promotions system to use the MVT process to achieve breakthrough results. Newsletter articles, bulletin materials, and the like should praise those who make breakthroughs using the MVT process. Even compensation should be tied in, and whether a person is promoted or not should rely to some extent on the person's successful participation in the MVT process. The system should require proper use of the MVT process in regard to important objectives and the achievement of truly breakthrough improvement in results.

19. *Managers must monitor and control the MVT projects effectively.* At all levels, managers, need to monitor and control the use of the MVT process within their portions of the organization. A system should be executed that tracks MVT plans, activities, and results for every manager in his or her part of the organization.

20. *Every person should understand his or her role in the MVT process and how to execute it.* The MVT process can involve virtually everyone in the organization. It also can be used in a way that minimizes employee involvement and time commitment. A communication and training plan should be constructed that ensures that every employee understands how he or she will interact with the MVT process. The plan also

must provide for appropriate and timely training to equip employees with the knowledge and skills to accomplish their roles.

21. *Training should be industry-specific, role-specific, and timely.* Training in the MVT process must be done properly if it is to be effective. Training should be appropriate to the roles that the employees will perform, so it needs to be customized to reflect the industry and the functions of the trainees. The training should be done on a just-in-time basis; no training should be provided that will not be used by the trainees in the very near future.

22. *Training should be done only by experts.* Only a true MVT expert can effectively provide MVT training. With other approaches, trainers may provide classes after only a few weeks of their own training and virtually no experience. In MVT, executing a blind-leading-the-blind strategy is very likely to provide inconsistent and inaccurate knowledge that can derail your entire effort.

23. *During the rollout of MVT company-wide, expert MVT consultants must be available to provide help.* If the organization plans to teach its employees to use the MVT process, it is critical that they work side by side with an experienced MVT consultant. Even if employees have received classroom training, there are thousands of practical issues that cannot be anticipated in the classroom. Guidance by a true expert is necessary for MVT projects to succeed. This guidance usually is provided by outside experts unless or until an organization develops internal expert support.

24. *Internal MVT consultants must be developed properly.* Internal MVT consultants can be developed successfully. It is important, however, to have an appropriate training plan with a realistic timetable. Development of the expertise to reliably guide successful MVT projects requires the following: (1) Participation in at least two MVT projects as a project leader, factor owner, or data owner; (2) At least nine weeks of classroom training; (3) Serving an apprenticeship under an expert MVT consultant during at least four MVT projects. Attempting to shortcut this

process could result in poor leadership and disastrous results for MVT projects. It could risk "poisoning the well" for the MVT process within the organization and also could kill the chances of obtaining millions of dollars worth of potential MVT benefits.

25. *MVT projects should focus on existing processes and on the development of new processes.* The MVT process is amazingly effective at improving the results achieved from existing processes. It is surprising to many, however, to learn that it is equally effective at developing new processes. MVT experiments can make new-process development go much faster and can dramatically reduce start-up issues.

26. *MVT projects are best when they combine the organization's process with the customer's process.* Great benefits can be derived from using the MVT process on the organization's processes and its customers' processes at the same time. By experimenting with the integrated processes, you can identify actions that you can take that make the customers' results better. You also can identify easy, cost-free actions that your customer can take that will make your product even more effective.

27. *Suppliers should be involved in MVT process efforts.* MVT projects should be performed that involve both the organization's processes and its suppliers' processes at the same time. This can provide large rewards for both. You can also benefit greatly by sharing your learning about what is important in your process with your suppliers, so that they can work more effectively to meet your needs. Encouraging suppliers to initiate their own MVT experimentation will also reward your organization in the long run.

28. *MVT success stories should be communicated to customers and suppliers.* As the organization's MVT successes pile up, it is a good idea to communicate the stories to your customers and suppliers. Customers will be impressed with your use of cutting-edge technology and consistent efforts to improve. They will become even more amenable to joint MVT projects that strengthen your relationship with them. Suppliers will be encouraged to strengthen their own improvement programs as well as to participate in cooperative MVT projects.

29. *External MVT experts periodically review the organization's efforts to achieve breakthrough improvement.* Even if your organization develops internal MVT consultants, you should arrange periodic reviews by an external MVT consultant. Such independent observations can pay great dividends by pointing out areas in which your efforts may have slipped, by informing you of new techniques, and by providing objective assessment of possible areas of improvement.

30. *Every manager needs to exhibit perseverance.* Every manager, especially those at the top of the organization, must persevere in his or her improvement efforts and never lose track of the current status of key measures. Managers must never relent in their efforts to keep MVT processes focused on important objectives and must never accept the idea that any portion of the organization has become as good as it can be. More improvement is always possible. Managers must always demonstrate the expectation that the MVT process will be used effectively and continuously.

THE QUALPRO PROCESS FOR IMPLEMENTING MVT ON AN ORGANIZATION-WIDE BASIS

Using the key elements of success described above, QualPro has constructed a standardized process that we use to help clients implement MVT on an organization-wide basis (Figure 23.1).

Phase I: Complete two high-impact MVT projects with breakthrough results. The purpose of Phase I is to prove to senior management and the rest of the organization that the MVT process will work in that particular organization. Phase I consists of the completion of two, high-priority MVT projects that will clearly demonstrate the benefits of the MVT process to the organization. Project teams, guided by MVT consultants, apply the MVT process to financially significant opportunities. These initial successes pave the way for improvements on a broad scale. Often, the financial benefits from these Phase I projects more than

Figure 23.1   The QualPro Process

The QualPro Process©

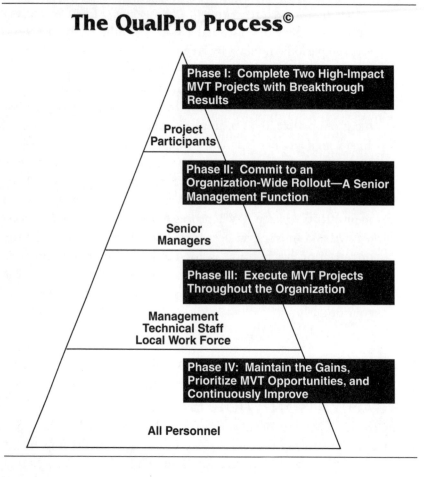

fund the organization-wide MVT process efforts for the first several years.

Phase II: Commit to an organization-wide rollout—a senior management function. The purpose of Phase II is to plan the organization-wide rollout of the MVT process. During Phase II, senior management creates and communicates an action plan that (1) prioritizes MVT projects to align with corporate objectives, (2) provides appropriate training, resources, and involvement to management, technical, and front-line personnel, and (3) monitors process-improvement activities to ensure that success is rapid and quantifiable. MVT consultants support Phase II efforts through assessments and executive sessions.

Phase III: Execute MVT projects throughout the organization. The purpose of Phase III is to expand the benefits of the MVT process across the entire organization. MVT projects are launched to address every major improvement opportunity. The objective is to produce results like those achieved in Phase I and to achieve dramatically improved results in all the organization's priority processes. Often, this broad application of MVT process-improvement techniques rapidly improves corporate financial performance.

Phase IV: Maintain the Gains, Prioritize MVT Opportunities, and Continuously Improve. The purpose of Phase IV is to involve all personnel in maintaining the gains made in Phases I and III while also working to further improve results. As new challenges and opportunities are identified, additional projects are initiated. New hires and promoted personnel are involved appropriately in new or existing MVT efforts.

The need for MVT consultant involvement decreases as line personnel participate in numerous projects and gain increasing competence in the MVT process.

Corporate financial performance continues to improve, shareholders enjoy an enhanced stock value, and the company's culture is transformed into one never satisfied with the status quo.

SUMMARY

Implementing the MVT process on a broad basis can transform an organization—competitively, financially, and culturally. The QualPro process is described in detail in the following chapters.

CHAPTER 24

PHASE I

Complete Two High-Impact MVT
Projects with Breakthrough Results

The purpose of first using the MVT process to generate two high-impact successes is to prove to everyone in the organization, especially the senior managers, that "this stuff works here." The projects selected for Phase I of the QualPro Process are ones that are capable of generating highly visible successes. The criteria for selecting the projects are:

- They are significant to the bottom line.
- They can be done in about two months.
- Most people in the organization can relate to them.

Furthermore, to ensure a high probability of project success, senior management controls the selection of the project leader and project participants. This approach has proven to be very effective for generating dramatic results very quickly.

INITIAL SUCCESS IS CRITICAL

At QualPro, we have done comprehensive studies of our clients, of companies that have used other process-improvement approaches, and of companies that have tried to do process improvement on their own.

The one conclusion that stood out more than any other was this: If a long-term, company-wide improvement effort is to be successful, there must be early, significant accomplishments. The evidence for this is overwhelming. Yet, for some reason, QualPro is the only process-improvement company that stresses early successes. Perhaps other process-improvement organizations have not compared the results obtained by companies that achieve early successes with those that do not.

Perhaps another reason that other process-improvement organizations don't talk about quick, initial success is that they don't know how to accomplish it consistently. At QualPro, we know that we can use MVT to improve any process. That's the basis of QualPro. You can't improve all the processes in a company if you can't improve an individual process. Better management, teamwork, more communication, and good attitudes are wonderful, but without the capability of improving whatever is weak, malfunctioning, or inefficient, you won't obtain breakthrough improvement. Good attitudes may make failure a little more digestible, but that's about it.

Using a process-improvement system that does not have the ability to quickly and reliably improve an individual process is like trying to make coffee without using coffee beans. You have the pot and the water and the cups and the spoons and the sugar and the cream. You can heat and mix and stir and pour but, without coffee beans, you aren't ever going to have coffee to drink.

THE TWO INITIAL PROJECTS MUST BE SIGNIFICANT

Something has to happen at first that significantly affects the organization's bottom line. Pete DeBusk, a friend of mine, owns DeRoyal Industries, a company that makes medical supplies. When I first started QualPro, Pete helped me with start-up capital and office space. In return, I helped him by doing process-improvement consulting. In thinking about our early work at DeRoyal, I realize that the only reason Pete stuck with the improvement effort was the success of the two initial projects. Their objectives were to improve efficiency in manufacturing operating sponges and to eliminate shipping errors. Both projects achieved dramatic results. Had we not been so successful, contributed immediately to the bottom line, and sharply reduced his problems in these areas, Pete would have abandoned the whole effort within a year, saying that it wasn't working, that we were wasting our time, and that we should be doing something more productive. But we solved two problems that were significant to him.

This story illustrates why senior managers have to be involved in the beginning of the improvement projects and why the projects need to be significant. I guarantee that the senior managers will stay involved if they see early successes that affect the bottom line in a positive way. If you can't show quick results that matter to them in some way, they are going to lose interest.

This story also underscores how important it is to select initial projects that allow for improvement, that will have bottom-line impact, and that can be recognized by everybody in the company. It is extremely important that people see the results and say, "Yes, that worked!" So the choice of projects to start with is critical. Some managers may want to select easy projects that they are sure they can do. However, if what is happening makes no real difference to the organization—if it is not significant, financially and otherwise—this leads to "ho-hum" attitudes and fails to generate the enthusiasm to carry further projects forward. This doesn't do much for the organization or its chances of widespread process improvement through MVT.

THE TWO INITIAL PROJECTS MUST BE ABLE TO BE DONE QUICKLY

The two improvement projects must be able to be done in the short term. We want to hit the ground running and show others that MVT works. We don't want to be working on either of the initial projects two years later.

That raises the question of what is possible to do quickly. The answer is that it depends on the capability of those involved in doing it. To some, it might seem that a 40-year-old problem couldn't possibly be resolved in two months, but that's exactly what we often want: a problem that appears insurmountable.

Of course, there are some projects that cannot be done in the short term. For example, attempting to reduce the time it takes the American automotive industry to move from design to production of a new model wouldn't be a realistic short-term project. Because this is a multiple-year process, it cannot be done in two months, so it should not be chosen as a Phase I project. (However, it might make a great Phase III or Phase IV project.)

PEOPLE SHOULD BE ABLE TO RELATE TO THE TWO INITIAL PROJECTS

It is extremely important to avoid choosing projects that a large portion of the employees cannot relate to. For example, top managers usually have lists of pet concerns. Maybe there is a need to improve forecasting, because a manager missed projections in the third quarter. That is important to the manager, but people in the factory can't relate to that problem. The results of the initial projects need to be things that everybody can understand and get excited about.

WHY THERE ARE TWO INITIAL PROJECTS

Early in the use of the QualPro process, we often worked on only one project. Even though we achieved success, many people within a company would claim that something other than the MVT process caused the improved results. For example, in a textile company, the initial project was to find a solution to a cloth defect problem that had existed for 45 years. The problem had cost the company more than $25,000,000 per year. The solution involved using the MVT process in three different plants, all part of the vertically integrated process. As a result of the use of MVT, the problem was completely eliminated in two months. Immediately, personnel from all three plants and corporate R&D claimed credit for solving the problem. Each group maintained that the success was not a result of the MVT process, but that the group's independent efforts caused the success. Fortunately, the senior managers realized that the MVT process had caused the success. A year later, the people in each of the dissenting groups were still trying to argue the point.

Our experience tells us that, if we do two initial projects, we will not have this problem. Even the most skeptical will realize that

Table 24.1   Selected Phase I Projects Performed by QualPro's Clients

Manufacturing	Sales/Marketing	Service/Administration
Increased first-quality carpet by over $5 million per year.	Increased sales by $1 million per year.	Accounts receivable days were reduced from 52 to 38, reducing average invested capital by $4 million and improving the division's return on investment by 3.5%.
Increased yield 10% and decreased cycle time 30%.	Increased the response rate by 0.40%, resulting in $30 million per year in annual profits.	
Throughput increased 10%, resulting in $1 million per year savings.	Increased per store sales by 150% and profits by 160%.	Reduced radiology report turnaround time by 70%.
Lamination rejects were reduced 20%, saving over $1 million annually.	Increased sales by 337% while saving $750,000 per year.	Reduced emergency department patient dissatisfaction by 78%.
Capability measures improved from 23% to 257%, contamination was cut in half, and cycle time per batch was reduced 25%, equating to $3 million per year in savings.	MVT experiments showed that sales could be increased 33%, an improvement that was worth $100 million.	Telephone repair time was reduced by 40%.
		TV installation lead time was reduced by 75%.
Spool waste was reduced by 83%, saving $3.25 million per year.	Sales increased over 10%, valued at over $4.5 million per year.	Increased on-time billings from about 60% to over 99%.
Increased process yield from 63% to 91%, saving $3 million per year.	Increased sales by over 25% and profits by $1.1 million.	Handle time was reduced an average of 17%, and productivity increases resulted in $15 million savings.
Decreased failure rate of a critical control valve from 50% such that the valve's life increased to 25 years.	Increased sales by 15%, resulting in an additional $18 million in profit per year.	Reduced credit memos by 40%.
		Reduced service order errors by 35%.
Increased paper machine efficiency from 92% to 99% by reducing flying splice paper breaks. Reduced splice consumption by 40%.	Increased sales and reduced print costs, resulting in a financial impact of $22.8 million.	Reduced repeat repair calls by 75%, with projected savings over all offices estimated to be $75 million per year.
	Increased renewals by over 50%.	
	Increased internet sales by 72%.	
	Increased response rate over 41%, resulting in a $7.2 million impact on the bottom line.	

arguing that two independent successes were both not due to the MVT process is futile.

Table 24.1 shows examples of Phase I projects performed by Qual-Pro's clients that met the criteria of being significant to the bottom line, being able to be done in about two months, and being relevant to most people in the organization.

THE RIGHT PEOPLE MUST BE INVOLVED

Carefully Select the People Who Will Work on the Phase I Projects

Having the involvement of the right people is incredibly important for initial projects. We have found that it is best to select a few special people who know the most about each process in need of improvement. These people will be the factor owners, data owners, and project leaders. They will come from the ranks of line managers, technical people, engineers, designers—the heavyweights. We also select people who are close to the process, those that do the actual work. They are needed to execute MVT recipes. Of course, many more than these select few are involved in the brainstorming process, we include everyone who could possibly have a worthwhile idea.

Companies sometimes want to maximize the number of people involved. However, except for the brainstorming activity, QualPro has found that no more than 10 people are needed on most projects. Think about committee work. Do you accomplish more with a small group or a large group? Which involves fewer distractions and side trips? We prefer to use just the best talent available, and we will check to see if they really know what they think they know. In fact, sometimes we shy away from selecting a particular project if the "right people" are not available to participate.

Use MVT Consultants to Guide the Initial Projects

In our experience, the most important factor in determining the level of success of initial improvement efforts is the use of MVT consultants to guide the projects. Early in QualPro's history, we tried to help companies perform MVT projects with only a few days' worth of support and guidance by MVT consultants. We found that this just did not work. There are too many tasks that require extensive expertise; there are too many judgments to be made; and there are too many situation-specific nuances in the MVT process for novices to be successful. Without the extensive involvement of MVT consultants, projects lasted five times as long and often required a great deal of rework. For initial projects, when internal experts have not yet been developed, MVT consultants must come from outside the company.

Even later, many of our clients insist that a SWAT team of MVT consultants be used to oversee all aspects of their initial, organization-wide MVT rollout projects. This is because the projects are so important to successfully launching the organization-wide improvement effort and the potential payoff is so great.

MONITOR AND CONTROL INITIAL IMPROVEMENT EFFORTS

Interest from the top of the organization conveys a sense of urgency that is the lifeblood to MVT-based process improvement. Senior managers get excited about dramatic improvements in results. Unfortunately, their interest sometimes fades fast. They get the effort organized and then they want it out of their offices, somewhere down the hall, so they can simply wait to hear about the payoff. Some managers sit back, fully expecting great results, without knowing how or when or why. Some managers show us lists of other things they feel are more important at the time. Some are afraid that they'll say something stupid in front of a knowledgeable team. All these ways of disengaging from the process-improvement effort can be deadly to the results.

Most of us look to the boss to set the tone, whether good or bad. If there is somebody in the top echelon who is really interested in what we are doing, we will be diligent and persevere.

We have to drive the managers we work with to stay on top of the MVT process-improvement effort. I have files full of personal memos to company presidents, urging them to monitor and control and to require their project leaders to report often on the status of their projects (at least every two weeks). We have conducted surveys to find out why managers try to escape this responsibility, and we have found many of the reasons listed above. Now we tell senior managers that we cannot guarantee the results unless they agree to monitor and control frequently the MVT process-improvement efforts. Their interest is the winning edge.

The details of how to monitor control will be discussed in Phase II.

IT'S IMPORTANT TO SPREAD THE WORD ABOUT SUCCESS

It is important not to rush past the early successes. After you fix something that wasn't working right, show everybody in the company how it was done. Tell everybody that this is just the beginning—that more improvements are to come. As the saying goes, "Nothing breeds success like success."

The reverse also is true: failure breeds failure. Leaders can declare a false start and try again. Even those embarrassed by failure tend to go on down the same road and conclude much later that what they are doing isn't working. By then, the people who are looking to the top for leadership will have lost their enthusiasm. The net result is nothing or, worse, negativity. As we have said, there is no substitute for early success stories.

THOROUGHLY DOCUMENT INITIAL SUCCESS STORIES

QualPro receives some wonderful reports about how the MVT process resulted in increased productivity and larger profits and greater shares of a market. We get thank you notes from company presidents who have received thank-you notes from more satisfied customers. This is good. We thoroughly enjoy success stories. But that isn't enough to inspire greater process improvement within companies and throughout larger organizations. We want every success story to be documented. Well–documented success stories can convince skeptics. They add fuel to the fire of those who already believe. This is absolutely crucial. Six years from now, people won't remember even a $30,000,000 savings unless there is documentation. Even next month, some of the impact is lost unless there is sufficient supporting detail to convince everybody that the gains are real.

It takes very little effort to document the MVT process success stories. That effort will still be paying big dividends years later.

CHAPTER 25

PHASE II

Commit to an Organization-Wide Rollout—A Senior Management Function

The purpose of Phase II is for the organization's senior managers to create and communicate an action plan for the organization-wide rollout of the MVT process. The action plan will specify ways to:

- Prioritize MVT process improvement initiatives to align with corporate objectives.
- Provide appropriate training and resources to management, technical, and front-line personnel.
- Monitor MVT process improvement activities to ensure that success is rapid and quantifiable.

This chapter discusses the roles of senior management, including development of the action plan, and the infrastructure elements that are important as part of that plan.

THE ROLE OF TOP MANAGEMENT

Top managers have several tasks and responsibilities in preparing the organization for implementation of the MVT process and in helping to guide it through the process. These include the following:

- Develop the customized action plan, the Plan for Breakthrough Results.
- Gain knowledge of the MVT process.
- Insist that the 12-step MVT process be used throughout the organization.
- Demand a consistent approach throughout the organization.
- Expect dramatic, not incremental, improvement.
- Ensure that line management takes responsibility for MVT use and that the workforce takes responsibility for process execution.
- Develop and communicate the "Proof of the Need" message.
- Visibly support the plan and its execution.

DEVELOP THE CUSTOMIZED PLAN FOR BREAKTHROUGH RESULTS

If you are going to go for organization-wide improvement using the MVT process, you should have a plan designed to fit your organization. For many years, U.S. business leaders have been enthusiastic about benchmarking. They look at what General Electric or Motorola is doing; they collect a number of bright ideas and then hurry home to copy them. That won't work with process improvement. Different companies have different problems and are starting from different places. It isn't enough to copy the winners, even if you understand what went into a successful process improvement effort. You would not take some off-the-shelf medicine that might not cure your ailment, and you certainly wouldn't take cough medicine to cure arthritic knees. In the same way, you do not want to risk your company's economic future on an off-the-shelf process improvement effort that is not customized to your company and its specific situation. Half of QualPro's new clients are companies that are on the rebound from piecemeal plans for continuous improvement. In too many cases, they were taking cough syrup for bad knees.

You need to have a customized Plan for Breakthrough Results. Unfortunately, a significant number of organizations don't have any kind of plan. There may be one in the president's mind or maybe in the quality manager's office, but when you ask around the organization, people have no idea what the plan is or even if there is one. We have even seen Baldrige Award-winning companies that did not have process improvement plans—or that did have plans but had not explained them to the employees. When we ask about the organization's plan at different levels, the most common answer is, "I don't know." Invariably, these organizations have been disappointed with their process improvement results—if there were any. Eventually, they realized that they needed something more.

So, starting at square one, aside from the desire to improve, an organization should develop a carefully thought-out, customized plan that can be understood by all concerned—all those who work within the organization and will help to implement, or be affected by, the plan.

A real-life example of a utility company's Plan for Breakthrough Results is shown in Figure 25.5 at the end of this chapter. This plan differs somewhat from typical in that: (1) they developed the plan while Phase I was still underway (discussions with other QualPro clients had already convinced them that they would be rolling out the MVT process company wide) and (2) they chose to execute four Phase I projects rather than two (the senior managers of all four major company divisions wanted to participate in Phase I).

The Plan Should Be Developed by Senior Management

The organization-wide, MVT process improvement effort has to be managed from the top. If it isn't, senior managers won't understand what is in it. Even if they do understand but they haven't put time, effort, and thought into the plan, they won't have the personal interest to make it happen. Even though I am convinced that no company is better than QualPro at studying organizational needs, assessing problems, and surveying customers and employees, we cannot develop the Plan for Breakthrough Results for your organization. We can do the best needs assessment, but there will be things that are missed, because we are not aware of everything that goes on within your organization.

We are happy to offer advice and give general direction. We can help an organization's leaders to find their way, but those leaders need to be involved in developing their own plan.

In many companies, if the subject were anything but process improvement, there would be no discussion about whether the senior managers would be involved. If we were talking about investment or expansion, the CEO would be sitting at the head of the table. Too often, however, process improvement plans are developed by the quality-control manager or another staff member. Senior managers may think they don't have time for it, or they may not be comfortable with the concept if they didn't learn about it in business school. Maybe they think the results are too far down the road. In some cases, they simply haven't recognized the need.

The good news is that creating the plan is not that difficult, and the benefits are great. A little bit of time and thought will result in a big payoff and make life much easier on down the road.

The problem is that if top managers are not involved in developing the plan, they will not understand it well, and it may not reflect their views of what needs to be done in the organization and how that might be achieved. When an action plan is to be implemented by thousands of employees, all supposedly working to make things better, you can rest assured that their managers, and the managers above them had better know what parts of the organization will be involved and when, what will be done, what to expect, and how to lead the effort. There might be some initial improvement without true participation by senior managers, but the plan will not thrive, and long-term results will fall short of expectations.

An action plan should be a page or two, three or four at most. It should be stated in simple, concise, easy-to-understand words. The senior managers must decide what the objectives are, and who will do what and when. The senior managers also need to decide who will lead, manage, and nurture the process improvement efforts. The right answer is—themselves. This is a big part of their job. Remember, we are talking about the potential for spectacular, breakthrough results as a result of the effort.

GAIN KNOWLEDGE OF THE MVT PROCESS

Top managers must have some knowledge of the MVT process before they can develop a Plan for Breakthrough Results. This book

provides an understanding of the process. In addition, QualPro typically teaches senior managers the essentials of the MVT process in a
one-to-two-day executive briefing. The briefing utilizes customized
training materials containing examples to which the managers can relate.

INSIST THAT THE 12-STEP MVT PROCESS BE USED THROUGHOUT THE ORGANIZATION

To achieve breakthrough results, you must use a process improvement
procedure that has been designed for your particular business, whether
it involves putting caps on bottles or selling more to your customers.
Improved communication is a good thing, teamwork is a good thing,
and better performance appraisal is a good thing, but the bottom line
is the organization's competitive position in its marketplace. Things
that matter to your customers and shareholders can be improved.
Brainstorming can help to elicit suggestions that help, but unless you
test those suggestions in a controlled way, you will not know which
will truly help, which will make no difference, and which will hurt.

MVT is a 12-step means of testing suggestions that produces improvements every time, whether the problem is the amount of time
between when a customer walks in the door of your restaurant and
when that person is served or how to improve the strength and flex-
ibility of a complex, high-tech plastic. And, as I have described in this
book, the kind of improvement you can expect is dramatic.

DEMAND A CONSISTENT APPROACH THROUGHOUT THE ORGANIZATION

Simply said, it is disastrous to allow different segments of an organization to use different approaches to process improvement. A few years
ago, I was called in by the president of an organization that had nine
companies under its umbrella. Some of the companies were inter-
twined; some supply value-added materials and products to others.
The president had allowed each company's CEO to choose his or her
own process improvement approach, although he had told them all
that they were responsible for the success of their plans. The president

described the problems he was encountering. The CEOs chose very different approaches. They could not communicate about process improvement with one another. When he tried to move a manager from one company to another, all kinds of problems erupted.

In 1982, a large automobile manufacturer's divisions were told to do continuous improvement. Some did one thing and some another. They also ended up trying to talk to one another in unknown tongues. In time, the company reorganized. Some of the divisions were thrown together, and their members found it very difficult to communicate about quality improvement. There was no common understanding.

The problem also exists when a company's supplier does process improvement with one approach, and a major customer uses another.

When we study what is happening across the United States in continuous-improvement efforts, we find that some segments of an organization make dramatic improvements, and other segments make none. The intentions are fine, in that top management wants everybody to feel responsible. But the results often are chaotic—another example of good intentions being implemented without adequate testing. The solution is for somebody at the top to insist that a common approach be used throughout the organization.

EXPECT DRAMATIC, NOT INCREMENTAL, IMPROVEMENT

Some improvement approaches strive for small, incremental improvements over a long period of time, but this is not what the MVT process is about. Senior managers need to establish a new paradigm for the organization. Slow incremental improvements should be viewed as inadequate. MVT projects should target large levels of improvement: for example, "increase manufacturing throughput by 25 percent" or "increase sales results by one-third."

MVT projects should be of broad scope, experimenting throughout vertically integrated processes. Factors from every major step of a process should be included in MVT projects. Projects should include factors in both the organization's and the customer's operations. Suppliers also can be involved in MVT projects.

MVT projects should be executed with a great sense of urgency in very short time frames. Rather than having the typical, 18-month time line, in most situations, MVT projects can identify solutions within a few months, or even a few weeks. If a proposed project cannot be performed in a timely fashion, challenge the selection of that project. Choose other projects that can help the organization sooner.

ENSURE THAT LINE MANAGEMENT TAKES RESPONSIBILITY FOR MVT USE AND THAT THE WORKFORCE TAKES RESPONSIBILITY FOR PROCESS EXECUTION

Senior management should very clearly communicate the role of management and the role of the workforce in process improvement. Management is responsible for defining the process. The workforce is responsible for executing the process as it has been defined.

If the workforce does its job of executing the process as defined, the results will be consistent within the range that represents the normal "noise" of the process. The members of the workforce should be expected to follow the process as defined and they should be the primary investigators of unusual results that may represent special causes. The workforce should not be expected to make the process produce results beyond its capability.

Managers must take responsibility for increasing the capability of the process, and the only way to increase capability is to take action that changes the way in which the process is performed. The only way to change the process, and truly know that results will improve, is to test the changes before implementing them. The MVT process is a management tool, and line management should take ownership of this tool and drive its use in the organization. Managers must clearly communicate responsibilities and lead the use of MVT in order to improve both financial and cultural results for the organization.

DEVELOP AND COMMUNICATE THE "PROOF OF THE NEED" MESSAGE

Senior managers should develop and communicate a "proof of the need" message. Often, management assumes that everybody within the organization understands the need for process improvement. However, if others don't see or understand why a process needs to be improved, their efforts will be less than is needed and will compromise the results. For a process improvement effort to be successful, the message about "Here's why we must do this" must get through.

QualPro surveys find that employees generally think that their companies are doing well. In most companies, employees do not see or do not understand actual performance statistics. For example, I worked with a company that had about 25,000 employees. I held an executive briefing with the top manager and his top 20 people. I did a little internal survey, which revealed that everybody thought the company was doing fine and that there was no need to improve. At dinner, I told the company president that most of his top people thought they were already doing fine. The president was astounded—and appalled. He said that the company's return on assets was the worst in the industry. He talked about seven years of investments and the pitiful return. He couldn't believe that the people most important to the success of the business didn't understand its poor performance. Two months later, he delivered a serious proof-of-the-need message. Even those on the plant floors then understood the need for improvement.

This kind of communications gap exists in many organizations, even though the top executive doesn't realize it. We can never assume that the masses of employees in a company understand that there is a serious and urgent need to improve. A proof-of-the-need message will tell them what the problem is, how serious it is, and why improvement is necessary, now.

VISIBLY SUPPORT THE PLAN AND ITS EXECUTION

With some process improvement plans, some top managers just go through the motions. They may pay lip service to the company's plan, but they don't really believe that it will lead to a result that will significantly improve the long-term well-being of the business. If senior managers don't believe in the plan, stop. The next step is to back up and develop a plan they can believe in—or explain the one on the table well enough that the managers are comfortable with whatever was misunderstood. Top managers must strongly believe in the Plan for Breakthrough Results before they can effectively support and execute it.

There will be times when even organization–wide MVT process improvement efforts require all the faith that can be mustered. At such times, managers must remind themselves of the payoff that the MVT process can bring to the company and them personally, and remember the Phase I successes that they have already seen.

ESTABLISH THE INFRASTRUCTURE TO SUPPORT AND REINFORCE EXECUTION OF THE PLAN FOR BREAKTHROUGH RESULTS

To establish the infrastructure to support and reinforce execution of the action plan, the organization's top management must do the following:

- Build a process for identifying and prioritizing MVT projects.
- Ensure that the reward, recognition, and promotion systems provide incentives for executing the Plan for Breakthrough Results.
- Establish a system to monitor and control execution of the Plan for Breakthrough Results.
- Provide customized, role-specific training for everyone involved in MVT projects.
- Provide MVT consultant support to guide projects and/or develop internal expertise.

BUILD A PROCESS FOR IDENTIFYING AND PRIORITIZING MVT PROJECTS

Identifying Potential MVT Projects

The first thing that needs to be accomplished is the development of a long list of potential MVT projects. This should include potential projects that can contribute to the organization's profitability as well as potential projects that can contribute to improved customer satisfaction.

To identify potential projects to improve profitability through increased sales and/or reduced costs, a number of sources should be used. Executive managers should share and discuss their ideas for projects.

Managers of segments of the organization and managers of specific processes should submit their ideas. They should all ask themselves: "What activity can we improve that can influence the sales, costs, and, therefore, the profitability of the organization?"

Similarly, several sources should be tapped to identify potential projects to improve customer satisfaction. These include customer surveys, input from those that have direct interaction with customers, and customer-complaint data. Again, each potential project should be assessed in light of the question: "What changes in our service or product characteristics could increase customer satisfaction?"

Prioritizing Potential MVT Projects

Not all opportunities for improvement deserve attention. For example, the projected savings may be too small, the proposed project may not have a sufficiently large ROI, or the project may have nothing to do with what's really important to the customer. Because the ability to improve is limited by the resources available to train people and manage the effort, you must prioritize. The goal is to make an intelligent assessment of where first to direct the improvement effort. The highest priority improvement projects should reflect the highest priority business objectives.

Effective prioritization of processes comes from an understanding of how the improvement contributes to organizational efficiency and profitability and/or how the improvement impacts customer satisfaction.

Our experience is that, if senior management stays involved in the ongoing identification and prioritization of MVT projects, we continue to get breakthrough results and huge payoffs. If senior management withdraws from the identification and prioritization process, the payoff diminishes.

Prioritization Based on Contribution to Organizational Efficiency and Profitability

It makes good business sense to focus on those processes that have the highest potential return on investment. In this case, the desires of the board of directors and stockholders may offer guidance. The final

Figure 25.1   Pareto Chart for Prioritizing MVT Projects
Based on the Potential Dollar Return

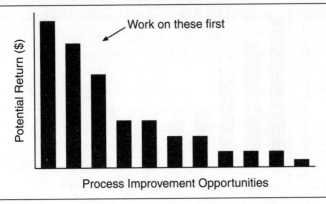

prioritized list of projects should be compatible with the organization's overall business strategy. Any incompatibility will only be counterproductive.

The Pareto chart in Figure 25.1 will help to identify the processes that will have the most effect on the bottom line.

Prioritization Based on Impact on Customer Satisfaction

In addition to focusing on processes that are important to organizational efficiency and profitability, it makes good sense to focus on those processes that have the most impact on customer satisfaction. An accurate understanding of what is important to your customers and how your products and services compare to your competitors' products and services is vital to targeting the improvement effort on those areas that directly impact your competitive position. A system for measuring customer satisfaction is critical to this understanding. Not only will this survey instrument help to identify the key measures, it also will help quantify the relative importance of each. Data generated from customer feedback are helpful in prioritizing when they are presented in the form of a Pareto chart (Figure 25.2) or a quadrant analysis (Figure 25.3).

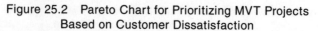

Figure 25.2   Pareto Chart for Prioritizing MVT Projects
Based on Customer Dissatisfaction

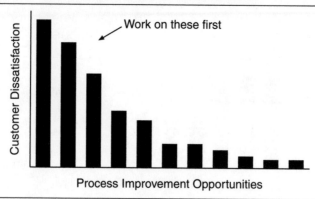

The second technique, quadrant analysis, involves displaying customer feedback in two dimensions: importance and performance. The highest priority projects are those that are high in importance and low in performance. Figure 25.3 is an example of a quadrant analysis for prioritizing process improvement opportunities for a sneaker manufacturing company.

Identifying and prioritizing MVT projects must be an ongoing process. The prioritized list of projects should be updated quarterly. It is

Figure 25.3   Quadrant Analysis for Prioritizing MVT Projects

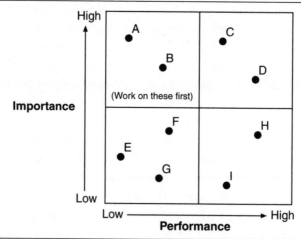

best to make the MVT project-selection process part of the formal planning process of the organization. The CFO and his or her organization should confirm the size of the financial opportunities before projects are undertaken, and the benefits achieved should be confirmed after projects are completed.

Survey Customers Periodically

Customers should be surveyed periodically to determine their wants and needs. I was surprised to discover that most big companies do not survey their customers to discover what the customers want to have improved. Process improvement related to customer satisfaction is like blowing in the wind if you don't know what satisfies your customers in the first place. There is no way an organization can know what its customers want if it doesn't ask them.

Some companies spend a tremendous amount of time and effort in attempting to survey a long list of customers. Yet pollsters have taught us that a small sample, properly selected, will provide inferences about very large numbers of people. It is possible to talk with a very few people, if we ask the right questions, and still come up with sound conclusions that have very small margins of error. If you ask the right people the right questions in the right manner, you only have to talk with a few to get the information that tells what you need to do to get better.

Most customer surveys are designed to provide favorable numbers or statements to be used for marketing messages. They are not designed to obtain essential information on which to base an improvement effort. Customer surveys should focus on what the customer would like to see improved in the organization's products and services and on what the customer prefers about the competitors' products and services. This is essential information to have before attempting to plan an organization-wide MVT process improvement effort.

Survey Employees

You also should survey your employees to get ideas for improvement and to identify obstacles to improvement. Dr. W. Edwards Deming talked of creating the correct environment for continuous improvement. One of his mandates was "drive out fear, so that everyone may work effectively for the company." When fear is driven out, employees aren't afraid to make suggestions or to report a problem.

In some companies, improvement efforts will suffer if steps are not taken to drive out fear. In other companies, however, fear is not a problem. In a survey I conducted in one company, large numbers of employees made negative comments about the top manager. Some called him a "gutless SOB." Even though it was an anonymous survey, some signed their names. I concluded that there wasn't any need to drive out fear in this company. This was proof that all-purpose solutions don't work in every organization.

Different companies have different cultures and characteristics. They suffer from different ills. There are hidden obstacles to improvement. We can uncover them with employee surveys. Rather than discovering too late that what you are attempting to fix isn't broken, you can use customer-survey techniques to survey employees. What do employees feel they need in the way of resources, support, and changes so that they can do their jobs better? Use of a proper survey instrument can provide absolutely essential information. In the more than 300 companies in which we have conducted employee surveys, in every case, top managers were surprised by some of the findings.

There are always some problems we never would have guessed. Many times what we thought were problems weren't problems at all. In one company, employees said that managers kept harping about more and better quality, that everybody had to be involved, and that everybody had to contribute. But no time was allowed for people to participate in process improvement activities or to get together in groups to talk about it.

The biggest problem we find that affects process improvement is apathy. It is the major problem in U.S. companies, and we have the survey results to prove it. Before an organization begins a process improvement program, it should know if employees are convinced that there is a need to improve. If employees see no reason to improve, the action plan must address how to convince the employees that the company needs to improve and can improve. We have seen many companies in which top managers were very serious but the employees missed the message. Or employees may think that process improvement is just another fad. If that attitude prevails, the plan must address how to overcome the misconception that top management is not really serious.

Ensure That the Reward, Recognition, and Promotion Systems Provide Incentives for Executing the Plan for Breakthrough Results

To be effective, process improvement efforts must provide true incentives to drive success. It must be clear to everyone that process improvement is a vitally important part of every manager's job. The people who get the biggest raises, the people who get recognition by senior management, the people who are promoted, the people who get the largest stock options, these should be the ones who get breakthrough results. This needs to be communicated up front and then followed through. Rewards and recognition systems that reinforce continuous process improvement can double the payoff of the MVT process improvement effort.

Establish a System to Monitor and Control Execution of the Plan for Breakthrough Results

Once process improvement efforts have begun, it is critical that they not be ignored, forgotten, or allowed to die. Clear definition, assignment, and communication of process improvement efforts are essential to their effective management but are not sufficient by themselves. All levels of management will obtain a great return on the energy they invest to ensure that MVT process improvement efforts make progress and succeed.

While we definitely want to tap the knowledge of the local workforce, management has a key responsibility in process improvement that cannot be delegated. This responsibility is ongoing monitoring and controlling. If the organizational culture requires softer terminology, the terms reviewing and nurturing can be used.

Monitoring and controlling of process improvement are critical to long-term success for many reasons. Some of them are:

- To ensure efficient progress through the MVT process.
- To provide access to employee ideas.
- To identify barriers to implementation.
- To identify employees who are natural process improvement "champions."
- To enable you to change priorities when appropriate.
- To identify new improvement opportunities.

Ensure Efficient Progress

Monitoring and controlling functions provide the forum for top management to stay involved and ensure efficient progress through the MVT process. For example, if efforts stall, top management can encourage innovation by asking questions, such as:

- Why have we not finished categorizing our factors?
- When is the MVT screening experiment going to start/end?
- Do we have a Pareto chart of factor effects?
- What's the control limit?
- What surprises have been identified by the MVT experiment?
- What factors will be implemented?
- How soon?
- How much is this improvement worth?

It becomes clear that senior management views MVT as being too important to ignore. The message spreads that management is really interested and participating.

Provide Access to Employee Ideas

Monitoring and controlling gives managers access to employee ideas that can lead to reduced costs and better products and services. These ideas will emerge naturally during regular management reviews. Some of these ideas will result in factors for future MVT experimentation, and others will result in potential projects to be prioritized.

Identify Barriers to Implementation

Regular management reviews provide the forum for managers to identify barriers to implementation. Managers can fulfill their responsibility to remove barriers only if the barriers are first identified. A few minutes of management review can prevent weeks of wasted effort, delays, or suboptimal improvement results.

Identify Employees Who Are Natural Process Improvement "Champions"

Monitoring and controlling enables managers to identify employees who are risk takers, who are interested in innovation, and who want to understand cause-and-effect relationships in their processes. Once identified, these "champions" should be utilized to their fullest potential and given opportunities to demonstrate their capabilities.

Change Priorities When Appropriate

Because of regular employee input, customer feedback, and ongoing process improvement successes, priorities will change over time. Management reviews will help to highlight these appropriate updates in priorities.

Identify New Improvement Opportunities

By being actively involved in regular reviews, managers will learn about the complexities of their processes. This understanding often leads to previously unknown, unidentified problems and great opportunity for improvement. For example, one MVT project team that was working to increase machine efficiency did so by combining two processes into one, freeing up time for a considerable amount of staff. At the same time, another MVT project was focusing on reducing defects in the product. The primary reason for defects was eliminated by utilizing the available staff members who were freed up by the machine-efficiency project. The production manager, through regular monitoring and controlling, saw this opportunity and took action.

The opportunity would have been missed by individuals working within the processes.

Monitoring and Controlling Requires Management Reviews

Monitoring and controlling is accomplished through regular management reviews. The first type of regular review should be a closeout session at the end of each week, to utilize the capabilities and experience of the lead MVT consultant, in order to help prepare the team to lead and manage the effort effectively.

Second, staff meetings should be used to begin to nurture the transition to using MVT process improvement. The agenda for each staff meeting should include a set period of time for process improvement reports, coordination, and oversight.

A standard format for reporting on MVT projects is very useful. We recommend the use of an "MVT Process Control Book." This is simply a collection of one-page status reports on each project. The most crucial component is the updated control chart on the key measure(s) and a statement as to what step of the MVT process that we are currently performing. Figure 25.4 shows a real-life example of a control book format.

Provide Customized, Role-Specific Training for Everyone Involved in MVT Projects

Training must be provided, as appropriate, to those who are involved in MVT process efforts. Some organizations choose to learn the MVT process and, over time, build the internal expertise to perform MVT experimentation with little external support. Other organizations choose to minimize the expenditure of time and effort by their own personnel and rely heavily on external resources.

Regardless of which approach is taken, training should be provided that is:

- *Timely:* It is provided just in time for participation in MVT projects.

Figure 25.4   Example of Control Book Format

Control Book
January 15, 2003

1. Project Name	Good Jobs In Eight
2. Objective	Increase efficiency of techs as measured by the number of good jobs in 8 hours per tech
3. Key Measure(s)	Good Jobs In Eight (GJi8)
4. Potential Payoff	10% Improvement = $100 Million
5. Start Date	December 1, 2001
6. Implementation Date	April 15, 2002
7. Current Step in QualPro's Twelve-Step MVT Process	Step 12

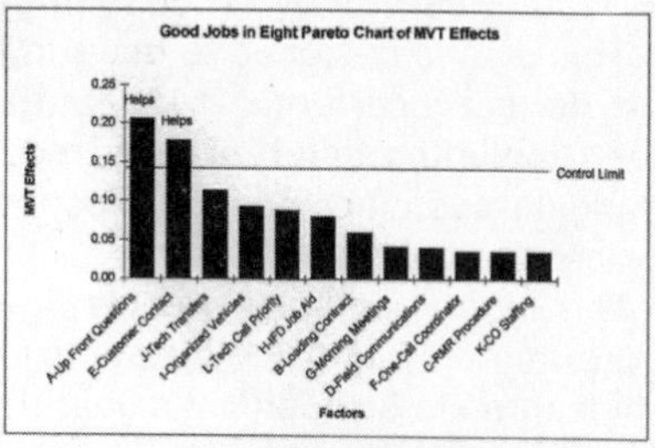

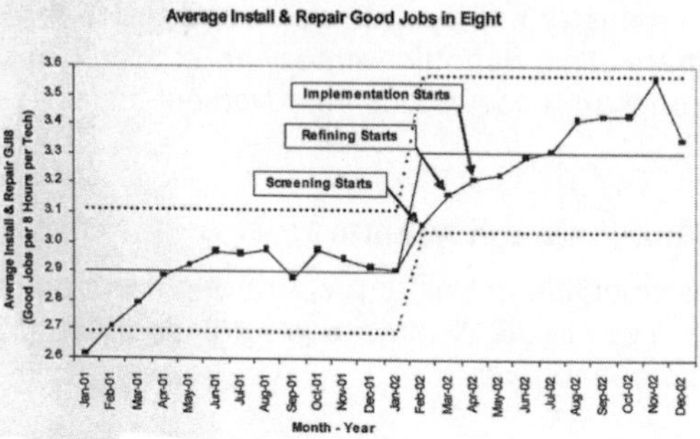

Good Jobs in Eight Pareto Chart of MVT Effects

Average Install & Repair Good Jobs in Eight

Implementation Starts

Refining Starts

Screening Starts

Month - Year

MVT Factors		- Level	+ Level
A	Up Front Questions	No	Yes
B	Loading Contract	No	Yes
C	RMR Procedure	No	Yes
D	COG/Field Communications	No	Yes
E	Customer Contact	No	Yes
F	One-Call Coordinator	No	Yes
G	Morning Meetings	No	Yes
H	IFD Job Aid	No	Yes
I	Organized Vehicles	No	Yes
J	Technician Transfers	No	Yes
K	CO Staffing	No	Yes
L	Tech Call Priority	No	Yes

Winning Factors		- Level	+ Level
A	Up Front Questions	No	Yes
E	Customer Contact	No	Yes

- *Role-specific:* It provides only the knowledge necessary for the specific MVT process tasks that a person will execute.
- *Customized:* It uses examples from the organization's industry/function to which the trainee can easily relate.

In Chapter 26, which describes Phase III, the appropriate training for different situations is discussed in greater detail.

Provide MVT Consultant Support to Guide Projects and/or Develop Internal Expertise

As the MVT process is spread across the organization in Phase III, it is critical that every project be supported by an MVT consultant. This is an investment that will pay for itself many times over and provide tremendous dividends. Any attempt to save a few dollars here is almost certain to result in less-than-desired results. Some companies choose to train internal MVT consultants during Phase III, to support Phase IV MVT projects.

Figure 25.5   Utility Company's Plan for Breakthrough Results

---

QualPro Process Plan for Breakthrough Improvement in Competitive Position by Process Improvement at Utility Company.

This plan is designed to use the MVT process to position the utility company for early performance breakthrough then continuous process improvement (including safety, waste reduction, superior service, adaptability to changing customer needs, expense reduction, financial performance, and competitive rates).

The utility company provides gas, power, water and waste services to approximately 3,000,000 accounts for area businesses and residents. Growth rate is three to five percent a year through building and some re-zoning. Residential customers comprise 65 percent of the total.

Deregulation in the utilities industry has opened new competitive threats and opportunities in recent years. This directly defines the strategic importance of this process breakthrough and continuous improvement plan.

Phase I: Initial Projects for Breakthrough Results

Immediate high priorities to accomplish dramatic breakthrough and demonstrate the power of the MVT process to the organization were identified (from data and interviews with key personnel) as:

- Reduce traffic into field offices
- Reduce power consumption at waste treatment plant
- Reduce installation time for gas service
- Reduce power outages

All four MVT projects are system-wide and meet the criteria of:
- Significant
- Relatable
- Doable

Each project will be sponsored by an executive. Involved personnel will attend working sessions the week of August 5 through 9. Projects will then be managed daily, on-site to achieve completion deadlines in the fourth quarter as detailed in the attached Gantt chart. The output will be a list of what actions have been proven helpful by MVT and a calculation of how much improvement will occur at implementation.

When the implementation is executed, the breakthrough will be confirmed (with control charts and control groups). Implementation will then be monitored to ensure improvement to calculated levels is maintained, using compliance sampling/audits and control charts on key measures.

Finally, the annual return from each project will be calculated and approved by accounting. Project success documentation will then be created for each project that is suitable as a template for future projects.

(continued)

Phase II: Commitment to Company-Wide Rollout

During Phase II, preparatory analyses for Phase III will be conducted as follows:

- Historical data specification and analysis to identify improvement priorities, special causes, and potential factors for experimentation.
- Customer and employee surveys to identify potential needs, wants, and competitive niches.

A year-end session with the executive team will review the Phase I successes, the historical data analysis summary, and the customer and employee survey results. During this work session, the Phase III plan will be constructed. The Phase III plan will then be communicated to the entire organization along with responsibilities and accountability for continuing success. Notice that this is the first formal communication to the organization (whereas Phase I was accomplished without announcement). In this way, the initial management communication is a statement of what has already been accomplished.

The crux of Phase III will be a series of improvement efforts in priority order. Priorities will be established by financial/survey data, overridden as needed by the executive team given strategic considerations.

The Phase III plan will also include a carefully constructed, logistically sound schedule for selected management, technical, and front-line personnel to become involved, beginning with MVT process training/work sessions and first project(s). The master plan for project execution and implementation will also be included. Resources and facilities for the working sessions will be outlined.

Management controls will be established as part of the Phase III plan. These will revolve around a single page per project showing objective, ROI anticipated, chart of key measure (ultimately showing the improvement as it happens), and a list of the MVT factors and results. This "control book" will support easy executive management of the overall improvement effort. It will be reviewed during a one-hour portion of the monthly staff meeting.

Twenty training/work sessions (at an intensity of about one per month) are planned under Phase III with one to four projects initiated in each.

Initial assessment indicates the following are viable Phase III MVT project candidates, subject to confirmation with data and management review:

- Call center productivity
- Line breaks ("dig-ins")
- Laboratory accuracy and precision/measurement control program/calibration management
- Billing accuracy
- Accounts receivables
- Credit decision process
- Safety for craftspeople
- Liabilities and claims (for example, broken curbstones)

(continued)

Figure 25.5 *(Continued)*

- Construction/engineering cycle time (gas, power, and water services).
- Inventory accounting, management, and reduction.
- Maintenance cycle time for customer repair jobs.
- Preventive maintenance effectiveness.
- Chemical costs.
- Customer satisfaction (all services and by service).
- Sales of appliances and supplemental services.
- Meter accuracy and replacement/refurbishment.
- Prescription drug costs.

Phase III: MVT Projects Throughout the Organization

Phase III is outlined in Phase II discussion above. The specific tasks and milestones are as follows:

1. Preparation—Prepare Phase I success documentation and transfer responsibility for maintaining the improvements to line/staff in each area.
2. Key measures—establish in each area so that improvements are measurable and accountable.
3. Communication—publicize Phase I successes and officially release Phase III plan/schedule throughout the organization.
4. Launch MVT Projects—Approximately 40 Phase III improvement projects over two years.
5. Manage, monitor and control the MVT Process improvement effort using the "control book."

Phase IV: Maintain the Gain and Continuously Improve

Phase IV will establish continuous improvement as routine and relentless at the utility company. It will continue processes established in Phase III but with no further need for the training, except for new hires. Executive controls will continue unchanged but will also add a mechanism for selecting additional new projects each year, using repeated analyses of historical data, customer surveys, employee surveys, and financial analysis. Of course, a fundamental component of Phase IV will be the continued maintenance of the gains established in Phases I through III, for each and every process improved, and for the long term. Selected processes will be subject to further improvement through additional refining MVT especially where markets, needs and/or technologies change.

(continued)

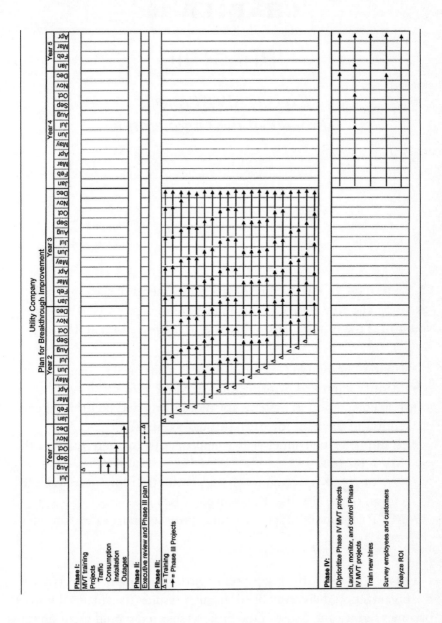

Utility Company
Plan for Breakthrough Improvement

Phase I:
MVT training
Projects
    Traffic
    Consumption
    Installation
    Outages

Phase II:
Executive review and Phase III plan

Phase III:
Δ = Training
→ = Phase III Projects

Phase IV:
ID/prioritize Phase IV MVT projects
Launch, monitor, and control Phase IV MVT projects
Train new hires
Survey employees and customers
Analyze ROI

273

CHAPTER 26

PHASE III

Execute MVT Projects Throughout the Organization

The purpose of Phase III is to have all segments of the organization using the MVT process on high-potential projects. To do this, you utilize the infrastructure that was developed in Phase II.

- Communication and execution of the Plan for Breakthrough Results.
- Identification and prioritization of MVT projects.
- Implementation of systems for monitoring and controlling execution of the Plan for Breakthrough Results.
- Training of personnel that is appropriate to their roles in the MVT process.
- Use of rewards, recognition, and promotion for successful execution of the Plan for Breakthrough Results.
- MVT consultant support to guide projects and/or develop internal expertise.

Phase III is where the big payoff begins. With many projects across the organization delivering breakthrough results, the financial impact becomes significant. Most of the projects selected should focus on improving profitability in order to generate senior management and shareholder interest and enthusiasm for the effort.

COMMUNICATION AND EXECUTION OF THE PLAN FOR BREAKTHROUGH RESULTS

Senior Management Must Communicate the Plan for Breakthrough Results

Phases I and II of the QualPro process primarily involve the senior management team and the personnel involved in the initial MVT projects. In Phase III, the time has come to show and tell everybody. The senior managers should tell everyone in the organization about the need for process improvement, the organization-wide Plan for Breakthrough Results, and the dramatic success of initial efforts. This communication is best conducted in person, by top managers speaking directly to all employees, even if this means that the boss has to come back to talk with the third shift. In very large organizations, the message may have to be videotaped.

In this important communication, facts must support the statements. Employees must understand that this is not just a pep rally, that process improvement is serious business, and that the potential benefits are enormous.

The first thing to be communicated is the proof-of-the-need message developed by senior management. This clearly establishes, for all employees, why the MVT process improvement effort is being launched.

Next, the Plan for Breakthrough Results is explained. It will not take long for employees to figure out that something is about to change. The worst that can happen is that the reasons for change are left to their imaginations. It is important that the employees know what change is occurring, why it is occurring, which results are expected, and what their roles in the change will be. The formal communication of the process improvement plan to employees also provides management the opportunity to establish expectations and to reinforce overall strategies and objectives. This reinforcement is important in developing a clear, consistent message.

Finally, senior managers should share the stories of the organization's initial successes. Communication to everyone in the organization about these successes is vital to initiating the change process. The success stories are the proof of why management is insisting on the use of the MVT process.

As an example, the following initial success stories were very effective in launching the expansion of Pactiv's MVT effort. Bill McBee, head of Pactiv's Hexacomb Division, shared the story of its two initial and significant successes.

The first project focused on the reduction of waste in the Trenton, Illinois, manufacturing facility. The project tested 24 factors in a screening design, followed quickly by a refining experiment on a subset of those 24. In just a few weeks, three winning factors were identified and implemented. They were able to reduce overall waste by 50 percent—which nobody had thought possible—and, at the same time, reduce setup time by 35 percent.

The second project focused on increasing the division's sales. Implementation of the findings from this project increased sales by 18.2 percent. Bill's salesforce tested 23 factors in a 24-run MVT screening experiment, followed by a 7-factor MVT refining experiment that used 16 runs. This project amazed many people, including Bill. It identified winning factors in only eight weeks of experimentation, even though the sales process had a more than 12-month cycle time. Bill summarized the reaction of his senior managers, who also are his lead salespersons: MVT works everywhere and on everything; it produces financial results. By being informed about the organization's Plan for Breakthrough Results, the senior managers could understand it and lead it to success.

IDENTIFICATION AND PRIORITIZATION OF PHASE III PROJECTS

In Phase III, we use the process for identifying and prioritizing MVT projects that was described in the previous chapter. As is true of all MVT projects, Phase III projects should be:

- Significant (deliver big dollars) to the bottom line.
- Able to be done fast—in about two months.
- Understood and related to by people in the organization.

Most Phase III projects should focus on improving profitability; that is, they should have the largest potential dollar returns. Therefore, most Phase III projects increase sales, decrease costs, and/or reduce waste and, consequently, increase profits. However, if the organization has significant problems related to customer dissatisfaction, projects to address those issues also should be included in Phase III.

Although many Phase III projects involve obtaining breakthrough results in existing processes, Phase III also should include projects to design and develop new processes. Many people in today's organizations are creative and can use their imaginations to invent things with exciting possibilities. However, organizations often can't get these things to market with even a fair degree of reliability in a reasonable period of time. The same MVT experimentation that was used to improve carbon foam at Union Carbide can be used to design and develop new processes to produce defect-free products and fast, reliable services. The focus should be on using the MVT process to develop capable, controlled, new processes in half the usual time. And, yes, this can be accomplished in a fraction of the time that design and development currently takes.

IMPLEMENTATION OF SYSTEMS FOR MONITORING AND CONTROLLING EXECUTION OF THE PLAN FOR BREAKTHROUGH RESULTS

Monitoring and controlling execution of the project plans is simple in Phase I, when there are only two projects. As the use of the MVT process is rolled out across an organization, monitoring and controlling require additional time, because more projects and more people are involved. Senior managers generally enjoy this activity; they often feel that they are finally focusing on their real job, that of making the organization better and more profitable.

It is time for the system that was developed in Phase II to be implemented. This almost always involves management reviews. Management reviews usually consist of weekly status and progress reports by each MVT project leader to the project sponsor. Sponsors typically update the senior management team on MVT progress on a monthly basis. In most companies, senior management arranges for a direct presentation of completed MVT projects on a quarterly basis.

The details of monitoring and control plans vary greatly from one organization to another; however, every successful MVT rollout effort has two things in common:

1. Every level of management is aware of MVT activity, progress, and results in its area.
2. Every manager has accountability for the MVT project activity, progress, and achievement of breakthrough results.

Monitoring Return on Investment

There is a definite relationship between process improvement utilizing MVT and financial gain. Senior managers should expect dramatic returns on investment from their improvement efforts. Therefore, each documented success should incorporate a financial assessment and return on investment (ROI) analysis. Ideally, the ROI calculation is the responsibility of the CFO (or his or her designated representative). This ensures that the documented benefits are true dollars going to the bottom line and not "funny money."

TRAINING OF PERSONNEL THAT IS APPROPRIATE TO THEIR ROLES IN THE MVT PROCESS

There is a wide range of training needs and desires in organizations that use the MVT process. Some companies, such as manufacturers, want many of their employees to learn the MVT process. They want those employees to develop the skills to use MVT experiments as part of their everyday work life. They want them to gain the expertise to execute MVT projects with minimal support and guidance from others.

Other companies, such as retailers, tend to be at the opposite extreme. They have no interest in having their employees learn how to use MVT. They want the employees to stay focused on doing their regular jobs. They use external resources to drive MVT projects in order to minimize any drain on the time and energy of their employees.

Most organizations fall between these extremes. They may want to develop moderate levels of skill among many employees and also to develop internal MVT consultants to support ongoing projects. Or they may provide minimal training to most employees and try to develop a cadre of MVT consultants to drive projects focused on specific opportunities.

Regardless of the approach taken, certain commonalities exist. All training needs to be:

- Top-down and just-in-time.
- No more than is needed for the role of each individual.
- Industry/company/function-specific.

Training Should Be Top-Down and Just-in-Time

Some organizations train everyone at once, whether or not all employees will use the learning in the near future. This is a mistake. What typically happens when people cannot immediately apply their learning is that they forget what they have been taught. Then they either become obstacles at a later time or require additional training investment. We have found that the learning is most effective when the employee is immediately assigned to an activity and assisted in the application of the MVT process. After completing two or three improvement efforts, employees generally understand their roles in the MVT process and are confident and competent in carrying them out.

Training must start at the top of the organization, with the CEO and his or her management team, and then cascade throughout the organization. The training must be applied first to work groups that can have the biggest impact on profitability and should be associated with specific MVT projects. The direction and timing of the cascade is determined by the priority of specific process improvement opportunities.

Provide No More Training than Is Needed for Each Individual's Role

As mentioned previously, some organizations have no desire to learn how to use the MVT process and, therefore, no formal training is appropriate. If an organization does intend to learn how to use the MVT process, it is wise to heed the training guidelines that follow.

During Phase II, senior managers are trained in the process concepts. The targets for training in Phase III are all managers, supervisors, technical staff, other professionals, and local workforce members who are involved in MVT projects. These people are responsible for managing, leading, and participating in the application of the MVT process. These also are the people who will take the message about MVT to the local workforce.

Basically, training is divided into five categories:

1. Executive briefings for senior managers.
2. Training in the essentials of the MVT process for mid- and upper-level managers.
3. Complete MVT-process training for project leaders, technical staff, and highly involved management and professional personnel.
4. Training in the basics of the MVT process for members of the local workforce.
5. In-depth, advanced MVT-process training for internal MVT consultants.

Table 26.1 shows the recommended training for the first four roles. Training for internal MVT consultants is described later in this chapter.

Training Should Be Industry/Company/Function-Specific

We have found that individuals at the tops of organizations and those at the lower levels have trouble relating to MVT process improvement efforts unless we provide training that uses materials that match their businesses. In short, senior managers and local workforce personnel do not tolerate generic instruction. If training materials are customized to use their language and their examples, they can learn. Although engineers can handle generic instruction, even they fare better if their training is in their company's or industry's language.

People in the chemical industry are making stuff; they don't relate to manufacturing examples of people making things. People in service industries have trouble with examples from paper or textile plants or steel mills. As a result of this finding, in 1985 we began to offer industry-specific instruction. It's like going to another country; you

Table 26.1   Recommended Training for Each MVT Process Role

Training	Senior managers and sponsors	Mid- and upper-level managers, factor owners, and data owners	Project leaders, technical staff, and highly involved management and professional personnel	Local workforce
Executive Briefing (1–2 days)	X			
Essentials of the MVT Process (3 days)		X		
Preparation for MVT (3 days)			X	
The MVT Process (3 days)			X	
Improving Measurement Systems (3 days)			X	
MVT for the Local Workforce (1 day)				X

get along better if you speak the language. There's no way to understand all the details if you must suffer through translation.

QualPro starts to customize its training materials by spending two or more weeks inside an organization. Our consultants observe, gather data, ask questions, listen, pick up buzzwords, and note all organization-specific language. Survey information also is used to customize training materials to fit the organization.

USE OF REWARDS, RECOGNITION, AND PROMOTION FOR SUCCESSFUL EXECUTION OF THE PLAN FOR BREAKTHROUGH RESULTS

In Phase III, we put to use the rewards, recognition, and promotions system that we designed in Phase II. The organization's senior management has communicated, through the action plan, that effective use of the MVT process to achieve breakthrough results will be an important component of job reviews, recognition, compensation, and promotions. Now comes the fun part: sharing the rewards and the glory. Those organizations that reward MVT-process successes have much greater returns on their investments than those that do not.

MVT CONSULTANT SUPPORT TO GUIDE PROJECTS AND/OR DEVELOP INTERNAL EXPERTISE

After employees have completed role-specific training, they know just enough to be dangerous. Every MVT project must have the guidance of an MVT consultant.

Just as you would not want a person who has completed flight training and effectively flown a simulator to pilot a commercial jet, or a person who has just graduated from medical school to be your primary heart surgeon, you would not want to put your business results, your reputation, and your career in the hands of a recently trained process improvement novice. People who are learning MVT expertise must have the guidance of an experienced expert to ensure success.

Training Internal MVT Consultants

Many companies want to develop their own MVT process experts to serve as internal MVT consultants. This is a practical objective and can reduce or even eliminate the need for external resources in the long term. The time and effort required to develop the expertise of an MVT consultant should not be underestimated. Substantial classroom training must be supplemented by an apprenticeship under the guidance of an experienced and successful MVT consultant.

MVT consultant candidates need strong quantitative capabilities (scoring in at least the 90th percentile in the Graduate Record Exam), outgoing personalities, strong work ethics, project-management ability, enough business experience to communicate with managers, and inherent curiosity. Table 26.2 shows the requirements of the Qual-Pro certification program to develop client MVT consultants.

Table 26.2   Requirements of the QualPro Certification Program for
Development of Client MVT Consultants

Trainee Phase

Required courses:
- Induction Workshop (1 day).
- Preparation for MVT Seminar (3 days).
- The MVT Process Seminar (3 days).
- Improving Measurement Systems Seminar (3 days).
- Team Process Seminar (3 days).
- Advanced MVT Preparation Seminar (3 days).
- Advanced MVT Process Seminar (3 days).
- Regression for the MVT Process (5 days).
- Multivariate Methods for the MVT Process (5 days).
- Management of the MVT Process (5 days).

Elective courses (choose any five):
- Strategic MVT Process Planning (2 days).
- MVT Process for Managers in Manufacturing Industries (3 days).
- MVT Process for Managers in Service Industries (3 days).
- Preparation for MVT Process for Manufacturing (3 days).
- Preparation for MVT Process for Service & Administrative (3 days).
- Preparation for MVT Process for Marketing & Sales (3 days).
- Preparation for MVT Process for Chemical (3 days).
- Preparation for MVT Process for Electronics (3 days).
- Preparation for MVT Process for Maintenance (3 days).
- Preparation for MVT Process for Paper (3 days).
- Preparation for MVT Process for Apparel & Textile (3 days).
- Preparation for MVT Process for Health Care (3 days).
- Preparation for MVT Process for Telecommunications (3 days).
- Preparation for MVT Process for Clinical Procedures (3 days).
- The MVT Process for Manufacturing (3 days).
- The MVT Process for Service (3 days).
- The MVT Process for Textile (3 days).
- The MVT Process for Marketing & Sales (3 days).
- The MVT Process for Paper (3 days).
- The MVT Process for Chemical (3 days).
- The MVT Process for Telecommunications (3 days).
- The MVT Process for Research & Development (5 days).
- Finding Special Causes of Uncontrolled Variation (3 days).
- Company-wide Quality Function Deployment (3 days).
- Customer Satisfaction Survey Techniques (3 days).

Two observation projects:
1. Written Success Story Reports.
2. Oral Presentation.

Comprehensive exam

(continued)

Table 26.2 *(Continued)*

Intern Phase

Supervised project #1:
1. Project initiation form approval.
2. Monthly written updates.
3. Written Success Story Report.

Supervised project #2:
1. Project initiation form approval.
2. Monthly written updates.
3. Written Success Story Report.

Oral presentation/defense of one supervised project

Two solo projects:
1. Project initiation form approval.
2. Monthly written updates.
3. Written Success Story Report.
4. Oral and Written Project Presentation/Defense.

Annual certification:
- Written Success Story Report.
- QualPro Leadership Symposium participation.
- QualPro Leadership Symposium presentation.

Requirements for QualPro's own MVT consultants are well beyond this curriculum.

Some may think that these requirements are extreme, but our experience tells us that this is the absolute minimum required to produce effective MVT consultants.

Obviously, organizations that have high turnover rates probably should not invest the time, effort, and money to develop MVT consultant skills in individuals who may take their expertise to other companies. But regardless of whether a company chooses to develop internal MVT consultants or use external resources, it is critical that this expert guidance be provided to support every MVT project.

CHAPTER 27

PHASE IV

Maintain the Gains, Prioritize MVT Opportunities, and Continuously Improve

In Phase IV, the gains continue to escalate. The benefits of Phase I and Phase III projects continue to be enjoyed. Previous successes are added to by refining previous learning and/or testing new ideas. New MVT initiatives are launched as additional, high-priority opportunities are identified.

PROJECT SELECTION

During Phase III, most projects are focused on improving profitability. As Phase IV unfolds, we continue to initiate projects that have large profit potential, but projects that strive to improve customer satisfaction and the organization's competitive position represent a greater portion of the project mix.

Focus on the Customers

During Phase IV, we begin to execute MVT projects that combine the organization's processes with those of its customers. This combination enables us to optimize the output of the customers' processes and, in turn, makes the organization a much more valuable supplier to its customers, greatly strengthening the bonds between the organization and its customers and building a whole new level of loyalty to its products. It often increases the perceived value of its products to the point that a larger share of the customers' business can be enjoyed.

MVT Process Improvement Program for Suppliers

If possible, the MVT process should be used on a combination of the organization's processes and those of its suppliers. This allows the optimization of the organization's output and identifies new ways in which suppliers can help improve the organization's results.

Note that this comes after the organization has gained experience in using the MVT process to improve its own existing processes and has launched some efforts to better satisfy its customers. The payoffs from instigating an MVT process improvement program with suppliers will not be quick. However, the payoff will be large. And it is a logical next step in the organization-wide MVT process improvement program.

Invariably, during its own MVT efforts, the organization will identify areas in which it requires improvements from a supplier in order to improve its own results. When that happens, the organization must insist on improvement from the supplier. The only way that the improvement can be achieved effectively and in time is to use the MVT process on a combination of the organization's process and the process of its supplier.

The organization should encourage, and possibly require, the supplier to begin its own, independent, MVT process improvement effort. This will pay great dividends for the supplier and the organization in the long run.

In some cases, big customers have simply dictated that suppliers embark on continuous-improvement programs. For example, in the early 1980s, large auto manufacturers demanded statistical evidence of quality at the supply level, and the payoff was remarkable. If they had been using the MVT process, the payoff would have been even greater. Much of what they told suppliers to improve did not really improve the automobile manufacturers' products.

QualPro worked with a company that supplied transmissions to auto manufacturers. The car builders provided all the specifications of transmission components and asked for statistical evidence of quality. They wanted that hole to be this diameter with this tolerance. They wanted control charts to show how much variation there was in a month's worth of production. The transmission company did what was demanded, yet complaints from automobile purchasers increased. "My transmission leaks." "My transmission makes strange noises." The supplier worked diligently to reduce variations, to meet exactly the requirements handed down by the manufacturers. The automobile manufacturers eventually learned that they had been working on the wrong things. They had developed the mandate for suppliers before they obtained information about what was important to their customers. A small effort with customers in the beginning would have provided the proper objectives. This, along with MVT experimentation on the combination of the auto manufacturers' and transmission supplier's processes, would have quickly led to transmissions that didn't leak or make funny noises. The auto manufacturers would have had satisfied customers and would have greatly reduced warranty costs. Instead, they spent years of their efforts and those of their supplier in vain.

Suppliers think that customers are important, yet some customers are reluctant to ask suppliers to do anything more than take their money. If customers need better performance from their suppliers, they often just need to ask for it. For example, I worked for a year trying to get a smaller company to tell a big chemical company what it expected in the products it purchased. Finally, a meeting was arranged. The big company sent a representative who said that he wanted to make his position clear, that the customer was very important and the big company was very willing to cooperate in any way possible to do what was wanted . . . that the smaller company's business was very important to the big company . . . that if the smaller company wanted the big company to change something to help improve the quality of a product, all it had to do was ask. I thought that I knew well in advance what the big company would say and do. I knew it had heard about satisfying customers. That's how the big company got to be a big company.

However, there were surprised expressions on the faces of the managers from the smaller company. They didn't believe what they were hearing. They expected the big company to say, "Take it or leave it; this is how it is." They had no idea that their company was so important.

This lack of communication really gets bad when related companies are in a customer-supplier arrangement and top managers don't enforce, from either direction, the customer's right to spell out what it wants and needs. This undoubtedly leads to products with severe deficiencies.

Use the MVT Process to Increase Your Customers' Sales

You can use the MVT process to determine what the customers of your customers want. Go to your customers and volunteer to use the MVT process to improve their sales. Brainstorm and select ideas that you can execute and that your customer is interested in testing. Include both organizations' ideas in the same MVT experimentation. The measurement is your customer's sales. Once the findings are in, both you and your customer should implement the helpful actions. Your customer's sales will go up, and, of course, your sales to the customer will go up, too.

QualPro helped a large commercial bakery to do exactly that. The bakery sold cakes, doughnuts, and pastries to supermarket chains that sold them in their delicatessen sections. The bakery's president went to a large supermarket chain and said, "I have something that will increase your sales by 5 to 25 percent. It's called MVT and it won't cost you a penny. Are you interested?" The supermarket chain said, "Yes."

The two organizations jointly tested over 20 ideas. Some originated with the bakery and some from the supermarket chain. Seven of the ideas increased sales of certain products or the overall deli operation. After the winning ideas were implemented, the supermarket chain's sales increased by $35 million per year, and its profits increased by $22 million per year. The bakery's sales to the supermarket chain also increased dramatically. Even more importantly, it cemented the bakery's relationship with its customer.

COMMUNICATE SUCCESSES INSIDE AND OUTSIDE THE ORGANIZATION

Success stories are necessary to get the MVT effort started, and they are necessary to keep it energized. People will try very hard for only a little while on the faith that something will work. Soon, they demand results. It is that way in football; practice intensity drops off quickly if the team fails to win. People need to see continuing success to be sure that it is still happening. Put the department, division, and organization-wide success stories in the company newsletter, on bulletin boards, and in a video message that is played in the lunchroom or at regular meetings. Recognize those who accomplish exceptional results. Give the others something good to see and talk about. Nothing begets success like success.

It also is important to extend communication about process improvement results to customers and potential customers. After the organization has advanced from limited MVT projects to a company-wide process improvement effort, talked about its MVT process improvement successes internally, offered proof of its progress to those involved, and everybody is working on continual improvement and good things are happening, it is time to advertise. The best thing that can happen after an MVT process improvement effort is for the organization's customers to brag about it to their colleagues and friends. There is no better advertising than to have customers tell potential customers about your products or services.

It is time to tell the organization's customers about the significant improvements and observe their reactions. For example: "We had Tide, but now we have Ultra-Tide. We know it works better and we want to prove it to you." "Look at these new towels; they are stronger and fluffier to better satisfy your needs. Try them and tell us what you think. Better yet, tell others."

This opens the door to some more surveying. Ask potential customers what they think about the samples and how they compare with what the customers have been using. What else could the organization do to improve its product or service? What would the customer like that nobody is offering yet? This information will help the organization to make even better products and improve its services. It will gain new customers and sell more to existing customers.

TRAIN PERSONNEL AND NEW HIRES

If the organization is working to learn the MVT process, the training effort will continue into Phase IV. Employees at various levels who will be involved in MVT projects but have not yet been trained should now be trained as their projects are initiated. New hires and persons whose roles have changed also should be trained appropriately.

Some organizations decide that those who have not been involved in MVT projects and do not appear to be likely participants in future projects should, nevertheless, be exposed to MVT "awareness" training. This training typically is short, maybe two hours, and provides a very brief introduction to the MVT process so that the employees can communicate with others in the organization.

HAVE INTERNAL MVT CONSULTANTS STEP IN

If, during Phase III, internal MVT consultants have been in training, they are able to begin fulfilling their roles in guiding MVT projects during Phase IV. They will continue to need support and guidance from external MVT consultants, but on a less frequent basis.

HAVE AN EXTERNAL MVT CONSULTANT PERIODICALLY AUDIT YOUR MVT PROCESS IMPROVEMENT EFFORT

Even after you have trained internal MVT consultants, you will need to have an external MVT consultant periodically audit your MVT process improvement efforts and suggest ways to improve them. Even the best companies get off track now and then. They may miss the obvious. They may forget to follow through on something. An outsider may catch a shortcoming that the organizational members have been looking at for months. And the payoff may be great. In addition, there will be new things to see, new things to try, and minor adjustments to be made.

CONTINUE TO SURVEY CUSTOMERS AND EMPLOYEES

There is great value in continuing to survey customers and employees. If you ask, you are likely to discover problems before they become monsters, when they can be treated simply and swiftly. The aim is to identify anything that helps or hurts the process improvement effort. Find the things that need to be done in order to make the push for breakthrough results go more smoothly.

There is another benefit from continuing to survey customers and employees. It tells all concerned that the organization is thinking long range, that it is in the MVT process improvement business for keeps.

We recommend surveying employees and customers annually. Some organizations that are really serious about doing things to better satisfy customers and gain greater shares of the market survey them more often.

Surveying the customer base annually might be enough, but there also is a case for doing special surveys. If you are considering a new product or service, ask some questions before starting design and development. An intelligent survey can prevent serious blunders. Responses to a customer survey also may reveal that surprising changes have taken place in a year. You may find that what satisfied a customer six months ago isn't enough to keep that customer satisfied now. Wants and needs can change rapidly. New needs arise. Something may have changed in a customer's business that nobody thought to tell you about. Even in our business, we may develop something that works perfectly for three years, and then a survey will show us several things that could be improved.

We have never done an employee survey without discovering some unexpected information. Often, those who do the work see problems that management is not aware of. The view from the top office may lead a boss to think that a process improvement effort is working flawlessly, but an employee survey may reveal major problems.

Workers also can offer suggestions that will improve efficiency and reduce costs. I remember one survey in which an employee said that the company should have a backup copy of a computer program that covered accounts receivable. The employee said that a computer crash would cause an enormous problem. Everybody knows this now, but the company hadn't thought about it at the time. Management ordered the backup copies to be made. It wasn't three months before there was a power problem and everything in the computer was lost. It would have been a disaster without the backup copies.

Common sense dictates that someone outside the organization must conduct the survey. Otherwise, employees will be reluctant to say what they really think.

CONTINUE TO PLAN, MONITOR, CONTROL, AND REWARD

In describing Phase III, I emphasized the importance of planning and choosing good projects, of monitoring and controlling to ensure proper execution of the MVT process, and of rewarding success to reinforce positive behaviors and results. In Phase IV, all these activities are still as important. It is crucial that they be maintained year after year. Selection of MVT projects should be an integral part of the annual planning cycle. Monitoring and controlling MVT projects should be an essential task and high priority for every manager. Rewards for achieving breakthrough performance using the MVT process should be built into the very fabric of the organization. If attention is paid to these critical activities, the MVT process will still be paying great dividends five years from now and 25 years from now.

CHAPTER 28

THE PAYOFF

*Higher Revenues, Lower Costs,
Improved Profitability, and Increased
Shareholder Value*

A t the beginning of this book, I said that I was going to make an outlandish claim—that the MVT process is the greatest business-improvement methodology ever devised. I hope that you now understand why I would make such a claim and that you agree that the statement is not really outlandish. This chapter summarizes some things about why that claim is true and adds further information to support it.

THE MVT PROCESS IS AN AMAZINGLY POWERFUL TOOL

- *It yields big results.* The MVT process provides breakthrough levels of improvement. Testing dozens of ideas at once and implementing the 25 percent that are winners generates astounding increases in sales, remarkable reductions in waste, and unheard-of improvements in profitability.
- *It works every time.* MVT users testify that the MVT process works without fail. In fact, if 20 ideas for improvement are tested, the odds are 1,048,576 to 1 that the MVT process will find one or more ideas that significantly improves results.

- *It improves any process.* The track record of the MVT process is excellent. MVT has demonstrated the ability to improve any conceivable process, in any company, in any industry.
- *It provides counterintuitive learning.* Testing large numbers of practical, fast, and cost-free ideas virtually always reveals surprising findings. Testing one idea at a time, as is done by many companies, will never uncover synergies between ideas or processes.
- *It translates to the real world.* Findings from the MVT process always work when applied in the real world. Ideas that are helpful in both rounds of MVT experiments, while being tested along with dozens of other ideas, have at least a 400-to-1 chance of actually improving results.
- *It accomplishes fast improvement.* The MVT process accelerates learning by testing large numbers of ideas simultaneously. Fast improvement is ensured by testing only the ideas that can be implemented immediately.
- *It has a great track record.* MVT experimentation and implementation have been successful for over 13,000 processes in more than 1,000 companies during the past 23 years.

AN ORGANIZATION-WIDE ROLLOUT GENERATES INCREDIBLE ACCOMPLISHMENTS

- *It creates a can-do culture.* Everyone wants to be a winner, and almost everyone likes to be a part of a winning team. There is no better way to win at work than to be involved in an MVT-project success. People are always excited to accomplish breakthrough results that were believed to be impossible. The MVT process creates an environment in which employees are never satisfied with the status quo.
- *It creates greater customer satisfaction.* When organizations use the MVT process to improve customer satisfaction, they find that they delight customers well beyond the customers' expectations. Customer relationships are strengthened and that always results in increased business over the long term.

- *It generates higher revenues.* Invariably, when the MVT process is focused on projects that are aimed at increasing sales, remarkable improvements are achieved. Whether the sales channel is retail, business-to-business, a call center, a salesforce, the Internet, or direct mail, the MVT process always achieves breakthrough results.
- *It reduces costs.* Whether it is through reducing waste, increasing efficiency, or raising productivity, when the MVT process is directed at these objectives, dramatic progress is always the outcome.
- *It improves profitability.* If a company sells more, lowers the costs of doing business, better satisfies its customers, and has a more efficient workforce, the result has to be greater profitability. MVT delivers all these results.
- *It results in increased shareholder value.* Increased shareholder value is the ultimate objective of the MVT process. When improvements are implemented and profits increase, enhanced stock value is the inevitable result. When MVT process accomplishments are communicated to the business community, the value of the company is increased even more.

THE GREATEST IMPACTS OF THE MVT PROCESS HAVE YET TO BE REALIZED

- *MVT is an underutilized resource.* My employees and my directors kept asking me, "Why are you writing a book?" The answer is simple: I truly believe that the world needs MVT, and very few people know of its existence, much less its power. My hope is that this book will help to overcome the lack of awareness of MVT and that the increased use of this astounding technology will help people and companies throughout the world.
- *MVT should be used in every business.* Every business, no matter what its product or service, can benefit tremendously from using the MVT process. Every manufacturing plant needs to reduce defects, reduce waste, increase throughput, reduce environmental problems, decrease costs, improve maintenance, improve

measurement systems, improve sales, raise customer satisfaction, and improve profitability. Every service company needs to improve efficiency, improve customer satisfaction, improve marketing, improve sales, reduce costs, and improve profitability. You get the idea. Everybody has a lot to gain by learning how to get better at what he or she does.

- *MVT should be used for the public good.* Many of the problems that affect society could be solved by using the MVT process. If the MVT process were used extensively in the healthcare industry, we could reduce costs and dramatically improve outcomes. We could eliminate the healthcare crisis in this country. If the MVT process were used in developing prescription drugs, we could decrease development time by a factor of five and costs by a factor of two. At the same time, we could eliminate most of the undesirable side effects. If the MVT process were used in public education, we could improve learning tremendously and reduce costs while paying higher salaries to good teachers. The MVT process even could be used to make order-of-magnitude improvements in the most inefficient process in most countries: the judicial system. The time required to handle cases and the cost to society could be cut by a factor of 10 while, at the same, the justice dispensed could be improved. As with business processes, every public-interest process could be made more effective. The bottom line is that all of our lives could be better.

APPENDIX

PARTIAL LISTING OF PRESENTATIONS FROM QUALPRO'S ANNUAL LEADERSHIP SYMPOSIUMS

Company	Title of Presentation	Accomplishments
American Express	Outbound Telemarketing	Conversion increased 300% while several costly activities in the current process were eliminated. Profit impact was $11.7 million per year.
American Express	Transforming "Likely Attritors" into Loyal Cardmembers	Call center experiment leads to an 18% decrease in customer attrition worth over $1 million in fee revenue annually.
American Media	Improve Retail Sales	Changes in magazine placement in aisles, a large cover size, and a different display increased sales over 10% or $21 million in revenues.
American Media	Subscription Renewals	Direct mail MVT achieved a 50% increase in renewals and a large drop in mailing costs. Keeping clients was much cheaper than winning new ones.
BASF Corporation	By-Products Reduced 20% While Increasing Yield 1.5%	Moving a process operation from "near" optimum to "at" optimum results in savings of $150,000 per year (reducing by-product by 20% and increasing yield by 1.5%.)
BASF Corporation	Chemical Process Yields Increased	10% decrease in the amount of heavies formed, 20% increase in the conversion of heavies to product, savings in raw material alone close to $500,000.
BASF Corporation	Featured Speaker	MVT efforts have yielded tens of millions of dollars in accumulated benefits.
BASF-Freeport	Cost Savings and Capital Avoidance in Chemical Process	Increased production and improved yields result in manufacturing savings of over $600,000 while avoiding potential $750,000 capital expense.
BASF-Huntington, WV	Alkali Blue Color Reduced Rejects	Reject rate reduced from 15% to 7% with screening findings and further reduced to 4% with refining experiments.
Beaulieu	Carpet Soiling	Soiling claims were reduced 75% and a monitoring program was implemented to maintain the improvement.
Beaulieu	Machine Efficiency/ Maintenance	Scheduled maintenance was reduced from 60 minutes to 20 minutes, improved output per man-hour, increased throughput, and reduced seconds.

(Continued)

Company	Title of Presentation	Accomplishments
BellSouth	BBI	Company reduced every time measurement by 60% and reduced post office rejects by 50%. Bills went out quicker, customers paid quicker, resulting in savings of $1 million per year.
BellSouth	Phone Center Sales Yields $47 Million	Revenue per hour was increased 33%, contributing $47 million per year to the company's bottom line. Testing was done at the best performing center in the company to demonstrate the potential of MVT to gain improvement for even the best performers.
BellSouth	Reducing Circuit Outages	Repair time for circuit type A was reduced 20%, circuit type B was reduced 60%, and circuit type C was reduced 50%, thus protecting a $4 billion business.
BellSouth	Reducing Repeat Reports	Repeat trouble reports were reduced by 42%, while unexpectedly reducing the time per task by 10%. The total savings amounted to $1.3 million per year.
BellSouth	The Labyrinth of Customer Service	Service reps had over 800 suggestions. MVT identified those which helped reduce repeat calls by 50%.
Boise	Finding the Best Sales Force Incentive Program Increases Sales 20%	Understanding key drivers maximizes incentive program return with sales rep performance increasing by 20%.
Boise Cascade	Featured Speaker	Increased production, decreased costs, and improved product quality valued at tens of millions of dollars.
Boise Cascade	Wood Chips	With almost no additional cost, one small change improved chip quality 80%, which saved over $180,000 per year.
Boise Cascade, International Falls	Neighborhood Watch— Do You Know Where Your CE Is?	Increased pulp production results in an annualized savings of $1.6 million.
Boise Cascade, International Falls	Paper Mill Fiber Losses Down 60%	Fiber losses down 60%, valued at $997,920 per year.

(Continued)

(Continued)

Company	Title of Presentation	Accomplishments
Boise Cascade, Jackson	J-3 Surface Size	After four years of continuous process improvement success at this site, still achieved $1.3 million per year in savings.
Boise Cascade, Jackson	Optimizing for World Class Performance	Cost-benefit analysis on the J3 Paper Machine for a cost avoidance of $2 million.
Boise Cascade, Jackson	Pulp Mill Optimization	Reduced chemical usage in the bleaching process by 15%.
Boise Cascade, Jackson	Recycle Improvement	Production increased 110% while decreasing costs and improving quality. Achieved savings by avoiding equipment modifications and reduced raw material and energy costs. Bottom line showed a $4 million per year benefit.
Boise Cascade, Jackson	Recycle Plant	By focusing on factors influencing yield and furnish cost, the off-quality rate was reduced and saved the plant over $1.8 million.
Boise Cascade, Jackson	Reduction in Cost of Recycled Fiber	Reduced the cost-per-ton of recycled fiber for over $5 million in total savings.
Boise Office Solutions	Call Center Sales Increase by 50%	Call centers increase paper sales to mid-size customers by 50%.
Boise Paper	Change Times Reduced 19% and Energy Costs Lowered	Reduced change times by 19% and substantially lowered energy costs, worth more than a quarter of a million dollars.
Boise Paper	Paper Mill Generates Economic and Quality Benefits	St. Helens has generated economic benefits for the company and quality benefits for the customer.
Boise, Wallula	All Tied Up	Over 1,500 tons per year of waste was eliminated by solving a 20-year old problem.
Capstone Turbine	Introducing MVT Into a Start Up Culture	Production and reliability issues were resolved resulting in increased production and improved customer satisfaction.
Capstone Turbine	Featured Speaker	MVT helping to continuously improve reliability and efficiency in power generation equipment. MVT being used in product development and improved customer satisfaction.
Capstone Turbine	Manufacturing Streamlined While Failure Rate Reduced to Zero	Failure rate of a shaft was reduced to zero, while eliminating an entire production operation.

(Continued)

Company	Title of Presentation	Accomplishments
Capstone Turbine	Record Levels of Yield and Output Rates	A dozen MVT experiments drove total plant yield and output rates to unprecedented levels.
Capstone Turbine	Setting the Environment in a High Tech World	Product introduction time is being reduced from ten years to two months while revenues are increased 7X.
Cendant Corporation	Call Center Nets Highest Net Present Value	Travel service enhanced with continuously improved service and brought more value to members.
Champion International	Machine K Number	Testing determined high variability in the K-Number procedure itself. A new K-Number procedure was developed. Variability was reduced from 194% to 15% total, which permitted the plant to improve capability.
Champion International	Oxygen Delignification	Testing indicated that much of the problem was due to variability of the measurement system itself. Once that was corrected, several significant process factor changes yielded an improvement of $870,000 for each percent improved.
Cingular	Retail Outlets Increase Cellular Sales	Actions were identified which are expected to substantially increase retail sales.
Circuit City	Featured Speaker	Identified individual actions that have led to greater sales force productivity and increased store sales.
Citibank	Inbound Call Center Sales Increased 20%	20% increase in sales has the potential to deliver millions of dollars to the bottom line. An unexpected bonus was that employee satisfaction also improved.
Deluxe Corporation	Business NAK	A new business kit increased dollars per order by 28% with a predicted value of $8 million.
Deluxe Corporation	Client Partnership Yields 25% Accuracy Increase	Improving bank customer check printing accuracy saves Deluxe $106,928 per year and one of their banking clients $241,856.
Deluxe Corporation	Customers Retained and Costs Reduced Through Service Processes	Retention rates of "at risk" customers raised from 90% to 96% increasing retention revenue by $2.1 million to date. Customer use of voice response unit increased 15%, saving $500,000. Manual intervention in automated order entry system cut 75%, saving $750,000 per year.

(Continued)

(Continued)

Company	Title of Presentation	Accomplishments
Deluxe Corporation	FI Employee Credits	Testing indicated that zero credits was possible. Credits being issued immediately after the test were down 40% from previous levels and dropping steadily with an ultimate potential savings of $1.5 million per year.
Deluxe Corporation	Improved Call Center Sales Worth a Million	Establishing a selling environment with the right mix of elements impacts the bottom line.
Deluxe Corporation	More Clients Sign Contracts Without Account Manager Involved	Improved contract-signing rate while minimizing labor costs (number of contracts needing account manager intervention improved by 15%.)
Deluxe Corporation	Plant Throughput	Cost per production unit was reduced $0.23 per unit with an estimated worth of $19 million.
Deluxe Corporation	Reduce Rework, Improve Customer Satisfaction	Client data setup errors reduced 33% for an annualized savings of $512,000 in internal costs and improved customer satisfaction.
Deluxe Corporation	Reducing Waste	Reduced waste by 90%, saving $9.8 million per year.
Deluxe Corporation	Revenue per Order Increased 22% in Just Six Weeks	Increased revenue per order by 22% and annualized revenue gain of $457,000.
Deluxe Corporation	Selling/Marketing Mix Improved During Testing of New Product Viability	Identified actions to increase sign-up for a new product while revealing tactics that would be a non-productive investment
Deluxe Corporation	Software Errors Reduced in Half	Reduced by half the number of defects introduced in a newly developed software release.
DuPont	Apply MVT—It Just Makes the Process Run Better	Consistent application of MVT in the process creates more and more savings, well over $1 million per year of recurring improvement.
DuPont	Intricate Process Tackled by MVT Methods	After more than 30 years of frustrating experience, MVT identified improvements which increased capacity 5%.
DuPont	Maintenance as a Process	Pump failures were reduced by a factor of 5, which reduced maintenance cost $450,000 annually.

(Continued)

Company	Title of Presentation	Accomplishments
DuPont	Seaford Rug Product Process	First Pass Pounds and First Pass Yield increased 2.8%, which was worth $1.43 million.
DuPont Ag Products, Manati	Decreasing the Amount of Variation in Bulk Density	Variation was reduced by one-half, enabling savings of over $1 million and decreasing cycle time by 10 days for the product.
Du Pont, Cape Fear	Run Time Improvement	Run time was improved by 30% with no cost increase or capital expenditure. Capacity was increased by 40 million pounds.
DuPont, Chambers Works	Silane	$586,000 of direct product improvement, $250,000 waste reduction, and $2 million in downstream savings.
DuPont, Chattanooga	T31 Spinning	Over 20% improvement was achieved on the spinning process yield. Wound was increased over 18%.
DuPont, DeLisle	A Problem that Wouldn't Stay Solved	$5 million per year savings by virtually eliminating a constant problem.
DuPont Engineering Polymers	Featured Speaker	Problems that have been around 20 to 30 years solved in three to six months.
DuPont, LaPorte	Incinerator Capacity	Reduced measurement variation from 75% to less than 1%, tripled capacity, increased feed rate, and reduced cycle time resulting in an immediate savings of over $1 million per year without additional costs.
DuPont, LaPorte	Incredible Savings Using DOE with an Unstable Process	A "Hail Mary" design of experiments improves first grade material yield from 45% to 92%, saving over $1 million per year in product downgrading and unneeded blending.
DuPont, LaPorte	Lannate	Purchases of replacement product were reduced $9.1 million and additional sales with increased production were $1.7 million. Total value $10.8 million.
DuPont, LaPorte	Shutdown by EPA Averted	Averted a regulatory shutdown and saved the business unit $300,000 per day in product replacement costs and a potential $5 million business loss.
DuPont, LaPorte	Waste Water Contaminant Reduced	Decreased contaminant 98.8%, avoiding investment for a new waste treatment facility and without increasing other costs. Savings of $450,000 per year and no problem with future EPA compliance.

(Continued)

(Continued)

Company	Title of Presentation	Accomplishments
DuPont, Martinsville	Creel Waste	Stringout time was reduced 22% leading to a 2% increase in yield and a 59% reduction in creel waste worth over $770,000.
DuPont, Martinsville	Transfer Tail Rejects	Reject rate was reduced 43.3% on one machine and 32.8% on another to collectively increase yield 1.02%.
DuPont, Martinsville	Type 29 Yarn	A 15.4% increase in interlace with a 59.5% reduction in interface variance was achieved. This was worth $500,000 per year in reduced claims plus $100,000 saving in compressed air cost.
DuPont, Mobile	Catalyst Recovery	The process was fine-tuned to a point in which no further purchases were required. An additional $150,000 of catalyst was recovered.
DuPont, Mobile	Improve Quality in Product Expansion	A significant quality problem was eliminated within two months without increasing cost. Significant money was saved in rework cost and shipping delays.
DuPont PI	Along the Customer-Supplier Chain	A 40% reduction was achieved in customer problems, a 30% reduction in product defects, and $600,000 of increased annual revenue.
DuPont, Parkersburg	Reducing Catalyst Consumption	Implemented a no-cost action which reduced the amount of catalyst consumed by 20%, reduced the variation in consumption by 50%, and saved more than $750,000 per year.
DuPont, Parkersburg	Delrin Polymerizer Run Life	Run life of the polymerizers was increased 93%, saving $8 million per year in labor and increasing production $18 million per year.
DuPont, Parkersburg	Increased the Production of HFP to Avoid a $7 Million Capital Expenditure	Five factors were identified as significant and carried into refining. The capital expenditure was not necessary.
DuPont, Parkersburg	Teflon FEP	Increased production rate by 38% which improved earnings $5 million per year at one site alone.
DuPont, VESPEL	Parts and Shapes	Product yield improved from 80% to over 99% earning DuPont's Engineering Excellence Award.

(Continued)

Company	Title of Presentation	Accomplishments
DuPont, Victoria	$15 Million Improvement in a 25-Year Old Process	Over $15 million per year in improved yields and efficiencies in a 25-year old process. MVT upset conventional wisdom about several operating procedures that resulted in an immediate $4 million per year savings.
Dyno Nobel	When You Are Last, You Have to Work at Being the Best	Four factors in a decades old process were identified as creating great variance. Correction of these factors greatly reduced process variation.
Elo TouchSystems	Increased Yield	Yield was increased from 65% to over 90% in just a few months, improving profits by about $8 million per year.
Equipment Controls	Field Sales Margins	An improvement of $800,000 per year went to the bottom line.
Ethyl	Quality and Cycle Time	Key quality measures improved 23% to 257%, contamination decreased by 50%, and cycle times were reduced 25% for a total value of $2.5 million per year.
Evans Clay	Increased Throughput	10% increase in throughput was worth over $1 million per year additional revenue, with no extra capital expenditure. Awarded 1996 RIT/USA Today Quality Cup.
Foster Care Coalition, Greater St. Louis	Increased Inquiries into Adoption and the Numer of Licensed Homes	Inquiries increased 138% through weekly newspaper articles and increased communications to service organizations.
GAF Building Materials	Reducing Glass Fiber Breaks	A roofing shingles MVT produced a 15% reduction in the number of breaks per hour, improved process knowledge, increased troubleshooting tools, and gained experimental aggressiveness.
GAF Materials Corporation	Product Quality Raised While Costs Reduced	Reducing coating variation and improved color consistency, sheet construction, and granule adhesion, helping the plant realize an annual savings of $90K due to increased raw material loading.
GTE	Billing Inquiry	Reduced late payment accounts 14% to 22%, dropped unpaid balances 4% to 8%, reduced uncollectibles 12%, and reduced billing inquiries 8.8%.

(Continued)

(Continued)

Company	Title of Presentation	Accomplishments
GTE	Fortell II	New equipment reduced trouble call dispatches by 10% while no-cost methods changes reduced them by another 34%. Total reduction in dispatches was 44%, worth over $100 million.
GTE	Teaching Customers to Love Us, Not Leave Us	Process changes were discovered to increase the percentage of business customers rating its service as excellent by more than 7%.
International Paper	Optimize Business Performance, Gain Millions in Bottom-line Results	Targeted projects in paper industry lead to dramatic increases in employee involvement and tens of millions of dollars in improved bottom-line results.
International Specialty Products, Calvert City	Cycle Time Reductions and Capacity Increases in a Chemical Process	Chemical product cycle time was reduced 25% resulting in a sales increase of more than $1 million.
International Specialty Products, Calvert City	Improving the Ability to Control Viscosity	The improvements in viscosity control were worth $900,000.
International Specialty Products, Calvert City	Production Up and Costs Down on High-Value Chemical Process	Reduced distillation product losses, raised reaction and distillation capacity, increased unit reliability and other planned cost savings add $1.5 million to bottom line.
International Specialty Products, Calvert City	Reduce the Amount of "Out-of-Viscosity" Specification Material Produced	The measurement system required significant improvement before the MVT. In spec production improved from 80% to 95%, which was worth $4.5 million.
International Specialty Products	Capacity Increase 13%—$1 Million Additional Profit	Increasing production by 13% for more than $1 million in improved gross profit.
International Specialty Products	Reducing Variation Doubles Quality Improvement	An experiment was run on a key ingredient in a hair care product. The experiment reduced variation, lowered cycle time from 38 to 30 hours, and protected $8 million in sales.
Kieffer Paper	Improve Capability and Reduce Variability	Made significant increases in plant capability and substantial reduction in operating costs.
Knoxville Utilities Board	Avoiding Injuries and Damages	Reduced damages and injuries during construction to produce safer working conditions, uninterrupted service, and happier customers.

(Continued)

Company	Title of Presentation	Accomplishments
Knoxville Utilities Board	Billing Accuracy	Meter reading exceptions were reduced 26.17% and pre-billing exceptions by 30.3%.
Knoxville Utilities Board	Call Abandon Rate	The monthly call abandon rate was reduced 3.93%.
Knoxville Utilities Board	Installation Time	The average lead time for installing gas service was reduced by 75%, while missing no due dates.
LaRoche Chemicals	Teamwork Yields Big Benefits	Developing a team environment, reaching a common understanding of key measures, and resolution of a process conflict increased yield from 68% to 90% generating a significant bottom line impact.
Madison Paper	Spool Waste	Spool waste was reduced by 83%, enough paper to print 32 million copies of the New York Times Sunday Magazine. Savings were $3.25 million per year.
Maplehurst Bakeries	Featured Speaker	Boosted sales and profits for large supermarket chains while creating a revenue increase for Maplehurst from the added sales.
Merrimac Paper	Increasing Folder Speed	Increased run speed by 7%, saving $300,000 annually.
Mohawk Paper Mills	Reduce Scrap	More than two tons per day of production, which had been going to scrap, was improved and resulted in annual savings over $500,000.
Molycorp (Unocal)	A Successful Case of the Blind Leading the Blind	Several thousand pounds of highly valuable product was being held back each year as unsuitable. Identified and corrected measurement system problems and saved over $1 million per year.
Morton Adhesives	Increasing Red Dye Production	Production increased 50%, saved $450,000 in planned capital expenditures, and reduced labor and material cost over $150,000.
Morton International Specialty Products	Measurement System Havoc	Reduced variation, shortened cycle time, eliminated rework, and increased throughput to the tune of $5 million in additional sales.
Morton International Specialty Products	Process Improvement	A 15% capacity improvement was achieved which was worth $2 million per year in additional sales. An increase of 20% to 25% was projected which would add even more to the bottom line.

(Continued)

(Continued)

Company	Title of Presentation	Accomplishments
Oil-Dri Corporation	Box Leakage	Package sealing was improved to 90%, eliminating the leakage problem. Solving this problem avoided an expensive package redesign, saved $1.2 million in capital, and improved cost savings and production time.
Oil-Dri Corporation	Production Tripled to Satisfy a Customer	Increased output of clay granules 200% to 300% while improving product quality.
Olin Chlor Alkali Products	Capacity Increase Improves Annualized Profit by Nearly $800,000.	Production increased allowing a gain in market share adding $800,000 in annualized profit.
Olin Chlor Alkali Products	Featured Speaker	Introducing and managing a process improvement system in a geographically dispersed organization—with a contrast between his experiences with MVT and six sigma.
Olin Chlor Alkali Products	Major Saving in Power Utilization	Team has achieved approximately $435 thousand in annualized savings in power usage and expect to get another $200 thousand per year by the end of the first half of 2004.
Pacific Bell	Caller ID	Changes from complete blocking to selective blocking increased 85%. The resulting Caller ID sales improvement was 300%. Company estimated the value of this improvement at several million dollars annually.
Pacific Bell	Change for the Better and Have Customers Agree	Changing voicemail systems finds best communication elements while saving over $1 million in marketing costs while retaining customers.
Pacific Bell	High Capacity Circuit Revenues Saved	19% reduction in late installation of high capacity circuits that can lead to $11.95 million annually.
Pactiv Corporation	Featured Speaker	Organization is driving costs down and elevating sales through no-cost actions identified in the MVT process.
Pactiv Corporation	Set-up Time and Waste Reductions Worth Millions	Identified actions to improve set-up time and reduce waste with the potential to deliver millions to the bottom line when applied to all plants.
Pactiv Corporation	Tens of Millions of Dollars in Increased Technical Sales	Individual helpful actions increased sales by over 13%, while other actions increased sales by almost two new accounts per salesperson per month.

(Continued)

Company	Title of Presentation	Accomplishments
Progressive Insurance	Agent Sales	Sales of company policies increased 1.294 policies per week, potentially worth over $750 million in annual sales.
Progressive Insurance	Attorney Representation	Attorney representation rate fell from 36% to 28%, which was worth over $25 million per year in savings.
Progressive Insurance	Customer Retention for $8 Million in Profits and $200 Million in Sales	Improved customer retention resulted in $8 million in profits and $200 million in sales.
Progressive Insurance	Direct Mail Response Rates Up 15%	Increased direct mail response rates almost 15%.
Progressive Insurance	Featured Speaker	Various channels: retaining policy holders, reducing insurance claim fraud, increasing direct mail effectiveness, and optimizing advertising expenditures worth hundreds of millions of dollars.
Progressive Insurance	Optimization of Advertising Media Mix	Identified most effective use of TV, radio, billboard, and direct mail dollars. Resolved long-standing discussions and differing views.
Progressive Insurance	Targeted Marketing Mail Model Effectiveness Improved 25%	Reduced mail volume by 25% while maintaining virtually the same number of sales.
Riverwood International	Dramatic Improvements in Complaints, Scrap, Cost, and Production Rates with No Capital	Dramatic, simultaneous improvements in complaints, scrap, cost, and productivity rates with no capital investments.
RR Donnelley & Sons—UK	Bindery Efficiency	Bindery run time was increased nearly 25%, worth $1.25 million per year.
RR Donnelley & Sons	Flavor of the Month	Over $1.5 million in savings were identified in an existing process.
RR Donnelley & Sons	New Tools Cut Paper Costs	Savings of $1.4 million per year were achieved in a process which had been operating for decades.
RR Donnelley & Sons	Reducing Downtime	Press downtime was reduced by 58%, saving $500,000 annually. Bonus benefits consisted of increased revenue from extra press time, improved customer satisfaction, higher on-time delivery, higher quality, and increased employee job satisfaction.

(Continued)

(Continued)

Company	Title of Presentation	Accomplishments
Saks Fifth Avenue	Featured Speaker	The strategic value of MVT in the retail environment and the critical management tactics that ensure maximum organizational benefits and help achieve nearly immediate ROI.
Saks Fifth Avenue	Off 5th Increases Sales by 4.3% During MVT	During the test, the 24 stores participating out-performed the other stores by 4.3%, approximately $1 million in additional sales.
Saks, Inc.	Improving Sales and Changing a Corporate Culture	MVT has changed the planning process dramatically, testing has become an integral part of running the business.
Sauder Woodworking	Lamination Defects Cut in Half	Lamination defects were costing $4 million per year in wasted materials. Defects were reduced 50%. Defects were further reduced with more experimentation for a cost savings of over $1.5 million.
SBC Ameritech	Customer Care Center Repeat Calls and Unnecessary Transfers	Reduction of over 15% in nuisance calls that could result in more than $30 million in savings.
SBC Ameritech	Featured Speaker	Cut installation and repair backlogs in half and dramatically shortened customer response times, greatly enhancing customer service and satifsfaction. Helped avoid millions of dollars in labor costs.
SBC Ameritech	Productivity Increase for Telephone Technicians	Improving technician (GJI8) performance for a potental increase of 0.25 jobs per day.
SBC Ameritech	Repair and Installation Backlog Reduced 50%	Customer response times slashed and avoided millions of dollars in labor costs
SBC Communications	Billings	In just eight weeks, no-cost actions were identified and implemented which eliminated late billings. 0% late resulted in direct cost savings exceeding $2 million and a dramatic reduction in unhappy customers.
SBC Communications	Faster Installation of DSL High-Speed Internet Access	Order Flowthrough improved from below 50% to over 95% (i.e., order flows through without manual intervention.)
SBC Communications	Reduction in Telephone Installation Lead Time	Reduced the time interval from a residential customer to the successful completion of the installation.

(Continued)

Company	Title of Presentation	Accomplishments
SBC Communications	Use of MVT Throughout Critical Business Operations Brings Close to a Billion Dollars in Results	Improved customer service, billings, installations and repairs, data center operations, inventory management, and sales for close to a billion dollars in results.
76 Products	$3 Million a Year Difference	$3 million increase in crude oil throughput without taking the time and great expense to add pump stations.
SkillSearch	Increased Response Rate for Direct Mail Packages	Response rate rose by 39%. Changing the mailing procedures saved the company $2 million per year.
Southwestern Bell Telephone Company	$15 Million Sales Story	$11 million increased sales plus $4 million reduction in expenses.
Southwestern Bell Telephone Company	Bill Redesign	Designed a bill that was more appealing, easier to understand, and did not cost any more to produce. The customer satisfaction rating increased by 25%.
Southwestern Bell Telephone Company	MVT Triples Re-utlilization of Capital Resources Valued at $16 Million per Year	MVT found ways to recover more plant without using additional resources. Plant recovered was tripled for a value of $16 million per year.
Southwestern Bell Telephone Company	Necessary Work After MVT	Reduced failures by 20%, removing a big risk to this $1 billion revenue stream.
Southwestern Bell Telephone Company	PAC Contributions	Doubled participation in the PAC contribution process and increased contributions by 238%.
Southwestern Bell Telephone Company	Persistence Increases Sales	Overall improvement in annual sales was estimated at $3 million. This was accomplished with no additional staff while maintaining the same levels of customer satisfaction and center accessibility.
Southwestern Bell Telephone Company	Productivity Increases by Service Center	Increase in service center productivity results in a reduction of fines and reduced labor costs potentially valued at $1.5 to $2.1 million annually.

(Continued)

(Continued)

Company	Title of Presentation	Accomplishments
Southwestern Bell Telephone Company	QDD	On-time installations went from 84% to 98%, increasing customer satisfaction and retention.
Southwestern Bell Telephone Company	Right the First Time	Some pre-planning by repair personnel, prior to customer visits, dramatically improved customer satisfaction and saved over $1.5 million per year by reducing repeat visits.
Southwestern Bell Telephone Company	Teams + Customers = Win-Win-Win	MVT identified factors which reduced the critical interval from 32 days to 23 days. Not only were late charges avoided, projected corporate revenues increased over $1 million per year.
Southwestern Bell Telephone Company— Aladin	167% of Quota in Business-to-Business Sales	The worst performing district achieved a 300%+ increase in sales while the best performing district jumped over 50%.
Southwestern Bell Telephone Company— Houston	Excellence Through Service Guarantee	Missed appointments were reduced by 17.7% with an estimated value of $2.1 million.
Southwestern Bell Telephone Company— Houston	Sales Improvement	Sales were increased 12.4% with a predicted value of $1.9 million.
Southwestern Bell Telephone Company— Oklahoma	Plug Ins	Decreased total inventory value by 10%, a $2.3 million reduction in working capital.
Southwestern Bell Telephone Company— Pacific Bell	Coding Errors	Over 180% improvement in the accuracy of coding service orders. Number of customer claims reduced 89% and refunds reduced 36%. The estimated worth was $4.7 million.
Southwestern Bell Telephone Company— St. Louis	Employee Referrals	Increased number of referrals by over 40%, which resulted in increased revenues of $3.6 million.
Staples	Improved Circular Improves Retail Sales and Margin	Creating the most effective circular resulted in improved sales (up to 3%) and increased profits (up to 5%).

(Continued)

Company	Title of Presentation	Accomplishments
TELUS	Reduction in Service Order Errors	Realized an immediate 35% reduction in service order errors, worth $365,000 in annual savings, not counting the improved customer satisfaction.
Toys "R" Us	Store Remodeling and Advertising Changes	Optimizing innovative store remodeling program. Changes in newspaper insert, radio, and direct mail programs expected to significantly impact both revenues and costs.
TV Guide	What Makes You Buy a Magazine	Millions of dollars of increased sales.
Unocal 76, SF Refinery	Meet Regulatory Requirements While Maximizing Profits	Methods were found to know and hold constant the risk of producing any off-grade product while meeting all EPA and CARD regulations.
Unocal 76, Santa Maria Refinery	Removing Butane from Gasoline to Meet EPA Deadline	Vapor pressure reduction allowed butane to be removed from the product and improve capacity. Bottom line savings were $600,000 annually.
Wausau-Mosinee Paper	Going for Broke Saves $1.23 Million in Waste	"Broke" reduced by 30% which resulted in savings of $1.23 million annually.
Williams-Sonoma, Inc.	Brand Multi-Channel Sales Improved with Catalog Creative Testing	Restored sales growth in the catalog by 10%, worth $8 million per year while driving more incremental business to the internet and retail chains.
Williams-Sonoma, Inc.	Featured Speaker	The role of MVT as a tool for corporate turnarounds, as well as continuous improvement.
Witco	Capacity Increase	No-cost actions were implemented which increased plant capacity over 25% and improved profitability $3.2 million.
Witco	Sisterville Scum Reduction	Scum was eliminated completely which was worth $833,000 per year.
Witco Mapleton	Reliability and On-Time Delivery	Reduced cycle time by 10% and decreased late deliveries by 75%. Satisfied customers increased sales by $3.3 million.
Zep Manufacturing	Targets $30 Million in Sales Revenues	Improvement in sales results for an entire line of products is expected to be worth $30 million in increased revenue.

INDEX

Accuracy/precision, 74–75
Action plans, 133–134, 168–169
American Express, 44, 298
American Media, 298
American Society for Quality (ASQ),
    48
Ameritech, 5, 43–44, 207–219, 310
    empirical testing, three-pronged
        approach, 209–219
    direct MVT, 214–215
    implementation of MVT, 215–219
    indirect MVT, 210–214
    problems/background, 207–209

Barriers to implementation, identifying,
    267
BASF, 45–46, 298
Beaulieu, 6, 298
Bell, Jeb, 201–206
BellSouth, 299
Benchmarking, 53
Boise/Boise Cascade, 15, 299–300
Bouckaert, Carl, 6
Brainstorming (MVT Step 5), 28, 60,
    96–103
    case study, 101–103
    ensuring adequate quantity/quality of
        ideas, 99–100
    participants, 60, 96–98
    steps, 98–100

Breakthrough results plan, 234–235,
    252–254, 270–273
Bro, Darren, 195–196
Brown, Larry, 201
Burman, J. P., 9
Business decisions:
    MVT improving accuracy of, 21–24
    typical process, 20–21

Capstone Turbine, 300–301
Carbon foam example, 172–174
CarMax, 39
Case study, MVT (nationwide retailer):
    Step 1 (choosing goal and creating
        environment), 65–67
    Step 2 (measurement system),
        77–78
    Step 3 (control charts), 85–86
    Step 4 (data mining), 93–95
    Step 5 (brainstorming), 101–103
    Step 6 (selecting practical/fast/cost-
        free ideas), 108–111
    Step 7 (designing screening
        experiment), 123–126
    Step 8 (executing screening
        experiment), 138–141
    Step 9 (analyzing screening test
        results), 147–149
    Step 10 (designing/executing refining
        experiment), 155–157

Case study, MVT (nationwide retailer)
(Continued)
Step 11 (analyzing refining experiment results), 164–166
Step 12 (implementing most powerful ideas), 174–176
Cendant Corporation, 301
Champion International, 301
"Champions" of process improvement, 267
Check sheets, 135–136
Chemical process examples, 32–33, 73–74, 82, 83
Cingular, 301
Circuit City, 6, 39, 301
Citibank, 40–41, 301
Cluster analysis, 92
Cold War, 9–11
Communicating, importance of, 135, 170, 192–193, 275–276
Compliance, lack of:
implementation (factor execution), 170–172
screening experiment execution, 129–130
Consultants. See MVT consultants
Control. See Monitoring/control
Control charts. See Statistical process control (SPC) charts (MVT Step 3)
Control limits, calculating, 146
Cost-free (criterion for test ideas), 29, 106
Cost reduction, 38, 41–42, 295
Counterintuitive learning, 294
Creativity, 46, 192
Culture/morale, organizational, 26, 36, 41, 44–46, 294
Customer(s):
as brainstorming participants, 97
communicating MVT success stories to, 238–239
customers of, 288
MVT focus on, 238, 285–286
satisfaction, 38, 42–44, 261–263, 294
surveying/capturing wants/needs, 236, 263–264

Data collection, 137–138
Data mining (MVT Step 4), 28, 52–53, 87–95
case study, 93–95
methods, 89–92
cluster analysis, 92

discriminant analysis, 92, 93
multiple linear regression, 89–91
multivariate regression, 92
principle component analysis (PCA), 91
simple linear regression, 89, 90
outliers, 93
pitfalls/traps, 88–89, 93
pros and cons, 87–88
Data owner, 61, 133
Data review (monitoring process), 136
DeBusk, Pete, 243–244
Decision making ("seat-of-pants" versus MVT), 4–5
Deluxe Corporation, 42, 301–302
Deming, W. Edwards, 14–16, 263
DeRoyal Industries, 243–244
Design of experiments (DOE), 16–17, 31, 151–152
Direct mail response rate improvement, 128
Discriminant analysis, 92, 93
Dummy factors, 122
DuPont, xii–xiii, 41, 42, 45, 46, 194–200, 231, 302–305
Dyno Nobel, 305

Elo TouchSystems, 305
Emergency room example, 43
Employees:
getting ideas from, 264–265, 266
participating in MVT (see MVT participants)
Environment:
creating (MVT Step 1), 24–27, 57–67
optimal (not required), 235
Environmental emissions, real life results, 179
Equipment Controls Company (ECCO), 201–206, 305
Ethyl, 305
Evans Clay, 33–35, 305
Executive dilemma, 3–5
Experiment(s). See Refining experiment(s); Screening experiment(s)
Experimental units, 113, 115–120, 154–155
Experts:
conventional business wisdom, MVT undermining, 13–14
MVT (see MVT consultants)

Factor(s), 112
  compliance, 171–172
  dummy, 122
  effects, 143–144, 149, 159–160, 166
  levels, 107, 153
  owners, 60–61, 133, 139, 169
Fast (criterion for test ideas), 29, 106,
  294
Financial impact, 32–33, 38–44, 274
  improved customer satisfaction, 38,
    42–44, 261–263, 294
  increased sales, 38, 39–41
  profitability, 57–58, 260–261, 295
  reduced costs, 38, 41–42, 295
Foster Care Coalition, Greater St. Louis,
  305
Fractional-factorial experiments, 151
Full-factorial experiments, 151

GAF Building Materials, 305
General Electric, 49–50, 252
Glover, Dwight, 34, 35
Goal, choosing high-payoff (MVT
  Step 1), 24–27, 57–67
Googin, John, 17
Grabill, Vic, 218–219
Gray, Scott, 42
GTE, 305–306

Hammer, Art, 15, 187
Harris, Dennis, 5, 207, 208–209, 218
Healthcare crisis, using MVT for
  solving, 296
Historical data analysis. See Data mining
  (MVT Step 4)

Idea(s):
  categorizing as help/hurt/no-impact
    (MVT Step 9), 30–31,
    142–149
  generating:
    Step 3 (control charts), 27, 79–86,
      173
    Step 4 (data mining), 28, 87–95
    Step 5 (brainstorming), 28,
      96–103
  selecting for implementation (MVT
    Step 11), 31, 158–166
  selecting for testing (MVT Step 6),
    28–29, 60, 104–111
  statistics (percentage that help, hurt, or
    have no impact), 22, 193

Implementing selected ideas (MVT Step
  12), 32, 167–176
  action plan, 168–169
  case study, 174–176
  communicating, 170
  factor compliance target, 171
  factor materials and training,
    169–170
  fine-tuning earlier findings, 172–173
  recipe compliance,
    measuring/reporting, 170–171
  remedying execution flaws, 171
  results, unexpected, 171–172
  roles/responsibilities, 168–169
Infrastructure, establishing, 259
Innovation, promoting, 45
Interaction bar chart, 160
International Paper, 306
International Specialty Products, 45,
  306
Ismert, Neil, 6, 8
ISO, 53

Jahanshahi, Kamran, 41
Just-in-time training, 63, 279

Kieffer Paper, 306
King, Randal, 196
Knoxville Utilities Board, 306–307

LaRoche Chemicals, 307
Lean, being (versus MVT), 53
Learning the MVT process, 62–63. See
  also Training
Lee, Ron, 196
Lewis, Peter, 222
Linear regression (simple/multiple),
  89–91
Lowe's, xii, 22, 46, 185–193, 231

Madden, Tim, 220, 222, 226, 228
Madison Paper, 307
Management roles:
  brainstorming, 97
  committing to organization-wide
    rollout (Phase II), 240–241,
    251–273
  communicating plan, 234–235,
    275–276
  communicating proof of need message,
    234
  keys to success, 233–235, 239

Management roles *(Continued)*
  reviewing results of MVT process,
    161, 163–164
Manufacturing (examples of Phase I
  projects), 246
Maplehurst Bakeries, 307
Matrix. *See* Test matrix
McBee, Bill, 23, 36, 42, 276
Measurement system (MVT Step 2), 27,
  68–78, 235
  case study, 77–78
  components, 72
  evaluating ("guilty until proven
    innocent"), 72–76
  identifying key measures of success,
    68–69, 235
Measuring/reporting recipe compliance,
  170–171
Merrimac Paper, 307
Metal casting yield, improvement in,
  129
Mohawk Paper Mills, 307
Molded parts (surrogate measurement),
  77
Molycorp (Unocal), 307
Monitoring/control, 236
  Phase I, 248–249
  Phase II, 265–266, 268
  Phase III, 277–278
  Phase IV, 292
Monitoring process, measuring recipe
  compliance, 135–136
Monitoring return on investment (ROI)
  (Phase III), 278
Morale. *See* Culture/morale,
  organizational
Morton Adhesives, 307
Morton International Specialty Products,
  307
Motivating project participants, 63–64
Motorola, 50, 252
Mueller, Ed, 107, 207, 208–209, 218
Multivariate regression, 92
MVT (Multivariable Testing):
  business decisions, improved accuracy
    of, 20–24
  defined/overview description, 5–6
  expected improvement from, 177–180
  financial impact, 32–33
  history/roots, 8–16
  versus other approaches, 35–37,
    47–53

phases, organization-wide
  improvement effort *(see*
  Organization-wide rollout of
  MVT)
power of, 3–19
reasons to use, 38–46
  improved customer satisfaction, 38,
    42–44
  improved organizational culture,
    44–46
  increased sales, 38, 39–41
  reduced costs, 38, 41–42
refining experiments *(see* Refining
  experiment(s))
requirements, 180–182
as science, 33–35
screening experiments *(see* Screening
  experiment(s))
steps *(see* MVT process (12 steps))
MVT consultants:
  internal, 237–238, 282–284, 290
  Phase I, 232–233, 247–248
  Phase II, 269, 282, 283–284
  Phase III, 282–284
  Phase IV, 290
  Step 1 (creating environment), 61
  Step 8 (developing action plan),
    133–134
  training/certification, 63, 237–238,
    282–284
MVT participants:
  brainstorming, 60
  data owners, 61, 133
  factor owners, 60–61, 133
  idea categorization, 60, 106–107
  motivating for success, 63–64
  Phase I, 247–248
  project leader, 59–60, 133
  senior management *(see* Management
    roles)
  Step 1 (getting right people involved),
    59–61, 232
  Step 8 (action plan roles), 133–134
  Step 12 (final implementation) roles/
    responsibilities, 168–169
  training, 61–63, 236–237 *(see also*
    Training)
MVT process (12 steps), 24–32
  overview diagram, 25
  Step 1 (choosing high-payoff goal and
    creating environment), 24–27,
    57–67

Step 2 (defining measurement system), 27, 68–78

Step 3 (using control charts to find improvement ideas), 27, 79–86, 173

Step 4 (using data mining and other statistical techniques to find improvement ideas), 28, 87–95

Step 5 (brainstorming for improvement ideas), 28, 96–103

Step 6 (selecting improvement ideas that are practical, fast, and cost free), 28–29, 104–111

Step 7 (designing MVT screening experiment), 30, 112–126

Step 8 (executing MVT screening experiment and measuring test results), 30, 127–141

Step 9 (analyzing screening test results to categorize ideas as help/hurt/ no-impact), 30–31, 142–149

Step 10 (designing/executing MVT refining experiment), 31, 150–157

Step 11 (analyzing results; selecting high-impact ideas), 31, 158–166

Step 12 (implementing ideas and calculating bottom-line impact), 32, 167–176

National Enquirer, xiii, 187

Negative results (no factor helps), 162–163

Newberry, Alan, 196–197

Nuclear weapons manufacturing crisis, 9–11

Number-defective charts (*np* charts), 81

Oil-Dri Corporation, 308

Olin Corporation, 308

Organizational psychology-based approaches, 53

Organization-wide rollout of MVT: keys to success, 231–239

overview, QualPro process, 239–241

payoff, 293–296

Phase I (completing two initial projects), 239–240, 242–253, 270

Phase II (senior management commitment), 240–241, 251–273

Phase III (executing MVT projects throughout organization), 241, 272, 274–284

Phase IV (maintaining gains/prioritizing opportunities/continuous improvement), 241, 272, 285–292

Outliers, 93

Pacific Bell, 207, 209, 308. *See also* SBC Communications

Pactiv Corporation, 23, 42, 276, 308

Paper manufacturer (premium/nonpremium logs), 71

Payoff, 293–296

People. *See* MVT participants

Phases. *See* Organization-wide rollout of MVT

Physical audits, 136

Plackett, R. L., 9

Plastic containers, 43

Playing the Game, 122–123

Pond, Dale, 186–189, 190, 191–192

Practical (criterion for test ideas), 29, 104, 105–106

Precision/accuracy, 74–75

Predictive equation, 162, 166

Principle component analysis (PCA), 91

Prioritizing MVT projects, 259–269, 276–277

Problems (expected in screening experiment), 129–132

Process, QualPro's elements of, 59, 100

Profit impact. *See* Financial impact

Progressive Insurance, 220–228, 309

Project selection/prioritization, 57–58, 259–269, 276–277, 285

Proof-of-the-need message, 63–64, 257–258, 275

Proportion-defective charts (*p* charts), 81

Public good, using MVT for, 296

QualPro: annual leadership symposiums, xi, 297–313

Deming, and launch of, 14–16

elements of process, 59, 100

MVT services offered, xi

process for implementing MVT on organization-wide basis, 239–241

Quasi-interaction effects, 145, 146, 149

Ray, Rick, 45–46
Recipes, 113, 121–122, 154–155
Reengineering, 53
Refining experiment(s):
  design/execution (MVT Step 10), 31, 150–157
    case study, 155–157
    design, 153–155
    execution, 155
    full-factorial and fractional-factorial experiments, 151
    reviewing results of MVT screening experiments, 152–153
    versus design of experiments (DOE), 151–152
    purpose, 150–151
  results, analyzing (MVT Step 11), 31, 158–166
    case study, 164–166
    comparing results with screening results, 161–162
    factor effects, calculating, 159–160, 166
    management review, 161, 163–164
    negative results (no factor helps), 162–163
    predictive equation, 162, 166
Reflected designs, 121
Requirements, minimum, 180–182
Retail case study. See Case study, MVT (nationwide retailer)
Return on investment (ROI), monitoring, 278
Reward/recognition systems, 236, 265, 281–282, 292
Riverwood International, 309
Roles. See Management roles; MVT participants
RR Donnelley & Sons, 309

Sabotage, 167
Saks Fifth Avenue, 310
Sales:
  increased, 38, 39–41
  marketing and (examples of Phase I projects), 246
  retail sales graph example, 33
  sales rep performance example, 116, 118–119, 159, 160
Sauder Woodworking, 310
SBC Communications, 6–8, 231, 310–311. See also Ameritech

Science, MVT as, 33–35, 36
Screening experiment(s):
  examples, 113–115
  purpose, 113
  robustness of, 138
Screening experiment design (MVT Step 7), 30, 112–126
  case study, 123–126
  experimental units, 113, 115–122
  factors, 112
  Playing the Game, 122–123
  randomly assigning experimental units to test recipes, 120
  recipes, 113, 118–122
  reflected designs, 121
  size/duration, 122
  test matrix, 112–113, 118–119
Screening experiment execution (MVT Step 8), 30, 127–141
  case study, 138–141
  expectations, 127–131
  importance of, 132–138
  improved results, 127–128
  problems, 129–132
  steps, 132
    action plan preparation, 133–134
    collecting data, 137–138
    communicating plans/roles/procedures/ logistics/importance, 135
    creating/executing monitoring process to measure recipe compliance, 135–136
    factor materials and training, 134
    remedying execution flaws, 136–137
Screening experiment results, analyzing (MVT Step 9), 30–31, 142–149
  analyzing more complex designs, 147
  calculations:
    control limits, 146
    effects on variability, 146–147
    factor effects, 143–144
    quasi-interaction effects, 145, 146
  case study, 147–149
  examining the measurements, 142–143
  refining results compared to (in Step 11), 161–162
Secondary measures, 69–70
Selecting ideas for implementation (MVT Step 11), 31, 158–166
  case study, 164–166

comparing refining results with screening results, 161–162

factor effects, calculating, 159–160, 166

management review, 161, 163–164

negative results (no factor helps), 162–163

predictive equation, 162, 166

Selecting ideas for testing (MVT Step 6), 28–29, 60, 104–111

case study, 108–111

criteria:
  cost free, 29, 106
  fast, 29, 106
  practical, 29, 105–106
  factor levels, 107, 110
  participants, 60, 106–107

Selecting/prioritizing MVT projects, 57–58, 259–269, 276–277, 285

Self audits, 136

Senior management. See Management roles

Service businesses:
  applying MVT to service businesses, 15–16
  examples of Phase I projects, 246

76 Products, 311

Shareholder value, increased, 295

Sharp, Richard, 39

Six Sigma, 47–52

SkillSearch, 311

Small companies, 201–206

Soft drinks example, 43

Southwestern Bell Telephone, 6–8, 39–40, 207, 209, 311–312. See also SBC Communications

Special causes. See Statistical process control (SPC) charts (MVT Step 3)

Standard, 74–75

Staples, 312

Statistical process control (SPC) charts (MVT Step 3), 6, 27, 51, 53, 79–86

attribute data, 80

case study, 85–86

constructing appropriate chart, 79–81

count data, 80–81

identifying each instance of uncontrolled variation in the historical data, 81–82

investigating each special cause to identify its source, 82–84

number-defective charts (np charts), 81

proportion-defective charts (p charts), 81

special causes known with certainty are a "gimme," 84–85

steps, 79

types (two basic), 80

using suspected special causes as basis for MVT test factors, 84

variable data, 80

Statistical techniques. See Data mining (MVT Step 4)

Steps in MVT process. See MVT process (12 steps)

Success stories:
  communicating, 238–239, 249, 288–289
  documenting, 233, 249–250

Suppliers, 97, 238–239, 286–288

Surrogate measures, 76–77

Surveying customers/employees, 290–292

SWAT team approach, 62, 187

Synergies, identifying, 4

Tab weld strength example, 115, 121, 143, 144, 160

Taguchi, Genechi, 16

Taguchi, Shin, 16

Taguchi Methods, 16–17

Technical personnel (brainstorming), 97

Telephone audits, 136

TELUS, 312

Test factors. See Factor(s)

Test matrix, 112–113, 118–119, 124, 153–154

Tillman, Bob, 185–186, 188

Total Quality Control (TQC), 53

Total Quality Management (TQM), 53

Toys "R" Us, 313

Trade-offs, 163

Training:
  customized, 237, 269, 279–281
  experts providing, 237
  internal MVT consultants, 237–238
  just-in-time, 63, 279
  local workforce, 63
  management, 62–63
  MVT consultants, 63, 237–238, 282–284

Training *(Continued)*
  MVT implementation versus one-time
    fix for problem, 26–27
  Phase II, 269, 278–281
  Phase III, 279–281
  Phase IV, 289–290
  recommended (for each MVT process
    role), 281
  Six Sigma pitfall, 48
  Step 1, 61–63
  Step 8, 134
  Step 12, 169–170
  success factor, 237
  SWAT team approach, 62
  top-down, 279
TV Guide, 313

Unexpected, planning for, 192
Union Carbide, 9, 10–11, 15
Unocal, 307, 313

Utility company (example of Plan for
  Breakthrough Results), 253,
  270–273

Variability, calculating effects on,
  146–147
Variation, uncontrolled, 81–82

Wausau-Mosinee Paper, 313
Wells, Jeff, 6
Whitacre, Edward, Jr., 207
Williams-Sonoma, 39, 107, 313
Witco, 313
Workforce, local, 97, 233
Work required during MVT process,
  180–181
World War II, 8–13

Zep Manufacturing, 313